12/23/91

Joe—

Happy Holidays!
I hope 1992 is a prosperous
year for you!

Patti Neumann
Warfield's Business Record
The Daily Record

BALTIMORE

"Baltimore's Enterprises" by Joan G. Ford

Windsor Publications, Inc., Chatsworth, California

BALTIMORE
Jewel of the Chesapeake

A Contemporary Portrait by Neil A. Grauer

Windsor Publications, Inc.— Book Division
Managing Editor: Karen Story
Design Director: Alexander D'Anca
Photo Director: Susan L. Wells
Executive Editor: Pamela Schroeder

Staff for *Baltimore: Jewel of the Chesapeake*
Manuscript Editor: Michael Nalick
Photo Editor: Patty Salkeld
Editor, Corporate Profiles: Melissa Wells Patton
Production Editor, Corporate Profiles:
 Doreen Nakakihara
Proofreader: Michael Moore
Caption Writer: Mike Guiliano, Baltimore
Customer Service Manager: Phyllis Feldman- Schroeder
Editorial Assistants: Elizabeth Anderson,
 Dominique Jones, Kim Kievman, Michael Nugwynne,
 Kathy B. Peyser, Theresa J. Solis
Publisher's Representatives, Corporate Profiles:
 Phil Hernberg, Charles Hoddinott, Mary Whelan
Layout Artist, Corporate Profiles: Bonnie Felt
Designer: Ellen Ifrah

Windsor Publications, Inc.
Elliot Martin, Chairman of the Board
James L. Fish III, Chief Operating Officer
Mac Buhler, Vice President/Acquisitions

Library of Congress Cataloging-in-Publication Data
Grauer, Neil A., 1947-
Baltimore, jewel of the Chesapeake : a contemporary
portrait / by Neil A. Grauer. — 1st ed.
p.264   cm.23 x 31
Includes bibliographical references.
ISBN: 0-89781-369-3
1. Baltimore (Md.)—Civilization. 2. Baltimore (Md.)
—Description—Views. 3. Baltimore (Md.)—Economic
conditions. 4. Baltimore (Md.)—Industries. I. Title
F189.B15G73 1990   90-48361
975.2'6—dc20   CIP

Frontispiece: Photo by Walter Calahan/Folio

Right: Photo by Rich Riggins

Page 7: Photo by Greg Pease

Page 10: Photo by James Blank

Page 150: Photo by Greg Pease

CONTENTS

...

ONED
SHAD

SHAD
ROE

FINNAN
HADDIE

SALT
HERRING

C
M

OYSTERS

OYSTERS

LIVE
LOBSTER

OYSTERS

STANDARD 3 95 1/2 PINT

SELECT 4 10 1/2 PINT

QUART   PINT   1/2 PINT

CATCH OF THE DAY
CHIXS
7 95 EACH   2 FOR 15 00

CATCH OF THE DAY
SELECTS
1 1/4 TO 1 1/4 POUND
10 35 LB

CATCH OF THE DAY
2 POUND OR OVER
10 95 LB

CHIXS
1 1/4 1/2 M
2 1 LB M

SEAFOOD
Packaged For
TRAVEL
OR
SHIPMENT

COCKTAIL
CLAW
FINGERS
7 95

STANDARDS
7 80 PINT
3 95 1/2 PINT   13 95 QUART

SELECT
7 95 PINT
4 10 1/2 PINT   15 00 QUART

COUNTS
8 25 PINT
1 PINT   QUART
4 25   16 00

OLD BAY
SEASONING

SMOKED
HERRING
$4 25 LB

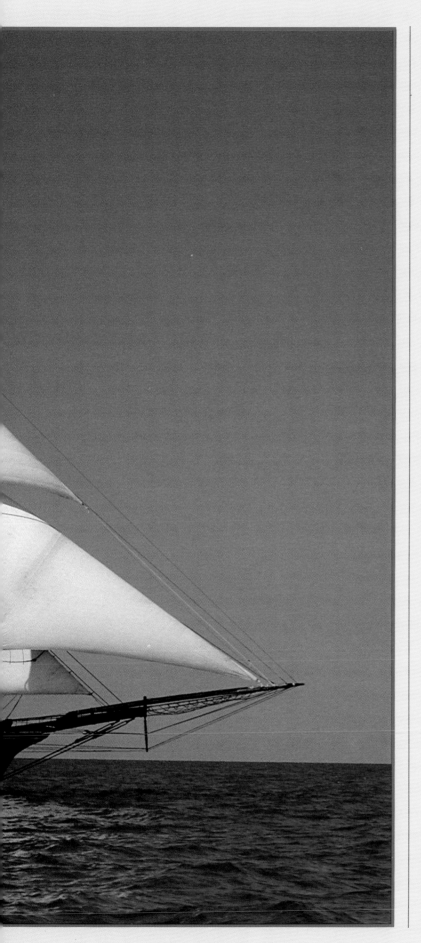

For Marc and Alice Davis, who allowed me to adopt them; and in memory of George J. Hiltner, Jr. (1914-1977), mentor, friend, a gentleman from The Sun and a gentle man.

ACKNOWLEDGMENTS

Writing, of necessity, is a solitary endeavor, but lucky authors are blessed with friends whose interest, expertise and support help ease the burden of writing a book and smooth the way to its completion. It has been my good fortune to have had the assistance of an extraordinary number of friends and colleagues while I worked on this book, but special thanks are due to Jonathan and Lucy Acton; John S. Bainbridge, Jr.; Russell Baker; James H. Bready; Neil L. Buttner; Robert D. Chessin; Thomas A. Cole; J. Joseph Curran, Jr.; Scott Duncan; Daniel Mark Epstein; John Fairhall; Charles S. Fax; Bailey and Stanley Fine; Graeme Fox; Henry M. Greenberg; Mike Guiliano; Edward Gunts; George H. Hanst; Joan Jacobson; Carleton Jones; Quint E. Kessenich; James R. Ledley; William Leibovici; Jon Morgan; Fred Rasmussen; Gilbert Sandler; Kevin Simpson; William Stump; Brian Sullam; Glen A. Thomas; Paul W. Valentine; and Brooke E. White.

Gliding majestically through the water, the *Pride of Baltimore II,* modeled after the famed Baltimore Clippers of the 1800s, is a spirited symbol of Maryland's maritime heritage. The 160-foot topsail schooner, which was handcrafted in Baltimore in 1987-88, sails to ports around the world sharing the glorious history of the Chesapeake Bay, before returning to home port in Baltimore's Inner Harbor. Photo by Greg Pease

9

PART ONE

...

"TIP OF THE SOUTH, TOE OF THE NORTH"

—OGDEN NASH

FROM THE BEGINNING

A replica of the *Dove*, the square-rigged ship that brought
Maryland's first settlers here, is among the sights to see in Saint
Marys City. Photo by Greg Pease

Water, the source of all life, was the reason for Baltimore's being.

Three swiftly flowing streams, coursing down from hills west and northwest of the site which would become Baltimore, emptied into a deep basin on the northwest branch of the Patapsco, an easily navigable river that itself flows into the nation's largest estuary, the Chesapeake Bay.

This convergence of streams, river, and bay—and thence from the bay to the Atlantic Ocean—provided just the proper mix of natural power and geographic location to give this town named Baltimore a chance to prosper after several earlier would-be Baltimores in Maryland had vanished without a trace.

The town that survived was by no means an instant success. Its site may have been splendid, but no settlement took root immediately or mushroomed overnight. Instead, baby Baltimore spent most of its long infancy in somnolence. It could be aroused—and would thrive—during times of international conflict, then return to its slumbers during periods of peace. A half-century after its founding it remained just a village; within another two decades, however, it would become a significant metropolis, one of the key cities of the new United States.

Baltimore's location would also account for its unique character, an uncommon blend of northern enterprise and energy with southern ease and gentility, of industry and insouciance. Poet Ogden Nash, a Baltimorean by choice rather than birth, deftly characterized the city's bipolarity with the couplet: "The tip of the South and the toe of the North, / It constantly teeters back and forth."

As Pulitzer Prize-winning critic Jonathan Yardley (also a Baltimorean by choice) has observed, "the history of Maryland is American history writ small." In the same way, it can be said that Baltimore could serve as a model for urban America, with its setbacks and triumphs—far more of the latter than the former.

Progressivism vies with conservatism in Baltimore's psychology. Baltimoreans, one out-of-town writer noted, "insist on change with continuity." They are as proud of their city's lasts as of its firsts; they not only relish the fact that in 1817 Baltimore became the first city in the world to have gas streetlights, but that it also was the last U.S. city to give them up—in 1957! The horse-drawn carts of produce vendors, a fixture of Baltimore's neighborhoods and downtown for generations, may soon be joined by a high-speed, light rail link to Washington, D.C. The latest international container cargo ships ply the same harbor waters that lap the wooden hull of the Navy's oldest surviving warship, the U.S. frigate *Constellation*, built in Baltimore in 1797 and now the centerpiece of its revitalized Inner Harbor.

Captain John Smith, the English explorer whose neck, legend has it, was saved by the Indian princess Pocahontas, was the first European to report visiting the present site of Baltimore. In 1608 he sailed up the Chesapeake and wrote in his journal that "a river not inhabited, yet navigable," divided into four branches at the end of the bay. The best branch, Smith wrote, "commeth northwest from among the moun-

tains," and he marked the spot on his map. The Piscataway Indians called the river the Patapsco, and when another map of the region was made in 1666, the Indian name was adopted.

George Calvert, a close advisor to Great Britain's King James I, was rewarded for his efforts first with a knighthood in 1619 and then, in 1623, with a 2,300-acre estate in County Longford, Ireland, which Calvert called the Manor of Baltimore, adopting the Gaelic name, meaning "place of the great house," from a small fishing village in County Cork. Calvert resigned his government posts in 1625, and the king, grateful for Calvert's service, gave him the title Baron of Baltimore.

Calvert later asked King James' successor, Charles I, for a royal grant, requesting the area surrounding the northern Chesapeake. King Charles signed the new charter in June 1632, two months after Calvert had died. His eldest son, Cecil Calvert, the second Lord Baltimore, thus became the first Lord Proprietary of the new colony, named Maryland in honor of Queen Henrietta Maria.

The new lord provisioned two ships, the *Ark* and the *Dove*, which set sail in November 1633 and landed in March 1634 near the mouth of the Potomac River at an island they called Saint Clement's, 72 miles south of today's Baltimore.

The second Lord Baltimore chose not to accompany the settlers of his new land (and never did see it himself) but sent instead his brother Leonard to serve as the new colony's governor. Among the instructions Calvert gave his brother was to create a colony in which "unity and peace" could be maintained between the Protestant and Catholic settlers. Consequently a 1649 law forbade derogatory references to the faiths of others and assured the informal, unfettered exercise of religion for all those who acknowledged the Holy Trinity and Christ as savior. Limited though it was—and later statutes, ironically, would deny Catholics and Jews the right to hold public office—this Toleration Act represented a major advance over the codified bigotry of Europe. It helped nurture an atmosphere in which religion could flourish, later enabling Baltimore to play a central role in the religious history of America.

More than a quarter-century would pass, however, between the founding of Maryland and construction of the first home on a site not far from what is now the center of Baltimore. In 1661 a certain David Jones is reputed to have become the town's first settler by building a house on a 380-acre tract beside the stream that still bears his name—the Jones Falls.

A growing demand for North American iron in England and for wheat to feed British colonies in the West Indies spurred interest in the splendid natural harbor adjacent to the Jones Falls. Along with two other streams, the Gwynns Falls and Herring Run, it provided ample waterpower for the iron furnaces and the mills that turned colonial wheat into flour. Such a mill was built beside the Jones Falls in 1711, and by 1729 the number of settlers on the banks of the falls and the Patapsco prompted planters and merchants to petition the Mary-

This early view of Baltimore is based on a drawing that John Moale made of Baltimore Town in 1752. Although its harbor was already appreciated, Baltimore was a small and sleepy town in the mid-eighteenth century. Courtesy, Maryland Historical Society

land General Assembly for a charter creating a town named Baltimore on "sixty Acres of Land, in and about the place where one John Fleming now lives."

Originally Baltimore Town was intended to be just a tobacco port, but its location proved more fortuitous than imagined. As the embarkation point closest to the wheat fields of Western Maryland and Pennsylvania, Baltimore also became a wheat port, and commerce began to flourish.

During the second half of the eighteenth century, the infant town grew to vibrant adolescence. Although it was not a pre-Revolutionary center of trade, business, or culture, Baltimore quickly responded to the distant disruptions in commerce caused by the cycle of conflicts that preceded and followed the American Revolution. The town advanced or marked time to the beat of the colonial war drum.

Many of Baltimore's merchants, tradesmen, financiers, and common folk began to chafe against British taxes and commercial policies, as did other Marylanders and a growing number of their fellow colonists. The push for independence gained momentum with the backing of such prestigious men as Charles Carroll, one of the wealthiest planters in the country; attorney Samuel Chase, a future Supreme Court justice; and John Eager Howard, a major Baltimore landowner and merchant who became a leading Revolutionary commander and later governor of Maryland and a U.S. senator.

Six months after the Declaration of Independence was signed in Philadelphia on July 4, 1776—with Charles Carroll and Samuel Chase among its signers—Baltimore found itself playing the unexpected role

of the would-be nation's capital. The Continental Congress, fearful of a possible attack on Philadelphia by British troops, adjourned and headed for a safer haven. Eventually it reconvened in a large, newly built Baltimore tavern that thereafter was known as Congress Hall. From December 20, 1776, through February 27, 1777, the delegates debated issues both momentous and mundane, conferring extraordinary powers on General George Washington to prosecute the war and ordering that geese and pigs be kept off Baltimore's unpaved streets.

Unseasonably mild and rainy weather had turned the town's thoroughfares into a sea of red, sticky mud. John Adams, the future president, grumbled about the dreary weather and impenetrable mud, calling Baltimore "the dirtiest place in the world." Virginian Benjamin Harrison, father of another president, also complained of the rustic accommodations and wrote to a friend, ". . . if you desire to keep out of the damndest hole on earth, come not here!" Yet despite the pigs, the mud, and the tendency of local tradesmen to boost the price of everything while Congress was in town, much was accomplished during its stay in Baltimore. Samuel Adams of Massachusetts, a distant cousin of the disgruntled John, wrote: "We have done more important business here in three weeks than we had done, or I believe should have done, in Philadelphia in six months." And it was while Congress kept its nose to the grindstone in a Baltimore inn that Washington was able to send it a report of his first victory, the audacious crossing of the Delaware River the day after Christmas and his rout of Hessian troops billeted by the British at Trenton.

Baltimore's sailors, shipbuilders, and merchants were ardent patriots, having harbored trade and maritime grievances against the British for years. The shipyards at Fells Point produced a number of warships commissioned by the Congress, but of far greater importance to the war effort were the exploits of a huge fleet of armed privateers, privately owned vessels and merchant ships that were granted government commissions called "letters of marque and reprisal." These gave them the power to capture enemy vessels they might encounter in the course of their trade, or in some cases pursue, capture, and sink any enemy vessel they could find. The booty that these ships succeeded in seizing was divvied up among the sailors, shipowners, and their financial backers.

Between 1776 and the end of the Revolution, about 250 privateers called Baltimore their home port. Many were the sleek, soon-to-be-renowned schooners known as Baltimore clippers, as well as smaller but equally maneuverable sloops with which a crew of skillful sailors could harass and plunder the enemy.

When the news of the climactic American victory at Yorktown reached Baltimore in October 1781, a new era dawned for the town as the nation's independence was won.

In 1787 a Constitutional Convention met in Philadelphia to revise the weak Articles of Confederation; ultimately, an entirely new federal constitution was drafted. Ratification of the Constitution prompted a massive celebration in Baltimore, including a parade, one of the city's favorite pastimes, then as now. About 3,000 people marched to the foot of a large, grassy hill overlooking the harbor and held a giant barbeque there. Ever since, the site of that feast has been called Federal Hill.

During the 1790s Baltimore throbbed with building and bustle. Since colonial days Baltimore had been governed by commissioners appointed by the Maryland legislature in Annapolis. As the town grew, however, so did the movement for home rule. By 1793 the town's business leaders were lobbying for a charter that would make Baltimore a city, run by officials it elected. On the last day of 1796, Baltimore obtained its charter, which created a mayor, a bicameral (now unicameral) municipal council, and its own courts. Baltimore Town had grown up: Baltimore City was born.

For a newborn city, Baltimore exerted an extraordinary influence on the affairs of great European leaders in matters private as much as public. As famed for their sleekness and grace as Baltimore's clippers were its beautiful women. The city developed what one historian has called a "cult of beauty," and the term "Baltimore belle" entered the language as an exemplar of feminine charm. Incredibly, a duo of these lovely ladies, sisters-in-law by one marriage, would later become the sisters-in-law of the two chief military rivals of the age, Napoleon Bonaparte and the Duke of Wellington. The glory, real or imagined, of these ancillary links to European nobility was relished for more than a century by those Baltimore social arbiters who were inordinately fond of genealogy, titles, and the trappings of privilege. Yet the stories they

savored did have a dash of romance, albeit bittersweet.

In 1803 Prince Jerome Bonaparte, youngest brother of Emperor Napoleon I, visited Baltimore and was entranced—some say entrapped—by Betsy Patterson, daughter of William Patterson, a prosperous city merchant believed to be the second-wealthiest man in the United States, with a fortune surpassed only by that of a fellow Baltimorean, Charles Carroll. Despite objections by her father and French officials in this country, the two were married. When Napoleon found out about the match he was appalled and ordered his errant sibling home. The would-be Madame Bonaparte gave birth in London to a son she named Jerome Napoleon, but neither she nor her son were ever acknowledged by the French imperial family. She lived to be 94, an eccentric, embittered but financially shrewd crone who once remarked ruefully: "My ruling passions have been love, ambition, avarice. Love has fled, ambi-

Above: A wealthy merchant anxious to win American independence from Britain, Charles Carroll of Carrollton served as a delegate to the Continental Congress and was a signer of the Declaration of Independence. Courtesy, Maryland Historical Society

Right: Samuel Chase practiced law in Annapolis before helping to spark the American Revolution by signing the Declaration of Independence. Chase would eventually be appointed to the Supreme Court by President George Washington. Courtesy, Maryland Historical Society

tion has brought disappointment, but avarice remains."

A happier outcome awaited her former sister-in-law, Mary Caton Patterson, who had married Betsy's brother Robert. After his death in 1822 she visited England and there met and married the Marquess of Wellesley, elder brother of the Duke of Wellington, conqueror of Napoleon at the Battle of Waterloo.

Baltimore's boom continued as the nineteenth century began. During the century's first 10 years, the city's population doubled, surpassing Boston to become the nation's third-largest city, behind Philadelphia and New York.

At first the disruption of European trade caused by the on-again, off-again war between Great Britain and Napoleon's France meant greater profits for the port of Baltimore. But Baltimore and other American ports slowly saw themselves becoming pawns in the deadly game between British orders of council and Napoleonic decrees that imposed conflicting blockades. Eventually Baltimore would find itself the "swordpoint of the republic" in what some historians later called the Second American Revolution—the War of 1812.

In June 1812 President James Madison called on a bitterly divided Congress to declare war on Great Britain, which it did by narrow margins in the Senate and the House. Baltimore was as divided as the nation about the war. Brutal riots erupted between the various factions,

giving Baltimore the sobriquet that would haunt its future: "Mobtown."

Nevertheless, privateers from Baltimore, sharpening skills already well-honed during the Revolution, almost took over the fight for the tiny U.S. Navy, which British frigates outnumbered by roughly 1,000 to 17. During the three years of war, 126 privateers set sail from the city, harassing trade virtually to the shores of England and seizing or sinking more than 550 British ships, one-third of all the vessels captured during the war and half of those claimed by private American craft.

The British understandably took a dim view of Baltimore's exploits. They denounced the city as "a nest of pirates" and "the great depository of the hostile spirit of the United States against England." The war became, as one historian has put it, "Baltimore's own," and Baltimoreans of that time knew it.

Once the British had temporarily defeated Napoleon and packed

Above: Not only does the patriotic spirit of the War of 1812 live on at Fort McHenry, but the look of that era survives through military re-enactments such as this one. Photo by Greg Pease

Right: Respect for the American flag is something visitors to Fort McHenry must feel keenly because the national anthem was born here during the War of 1812. Photo by Jed Kirschbaum

him off to Elba, thousands of battle-tested English soldiers and sailors were shipped across the Atlantic to seek a swift, decisive victory even as an Anglo-American peace conference got under way in Ghent, Belgium, in August 1814. The British expected military triumphs and planned to force a humiliating peace on the U.S.

The British ships of Admiral Sir George Cockburn, the greatest invasion fleet ever to enter American waters, held sway over the Chesapeake Bay, and in late August 1814 British forces under Admiral Sir Alexander Cochrane sailed up the Patuxent River, landed at Benedict, Maryland, and headed for Washington with Major General Robert Ross at their head. On August 24, 1814, they burned the Capitol, the White House, and other public buildings. Baltimoreans, standing on their rooftops 40 miles away, could see the fire's glow on the horizon and knew they would be the next target. Major General Samuel Smith, a veteran of the Revolution, one of Baltimore's most prosperous merchants, and a popular political leader, took command of the irregular forces scrambling to defend the city.

Under Smith's forceful leadership, the derelict Fort McHenry at the mouth of Baltimore's harbor was repaired, and fortifications were dug around the city. More than 16,000 men, 90 percent of them amateur militia, awaited the British forces, the masters of Napoleon. Ross, told of Baltimore's preparations, scoffed at the ragtag defenders. He said he would capture Baltimore "even if it rained militia."

On September 12, British troops under Ross began going ashore on the west side of North Point, and an army of 4,700 crack troops prepared to advance on the city. Within 10 miles of Baltimore Ross stopped to have a late breakfast. When he was asked if he would return for dinner he reputedly replied: "I'll sup tonight in Baltimore or in hell." He set off on his conspicuous white charger to investigate the results of some initial skirmishes with the defenders. Within minutes he was shot through the chest and nearly knocked off his horse by blasts that were purportedly fired simultaneously from the rifles of two young militiamen, Daniel Wells and Henry McComas. Return fire from the British troops surrounding Ross snuffed out Wells and McComas' lives.

The ensuing battle of North Point raged for more than two hours. Untried American militiamen, under the command of General John

Stricker and outnumbered three to one, held their own against the battle-hardened British. The invaders were forced to turn to their naval power if they hoped to take the city.

On September 13, British warships began a relentless bombardment of Fort McHenry. It lasted all day and most of the night. The city literally shook when the heaviest barrage of rockets, bombs, and cannonfire battered the fort between about 1 a.m. and 4 a.m. on September 14.

Francis Scott Key, a Georgetown attorney, anxiously watched the bombardment while he stood on the deck of a truce boat about eight miles away. As dawn flickered through the fog and rain, he trained his small spyglass on Fort McHenry and was overjoyed to see that its mammoth, 30-by-42-foot flag, as he would write, was still there. In a high emotional mixture of relief and exultation, he hurriedly began to write a poem on the back of a sheet of letter-paper to express his thrill at the sight. Thus "The Star-Spangled Banner" was born. It was sung for the first time in Baltimore; soon it was heard around the country, and eventually it became the national anthem.

In Ghent, where word of Washington's burning stiffened the British negotiators' resolve, news of Baltimore's successful defense deflated the English position. The Treaty of Ghent, ending the war, was signed on Christmas Eve in 1814.

Baltimore emerged from the war brimming with confidence. Its leaders wanted the city to emulate the great historic and cultural centers of Europe, particularly in the creation of impressive edifices, such as the Roman Catholic Basilica of the Assumption, mother church of American Catholicism, and monuments that celebrated the city's glories. Chief among these were the Washington Monument, begun in 1815 on a lofty hill donated by John Eager Howard (who also had donated the land on which the cathedral was built), and the Battle Monument, also begun in 1815 on North Calvert Street. It is the first true war memorial erected in the U.S.

With both the Washington and Battle monuments to its credit, Baltimore was deemed worthy of a more dignified nickname than "Mobtown." No less a personage than President John Quincy Adams coined the one by which the city became widely known when at an 1827 banquet in Baltimore he offered the toast: "Baltimore, the Monumental City—may the days of her safety be as prosperous and happy as the days of her danger have been trying and triumphant."

A year later, on July 4, 1828, Adams turned the first ceremonial spade of earth to signal commencement of construction on the Chesapeake and Ohio (C&O) Canal near Georgetown—a potential rival to Baltimore's role as an outlet for trade to the west. On the same day, at practically the same moment, Baltimoreans—spurred to bold innovation by the C&O challenge—cheered as Charles Carroll, then 91 and the last surviving signer of the Declaration of Independence, also shoved a

Built in 1785, Otterbein Church is the oldest church in Baltimore. The bricks in its walls were previously used as ballast in the ships docked at the harbor just to the east. Photo by Greg Pease

spade in the ground to mark placement of the first stone (itself entirely ceremonial) of the Baltimore & Ohio (B&O) Railroad. This would be a completely new form of commercial transport that required not stones but long, sinewy rails and steam-powered locomotives.

It was a daring initiative, one that the venerable Carroll recognized as vital not only to his beloved city but to the nation he helped to found. He considered this act of his to be equal in importance to his signing of the Declaration of Independence.

Twenty-five years were to pass before the B&O's rails finally reached the Ohio River at Wheeling, but all during the course of that prolonged expansion, the railroad continually enhanced Baltimore's position as a major receiver and dispenser of raw materials, finished products, and people—including hundreds of thousands of European immigrants.

Even before the precedent-setting B&O ground-breaking, Baltimore had been the site of a number of notable experiments, innovations, and "firsts." On June 24, 1784, the first manned balloon ascension in the U.S. took place in town when Peter Carnes, a lawyer from Bladensburg, Maryland, filled a 30-foot-high, 35-foot-in-diameter balloon with heated gas and then, either because of excess girth or cold feet, chose not to go aloft in it as planned. Instead he sought a volunteer from the curious crowd, and Edward Warren, an intrepid 13-year-old Baltimore boy otherwise unknown to posterity, willingly went up with the tethered balloon and politely waved to the applauding onlookers below. On other technological fronts, painter and scientist Rembrandt Peale installed a gas lighting system in his Baltimore Museum in June 1816, making it the first public building in the U.S. to be illuminated in this manner. It prompted sufficient interest to warrant the granting of a franchise that month to the Gas Light Company of Baltimore, the first of its kind in the country, and installation the following year of the first gas streetlights in the world.

Over the years enthusiastic Baltimorephiles have enumerated more than 50 "firsts" for which the city is given credit. Some are of great significance, others amusingly trivial or entertainingly fanciful.

Spiritually and temporally Baltimore has played an important role in the nation's history. In addition to being the home of the nation's first Roman Catholic cathedral, it also claims the first black Catholic church; the founding church of American Methodism (the Lovely Lane Meeting House, 1784); the first Church of the United Brethren in Christ (the Otterbein Church, 1785); and the first congregation of Reform Judaism in the U.S. (Har Sinai, 1842). Lloyd Street Synagogue, the state's first Jewish house of worship, was dedicated in 1845 and is the third-oldest surviving synagogue in the country. The city can even claim a footnote in occult matters: Baltimore's Kennard Novelty Company introduced the Ouija board in 1890.

The American presidential nominating convention's birthplace was Baltimore. Ironically, the honor of holding the first of these conclaves did not belong to the forerunners of today's Democratic and Re-

publican parties but to a bizarre splinter group devoted to the abolition of the Masonic Order. On September 26, 1831, the Anti-Masonic Party called its convention to order in Baltimore's Athenaeum to nominate candidates for the presidency and vice presidency in the 1832 election. Not to be outdone, the National Republicans held their first convention in the Athenaeum's "splendid saloon" on December 12, 1831, nominating Henry Clay for president. And on May 21, 1832, the Democrats followed suit, also choosing the Athenaeum as the site of their first national convention, renominating President Andrew Jackson and choosing Martin Van Buren as his running mate.

In 1845 the nation's first horse-drawn omnibus lines began operation in Baltimore; in 1885 the first commercial electric streetcar line in the United States—and perhaps the world—was installed in the city. And a Baltimorean was not only the first American in the air with a gas-filled balloon but first under the water with a military submarine. Baltimore's harbor became the birthplace of the nation's military subs when two inventors, working independently, chose it in the 1890s as the place to demonstrate their machine-powered, underwater craft. Baltimorean Simon Lake had devised a vessel with a pressured hatch to prevent the bends and a pilot house that could hold between 10 and 15 passengers. Its first trial runs were made off Locust Point around 1898. About a year later rival inventor John P. Holland demonstrated a similar but more compact submarine in the harbor. Holland's craft was selected as the U.S. Navy's first submarine in 1900 and became the standard model for the British Navy, too. The Russian czar preferred the Lake model, which had made maritime history by taking to the open sea and cruising under its own power from Norfolk to New York harbor shortly after its Baltimore debut. The czar ordered six of them.

Baltimore was a pioneer in communications. On May 24, 1844, inventor Samuel F.B. Morse sent the first telegraph message—"What Hath God Wrought?"—from the Capitol building in Washington to Baltimore's old B&O Railroad station on West Pratt Street, and while *The Sun* was an early, enthusiastic employer of the new technology, the first telegraphic press report actually appeared in another Baltimore paper, the *Patriot*, on May 25, 1844—a one-line dispatch about the adjournment of a session of Congress.

Similarly, although in 1885 Baltimorean Ottmar Mergenthaler patented the Linotype, a machine for setting newspaper type automatically rather than by hand, Baltimore newspapers allowed the New York *Tribune* to become the first newspaper to use Mergenthaler's extraordinarily complicated but efficient machine in 1886. He had accu-

Facing: Union troops marching through Baltimore during the Civil War probably worried more about hostile Baltimoreans than about the Confederate armies massed elsewhere in Maryland. Although the state was officially on the Union side, Southern sympathy was strong in Baltimore. In fact, Union soldiers didn't just march through Baltimore; they occupied the city during the war. Courtesy, Enoch Pratt Free Library

rately, if a bit immodestly, declared the Linotype "the greatest advance in typesetting in the 400 years since Gutenberg," and soon every major newspaper, *The Sun* included, used it. *The Sun*'s evening sister (and fierce rival), *The Evening Sun*, was the first newspaper to employ another technological advance for news-gathering: On September 1, 1920, it hired a Curtiss biplane to help it score a scoop in the coverage of a train wreck at Back River.

Baltimoreans also are proud that their city can be given credit for doing much to make America's tummies happy and keep its heads dry, for it was in Baltimore that the nation's first ice cream factory was founded and where umbrellas—if not first made, as legend has it—certainly were mass-produced in mammoth numbers. The small-scale manufacturing of ice cream was common in Baltimore and elsewhere as early as the eighteenth century, but wholesale production of it began in the Baltimore milk dealership of Jacob Fussell in 1851. Baltimore claimed credit for popularizing umbrellas, originally imported from India by way of England in 1772, by launching this country's first umbrella-making business in 1828. Some scholars of business history contend that a number of umbrella makers were at work in Philadelphia as early as 1800, but that did not stop one major Baltimore-based umbrella manufacturer (perhaps by then the largest in the country) from proudly proclaiming that its specialty was "Born in Baltimore and Raised All Over the World."

The combination of a failed revolution in Germany and a potato famine in Ireland accounted for a flood of immigrants to Baltimore during the 1840s. In time the Germans became the largest immigrant population, numbering nearly a quarter of the city's population,

Above: The first deaths of the Civil War occurred in Baltimore on April 19, 1861, when local citizens rioted against the Massachusetts Sixth Regiment, which was passing through the city on its way to Washington, D.C. Courtesy, Maryland Historical Society

Facing: The Union soldiers stationed on Federal Hill pointed their cannons towards the city, thus ensuring that Baltimore's numerous Confederate sympathizers would behave themselves for the duration of the Civil War. Courtesy, Maryland Historical Society

supporting German-language newspapers and Germanophile societies. The Irish were the second-largest group.

Baltimore was not only a mecca for immigrants but a metropolis celebrated for its gracious hostelries and fabulous food. Charles Dickens considered Baltimore's Barnum's Hotel the "most comfortable of all the hotels . . . in the United States," and the treasures of the Chesapeake Bay—the crabs, oysters, clams, shad, terrapin, and other delicacies from beneath its water and the canvasback ducks that flew above it—caused Oliver Wendell Holmes, Sr., to proclaim Baltimore "the gastronomic metropolis of the Union" in 1859, an honor its citizens still endeavor to maintain.

On the eve of the Civil War, both Baltimore and Maryland were deeply divided, torn between their commercial links to the north and west and their emotional ties to the south. "Marylanders by and large wanted both to uphold Southern rights and to hold the Union together," historian Robert J. Brugger has written. It was an impossible balancing act, and events in early 1861 put Baltimore at the focal point of national division, earning it an unenviable "first" it would have preferred to avoid: the first bloodshed of the Civil War.

Slavery had been a part of Maryland's agricultural economy since the founding of the colony. Opposition to slavery and calls for its abolition were similarly long-standing in the state. A Baltimore chapter of the Maryland Society for Promoting the Abolition of Slavery was founded late in the eighteenth century, and one of the nation's most prominent early abolitionists, Benjamin Lundy, lived in Baltimore and published *The Genius of Universal Emancipation,* the county's only exclusively antislavery newspaper, in the city. Elisha Tyson, a wealthy Quaker merchant in Baltimore, was among the most prominent early abolitionists, and two of the antislavery movement's greatest black leaders, Harriet Tubman, commander of the Underground Railroad,

gotten wind of a plot to assassinate him.

Less than two months later, however, blood was shed in Baltimore when 1,200 members of the 6th Massachusetts Infantry, among the first to respond to Lincoln's call for troops, had to pass through the city on April 19, 1861, on their way to Washington. A mob of Southern sympathizers attacked the soldiers, assailing them with insults, cobblestones, and pistol shots. When the troops finally returned the fire, a full-scale riot erupted. Four soldiers and 12 Baltimoreans were killed.

Pro-Union Marylanders held a convention in the city to pledge the state's loyalty to the federal government, but Lincoln, fearing that Washington might be caught between Confederate Virginia to the south and a potentially secessionist Maryland to the north, clamped down. On May 13, federal troops under Massachusetts General

and Frederick Douglass, born a slave on Maryland's Eastern Shore but taught to read and write in Baltimore, had ties to the city. By 1860 Maryland was home to more free blacks—84,000—than any other state, with some 25,000 of them living in Baltimore, the most of any city in the Union. It was, according to one historian, the "black capital" of nineteenth-century America.

A substantial majority of Marylanders and Baltimoreans opposed the concept of secession, but many were equally reluctant to use force against the South to preserve the Union. Tension mounted in early 1861. President-elect Abraham Lincoln, on his way from Illinois to Washington to take the presidential oath, had to travel incognito through Baltimore, where detective Allan Pinkerton claimed to have

Benjamin F. Butler occupied Federal Hill and aimed its guns at downtown Baltimore—purportedly putting both the Washington Monument and the elite Maryland Club in their sights. Other federal forces later encamped elsewhere in town, barricades were erected, and for the remainder of the war, Baltimore was an occupied city. A Marylander living in Louisiana, James Ryder Randall, wrote an impassioned poem, "My Maryland," decrying the "gore that fleck'd the streets of Baltimore" in the April riots. The lines were set to the German carol "O, Tannenbaum" and popularized as a suitable song for the Confederacy. It remains Maryland's official anthem.

Baltimoreans fought on both sides of the Civil War, and the dual legacy was preserved by monuments erected in the city to both Union

and Confederate veterans. While some prominent Baltimoreans of the Civil War era were decidedly pro-South, others were staunchly for the Union. Among these were some of the city's most successful businessmen: George Peabody, Johns Hopkins, and Enoch Pratt. After the Civil War ended in 1865, they launched what historian Sherry Olson has called "a magnificent era for Baltimore in private philanthropy." The benefits derived from the generosity of these men were realized not just locally but nationally and internationally. They spread Baltimore's name around the globe as swiftly, surely, and positively as the clippers of an earlier generation.

Peabody, a Massachusetts-born merchant, arrived in Baltimore in 1814 and during the next 20 years amassed his first million in the city before moving to London to multiply his fortune manyfold. Always grateful to Baltimore for his early success, he gave $1.5 million to the city to establish the Peabody Library and Conservatory of Music, which opened in elegant buildings he had erected on Mount Vernon Place between 1866 and 1878.

The example Peabody set impressed his good friend Johns Hopkins, a savvy, Maryland-born Quaker businessman whom Peabody had once said was the only man he ever knew more interested than himself in earning money. And Hopkins earned a lot of it, first as a wholesale dealer in commodities, then as a financier and one of the early

Top: This early twentieth-century view of the Peabody Institute shows how firmly it anchors Mount Vernon Place. The seated gent in the statue at the center of the picture is George Peabody. Peabody, a nineteenth-century mercantile prince, left a lasting cultural and educational legacy in Baltimore. He donated money in 1857 to establish the music conservatory that today remains dedicated to its musical mission. Courtesy, Maryland Historical Society

Right: The Homewood campus of The Johns Hopkins University has grown since this early twentieth-century view featuring jalopies cruising along a campus drive. But its Georgian-style architectural profile and woodsy setting remain largely unchanged. Merchant Johns Hopkins, who died in 1873, left his considerable fortune to found a university and hospital bearing his name. Today these institutions remain vital to the life of the city. Courtesy, Enoch Pratt Free Library, Maryland Historical Society (inset)

investors in the B&O Railroad. By 1867 Hopkins, a bachelor whose own formal education ended when he was 12, had decided to leave the bulk of his vast estate—some $7 million—for the creation of a university and hospital to bear his name. Hopkins died in 1873 and did not see his institutions flower, but his university, which opened in 1876, was the first true European-style university in this country; and his hospital, which opened in 1889, and medical school, which opened in 1893, profoundly affected medical education and health care in this country and overseas—from the time of their inception to the present.

Enoch Pratt, another Massachusetts native, was a merchant and banker who became one of the nation's leading hardware dealers. He also was one of the city's most civic-minded citizens. Serving as treasurer of the Peabody Trust, Pratt recognized that Baltimore needed more than the Peabody Library, magnificent as it was. He set about to correct this deficiency by donating some $833,000 in city bonds towards construction of an enormous free library bearing his name. When it opened in 1886, Pratt's library already had 28,000 books.

Following the Civil War Baltimore became the financial, clothing, and canning capital of the South, and in some cases of the nation. It supplied more canned produce and oysters—as well as manufactured more straw hats—than any other city. By the end of the nineteenth century, Baltimoreans had invested $100 million in rebuilding the battered South.

Symbolic of Baltimore's resurgence was its magnificent new city hall, a massive Victorian masterpiece, topped by a huge cast-iron dome. It was designed by George Frederick and completed in 1875 for $2,271,000—an astonishing $228,865 under budget.

Beneath this dome flourished a burgeoning city. Between 1868 and 1900 some 600,000 immigrants arrived in Baltimore harbor, disembarking at a Locust Point terminal maintained by the B&O Railroad, under an arrangement with the North German Lloyd Line. A significant Polish community began to develop in East Baltimore after 1870, and from about 1880 an Italian enclave that had begun around 1840 near the President Street station of the Philadelphia, Wilmington and Baltimore Railroad began to grow into a distinct Little Italy. Russian Jews, escaping persecution, also began to arrive in large

numbers. Many in the established Jewish community were distressed by the problems of these new immigrants and tried to alleviate them. Among the leaders of this effort was Henrietta Szold, daughter of Rabbi Benjamin Szold, who led the Oheb Shalom congregation for 34 years. She organized the Russian Hebrew Literary Society and a Russian night school, perhaps the nation's first such immigrant night school. In 1893 she was among the organizers of the Zionist Society of Baltimore, perhaps the first such organization in the U.S., and later, after she had moved to New York, she was the chief founder of Hadassah, the great Jewish welfare organization. (She subsequently moved to Palestine and became a leader of the World Zionist Organization; by

15,000 buildings and 2,500 businesses were gutted or completely burned down. The total damage estimate came to $150 million. The entire clothing manufacturing center was destroyed; 20 banks were burned out; the major portion of the produce and wholesale business area was gone; wharfs from Light Street to the Jones Falls were ruined. Eight hotels, nine newspapers—including *The Sun*'s famous Iron Building—and nine transportation businesses, among them the B&O Railroad's headquarters, were reduced to rubble.

It began innocently enough on a quiet, cold, blustery Sunday morning—February 7, 1904. At 10:48 a.m. an automatic fire alarm sounded at the six-story brick building housing the dry goods firm of

the time of her death at 84 in 1945, she was possibly the best-known Baltimore-born Jew.)

As Baltimore's ethnic areas took shape, older and more prosperous Baltimoreans began expanding the city's residential boundaries. Suburbs sprouted. Baltimore had always been a city composed of identifiable parts, but by the 1890s it had become "a confederation of neighborhoods," as historian Robert Brugger has put it, a jigsaw puzzle of communities where families tended to remain for generations.

Baltimore entered the twentieth century on a Progressive tide. A city service group, the Municipal Art Society (founded in 1899), endeavored to make the concept of comprehensive planning work in a city that had hitherto shown initiative and daring only in times of crisis. Ironically the comprehensive planning movement was gaining momentum when fate—and the kind of crisis to which Baltimore had always responded well—forced the concept over the line from theory to reality. The Great Baltimore Fire of 1904 wiped out the heart of the city.

The fire's statistics were awesome: Nearly 140 acres of prime downtown real estate, more than 70 blocks, were laid waste. More than

John E. Hurst and Co., located at Hopkins Place and German (now Redwood) Street.

Two alarms, then three, were sounded in rapid succession, as the fire spread quickly to the west and south, while winds from the southeast carried it to the northwest. The wind helped the blaze to play tricks on the embattled fire fighters, spreading the flames erratically. Dynamite was used in a futile effort to block the fire's progress. Forty miles to the south, Washingtonians could see the fire's glow flickering eerily on the horizon.

The fire finally was contained, and by 5 p.m. Monday it was under control. The rubble of what had been Baltimore's center continued to smolder for days. Miraculously, no one was killed, and only a few were left homeless.

Although offers of financial aid began pouring in, Baltimore declined them with thanks and vowed to rebuild on its own. Even as the fire's flames still sputtered, the *Baltimore News* proclaimed: "To suppose that the spirit of our people will not rise to the occasion is to suppose that our people are not genuine Americans. We shall make the fire of 1904 a landmark not of decline but of progress." So it

proved to be.

The Progressive tide in Baltimore and the nation crested at the 1912 Democratic National Convention, held in the city's Fifth Regiment Armory, where Woodrow Wilson's cause was championed by Charles H. Grasty, the crusading editor of *The Sun*. Grasty had long admired Wilson, a Johns Hopkins-trained Ph.D., and even offered him the editorship of *The Sun* in 1910, just after the future U.S. president had resigned the presidency of Princeton University. Wilson instead went into politics and was elected New Jersey's governor, and Grasty became determined to boost his presidential candidacy.

When the convention at Baltimore's bunting-festooned but sweltering armory bogged down in a stalemate between the forces of Wilson and a half-dozen other contenders, *The Sun* maintained a steady barrage of stories extolling Wilson's virtues. At last triumphant after 46 enervating ballots, Wilson gratefully telegraphed Grasty: "I want you to know how warmly and deeply I have appreciated the splendid support of *The Sun*."

Above: The daughter of a Baltimore rabbi, Henrietta Szold helped Jewish immigrants adjust to life in America by forming educational organizations for them. After she moved from Baltimore to New York, she became the chief founder of Hadassah, the Jewish welfare organization. She is depicted here in a painting by William Wachtel. Courtesy, Enoch Pratt Free Library

Facing: What Ellis Island was to New York City, Locust Point was to Baltimore. This immigrant pen at Locust Point was the first impression of America for many coming here at the turn of the century. Thousands arrived at the terminal, with many boarding trains for the Midwest and others remaining in Baltimore to form ethnic enclaves that still exist. Courtesy, Peale Museum

late May 55,000 Baltimoreans of military age had signed up for the Army draft. By war's end 16,000 Baltimoreans were in the military, with the 115th Infantry Division and 313th Infantry Division ("Baltimore's Own") fighting under General John J. Pershing in France.

Baltimore's unique location—100 miles west of the eastern seaboard and therefore relatively safe from submarines—left it "protected yet accessible," as one historian put it. Once again it was a vital military base, close to Europe by sea and to the midwest by rail.

World War I transformed Baltimore into a modern industrial center, according to historian Sherry Olson. Commercially Baltimore was again the chief emporium of the South. Its size had also tripled. In 1918 the city annexed 62 surrounding square miles in Anne Arundel and Baltimore counties, extending its area from 30 to 92 square miles in one fell swoop. And most of the newly acquired land was undeveloped. By the mid-1920s housing construction

Baltimore's reign as the king of national political convention cities may have ended with the 1912 Democratic blowout, but its role as a pivotal center for manufacturing and defense was highlighted once again in 1914, when war erupted in Europe.

Officially the United States was neutral during the first two-and-a-half years of the war, which had broken out in August 1914. With its large German population, however, Baltimore was torn. Other ethnic groups also had loyalties elsewhere and laid claim to the city's heart, while many of the city's social and business leaders were Anglophiles and supported the British.

As the U.S. inched toward participation in the war, Baltimore's strategic location as a center for steel-making and shipbuilding became increasingly important. Once the U.S. entered the war in April 1917, Baltimore exerted every effort to prove its patriotism. Within a month 3,000 Marylanders enlisted in the Navy, Baltimore clothiers began mass-producing military uniforms (as they had for the Civil War and Spanish-American War), factories worked around the clock, and by

reached a peak of 6,000 new homes a year, twice the previous record. The "suburban" building boom led to an exodus of the city's social elite from their traditional Mount Vernon Place and Bolton Hill townhouses, with many moving to the new developments of Roland Park, Guilford, University Parkway, and Homeland—or farther out to the Greenspring, Worthington, and Dulaney valleys.

Always renowned for its gracious hospitality, Baltimore now acquired an additional allurement as an acknowledged oasis in the desert of national prohibition. "Baltimoreans were solidly in favor of prohibition everywhere except Baltimore," as one historian put it. Neither the mayor of the city nor the newly elected (and often re-elected) governor of Maryland, Albert C. Ritchie, would authorize local enforcement of the federal Volstead Act, the law designed to give teeth to the constitution's 18th-Amendment ban on alcoholic beverages. *The Evening Sun* began referring to its home as "The Maryland Free State," a nickname still proudly employed, and Maryland claimed to be the wettest state in the Union during the parched period of the "noble experiment."

A scourge of Prohibition's folly—and indeed, of all idiocies, pomposity, and the "Booboisie" —was Henry Louis Mencken, Baltimore's most famous resident of the period and "the master craftsman of daily journalism in the twentieth century," in the view of his protégé and friend, Alistair Cooke.

Mencken, born in Baltimore in 1880 and occupant of the same unpretentious rowhouse on Hollins Street for most of his life, remained in and of the city despite attaining "the most fabulous fame in American journalistic history," as Cooke put it. Mencken felt that Baltimore's greatest attraction was that it was *not* New York, a city to which he commuted regularly as co-editor (with George Jean Nathan) of *The Smart Set* and of *The American Mercury*. He liked nothing better than to return to Baltimore and believed that if "the true purpose of living is to be born in comfort, to live happily and to die at peace, the average Baltimorean is infinitely better off than the average New Yorker."

The onset of the Great Depression following the stock market crash of October 1929 marked the end of Mencken's ascendancy, as well as of Baltimore's prosperity. Alistair Cooke observed—his keen eye for analysis undimmed by his affection for Mencken—that "the New Deal was Mencken's Waterloo and Roosevelt his Wellington." Mencken's orotund shellackings of politicians, government, and materialism rang hollow when millions were unemployed, destitute, and in need of government help.

The Depression's toll was especially grim in Baltimore, but the "alphabet soup" agencies of the New Deal made significant contributions to the city's development during the 1930s. With Johns Hopkins University Professor Abel Wolman, the world's foremost sanitary engineer, as its director, the Maryland branch of the federal Public Works Administration (PWA) spent millions to expand and enhance Baltimore's water supply system, building the Prettyboy Reservoir, among other projects. A new main branch of the Enoch Pratt Free Library was built.

Among the few bright spots for the city during the Depression era were two widely disparate events that paradoxically had a common theme: Baltimore's triumph over Great Britain—first on the field of battle and then in affairs of the heart. In 1931, after a lengthy, tireless lobbying effort by the tiny but formidable Mrs. Reuben Ross Holloway of Baltimore, Congress at last enacted legislation proclaiming "The Star-Spangled Banner" to be the official national anthem. Then five years later a Baltimore belle succeeded (perhaps against her wishes) where Betsy Patterson had failed; this time a reigning monarch relinquished the crown rather than give up his love. On December 10, 1936, England's King Edward VIII shocked the British Empire by renouncing his throne because he "found it impossible to carry the heavy burden of responsibility and to discharge my duties as King, as I wish to do, without the help and support of the woman I love . . .," the twice-divorced Bessie Wallis Warfield Simpson of Baltimore. He became just the Duke of Windsor, and she became his Duchess. They would make several trips to her old hometown, which

always gave them a royal welcome. (For a brief time her old rowhouse on East Biddle Street was a minor tourist attraction, where visitors were invited to pay a small fee to sit in what had once been the future Duchess' bathtub.)

The September 1939 outbreak of World War II in Europe mobilized Baltimore's industries, just as wars had done for generations. Long before the United States entered the war, it became, in President Franklin D. Roosevelt's phrase, the "arsenal of democracy," and Baltimore once more served as one of that arsenal's primary forges. The city's steel, copper, machinery, shipbuilding, and aircraft companies surged ahead with work orders, and employment swelled as the demand for goods increased.

Once the Japanese attack on Pearl Harbor brought the United States into the war on December 7, 1941, Baltimore's war machine, already humming, went into high gear. The steel, shipbuilding, aircraft, and transportation industries performed especially heroic deeds. According to historian Robert J. Brugger, the B&O Railroad handled nearly 3.8 million cars of freight during a single war year, equivalent to one car every nine seconds, day and night; Bethlehem Steel produced nearly 20 million tons of steel; and the ship-workers at the Bethlehem-Fairchild shipbuilding operations in Sparrows Point, Fairfield, and Locust Point exerted superhuman efforts, working around the clock, seven days a week to reduce the time it took to build a Liberty ship from 244 to 30 days. By war's end the city's 47,000 ship-workers had manufactured 384 Liberty ships, as well as 94 Victory ships and 30 LSTs (the "landing ship, tanks" used in the Normandy invasion and other amphibious assaults). The Glenn L. Martin Company transformed its celebrated, pre-war China Clippers into the Navy's twin-engine PBM patrol bombers, building more than 1,300 of them during the war. It also built the huge Martin Mars, at 77 tons the largest flying boat constructed in the U.S. These craft ferried enormous amounts of cargo across the Pacific. At Johns Hopkins' Applied Physics Laboratory in Silver Spring, near Washington, scientists invented the proximity fuse for "smart bombs," employing a small radio to detect the closeness of targets.

On European battlefields Baltimoreans and Marylanders joined Virginians in the fabled 29th Division, the first American troops to hit the code-named Omaha Beach on the Normandy coast on D-Day, June 6, 1944. The 29th Division ultimately suffered casualties totaling about 7,000 men killed or wounded, but Hitler's Fortress Europa had been breached, and victory in Europe was assured.

In the Pacific, Baltimore-born Admiral Raymond A. Spruance had overall command of the ships and Marines who sustained heavy losses in the furious February 1945 battle for the island of Iwo Jima. In August Army Air Corps Lieutenant Jacob Beser of Baltimore, a radar specialist trained to fly aboard the latest American bombers, the B-29s, went on two epochal missions: one to Hiroshima and a second to Nagasaki, where the aircraft he was on dropped atomic bombs that obliterated both cities and brought the war to an end.

Baltimore emerged from World War II as an "aging matron" of a city, in historian Robert Brugger's phrase; its war-bloated industries threatening to sag with postwar decompression; its work-worn downtown and harbor—unimproved since before the Depression—needing a facelift; its decaying, inner-city housing an acknowledged disgrace.

The task was overwhelming, but Mayor Thomas J. D'Alesandro, Jr., elected in 1947, was determined to find ways to solve the city's intractable housing woes. That summer a new Baltimore housing court—the nation's first—began cracking down on violations of Baltimore's new housing code. What became known as the "Baltimore Plan," and the city's methods for implementing it, received nationwide publicity—and acclaim. The Citizens' Planning and Housing Association (CPHA), founded in 1941, blossomed. In 1946 it had 800 members; by 1951 the membership had more than doubled, reaching 1,700. Business leaders, housing officials, and average citizens all became part of the group effort to improve Baltimore's housing.

In 1955, 83 business and professional leaders, seeing the need for an intensified, coordinated attack on Baltimore's problems—commercial as well as residential—formed the Greater Baltimore Committee (GBC) to wage the fight for the city's renewal, to battle what one GBC leader called Baltimore's "colossal inferiority complex."

The GBC had a vision that extended beyond housing, as vital as that is. It pushed for improved transportation within and around the city; a civic center, originally proposed by Mayor Theodore R. McKeldin, for conventions, sports, and entertainment events; creation of new industrial districts; and revitalization of the port through a new Maryland Port Authority, created in 1956 at the behest of the GBC and others.

In what Brugger called "a turning point in Baltimore architecture and attitudes," the GBC's planning council and representatives of another civic group, the Committee for Downtown, met with Mayor D'Alesandro in March 1958 and presented him with a plan for a nearly complete re-creation of a 33-acre area in the heart of Baltimore's downtown: Charles Center. A reporter for *The Evening Sun*, Colin MacLachlan, wrote that the plan, if implemented, would bring about a "dramatic renaissance" for Baltimore—and the word "renaissance" stuck. Twenty-three years and almost $2 billion later, Scott Duncan, another *Evening Sun* reporter, would write that from the paper's yellowing clips to a glossy *Time* magazine cover piece, "Baltimore's downtown 'renaissance' is arguably the city's proudest success story."

As historian Sherry Olson has noted, Baltimore was a "strategic place" in the civil rights movement, a segregated city south of the Mason-Dixon line that seemed receptive to change, albeit gradual. In September 1952, two years before the U.S. Supreme Court's ruling that outlawed racial segregation in schools, the Baltimore City School Board voted to allow 12 black students to enroll in the city's Polytechnic Institute, an elite vocational high school, ending segregation there and paving the way for its elimination through the school system. In May 1954 Baltimore-born attorney Thurgood Marshall (later the first black appointed to the Supreme Court) successfully argued for an end to all segregated public schools in the landmark Supreme Court case, *Brown v. Board of Education of Topeka*. Baltimorean Clarence Mitchell, Jr., chief Washington lobbyist for the National Association for the Advancement of Colored People (NAACP), was in the forefront of the civil rights movement through the administrations of eight U.S. presidents. His gentle but firm manner and powerful persuasiveness were instrumental in winning passage of the federal Civil Rights Acts of 1957, 1960, 1964, and 1965. He also helped bring about passage of the 1965 Voting Rights Act and the Civil Rights and Fair Housing Acts of 1968.

Yet the grim ghost of "Mobtown," Baltimore's nineteenth-century alter ego, reappeared in April 1968 when the city—along with Washington, Chicago, Detroit, and Los Angeles—burst into rioting following the assassination of Dr. Martin Luther King, Jr.

Much soul-searching—in both the white and black communities—followed the riots, but so did a renewed determination to improve Baltimore for all its citizens. The effort to rebuild the downtown, particularly the Inner Harbor, proceeded under Mayor Thomas D'Alesandro III—"young Tommy." The Baltimore Urban Renewal and Housing Authority, led by Robert C. Embry (later a federal housing official under President Jimmy Carter and now president of the A.S. Abell Foundation), encouraged citizen participation in the planning and implementation of a broad range of renewal projects. Among the innovations was the first Baltimore City Fair, held in September 1970. It brought an estimated 300,000 people of all races and cultural backgrounds to Charles Center and the Inner Harbor for an entire weekend to view community exhibits, savor ethnic foods, enjoy carnival rides, and generally revel in their diversity. It continues to be a September tradition.

In 1971 the city embarked on its most remarkable modern era with the election of then-city council president William Donald Schaefer as mayor—"the best mayor in the United States," in the view of *Esquire* magazine. Under the leadership of the dynamic, imaginative, tireless—and acerbic—Schaefer (newspaperman and historian Carleton Jones aptly called him "flappable but indestructible"), Baltimore became, in *Newsweek*'s words, "a model of urban revitalization."

Above: Baltimoreans have always loved a parade, and the First World War gave them plenty of opportunities to fly the colors. The soldiers in this parade along Mount Royal Avenue step lively past the reviewing stand. Courtesy, Maryland Historical Society

Facing: Journalist H.L. Mencken shocked and delighted readers with his columns in the *Baltimore Evening Sun* and with his many books. A scholar of the American language and one of the most important opinion-makers of the 1920s, Mencken loved the good life in his hometown and in turn enjoyed celebrating the repeal of Prohibition with friends. Courtesy, Maryland Historical Society

The foundation of Baltimore's renaissance had been prepared by several of Schaefer's predecessors, but once he became mayor, Schaefer not only built on what his predecessors had initiated but shifted the city's redevelopment efforts into high gear, becoming an exponent extraordinaire of Baltimore's revival and garnering national—even international—attention for the city's innovative urban homesteading

program, accelerated Inner Harbor revitalization, multifaceted charms, and spirited rebirth.

The homesteading program, announced in September 1973, offered dilapidated, city-owned houses to enterprising buyers for one dollar, provided they agreed to rehabilitate them within six months and live in them for another year-and-a-half. Over the next five years more than 500 homesteaders breathed new life into once-moribund city neighborhoods. Despite the inherent challenges and difficulties in erasing years of neglect and decay, century-old homes in the Otterbein neighborhood, on Stirling Street, Barre Circle, Washington Hill, Ridgely's Delight, and Reservoir Hill were turned into beacons of Baltimore's vitality. Other cities adopted similar programs, but in no other city did they achieve such success. In 1979 the American Institute of Architects gave Baltimore an award for its comprehensive city planning.

The pace of redevelopment around the city's Inner Harbor gained unprecedented momentum under Schaefer. New ethnic festivals and entertainment events drew enthusiastic crowds to the waterfront. New office buildings, hotels, retail centers, and recreational facilities sprouted each year. In June 1976 the $10-million, four-story Maryland Science Center, designed by famed architect Edward Durrell Stone, became the permanent home of the oldest scientific institution in the city, the Maryland Academy of Sciences, founded in 1797. With its Davis Planetarium, scientific exhibitions, educational programs, and state-of-the-art IMAX theater, featuring a 75-foot-wide screen and 38-speaker sound system, it draws thousands of visitors weekly. In July 1976 eight of the glorious "tall ships" from foreign lands, in American waters to celebrate the bicentennial of U.S. independence, glided into Baltimore's harbor, luring more than one million visitors downtown to see them. In February 1977 the city launched its own graceful sailing vessel and international ambassador, the $476,000, 90-foot *Pride of Baltimore*, a meticulous

replica of Baltimore's vaunted clipper ships of a century before. A month later ground was broken for the National Aquarium, judged the world's best when it opened in 1981. In September 1977 the Maryland Port Authority broke ground for its 28-story, pentagon-shaped World Trade Center, designed by I.M. Pei. In 1978 city voters OK'd creation of Harborplace, a 3.1-acre, $22-million complex of shops, restaurants, and food stalls that was a stunning success the moment it opened in July 1980. It became the dazzling centerpiece of an Inner Harbor that the American Institute

surrounding the Hyatt, to the quaint Admiral Fell Inn in Fells Point, to The Inn at the Colonnade that opened in 1990 opposite the Johns Hopkins campus, 15 minutes north of the harbor. And of the city's 25 largest office buildings, nine were built between 1980 and 1988.

The Inner Harbor became the "linchpin," as one economic reporter put it, of Baltimore's $625-million tourist industry. Baltimore was no longer, as Schaefer once groused, an unknown city between New York and Washington; it had become a city to which busloads of tourists from Washington, New York—and elsewhere—came in growing numbers.

Above: Victory in 1945 brought the servicemen home and resulted in many hug-filled reunions like this one on a pier in Canton. Courtesy, Baltimore Sunpapers

Facing: Internationally acclaimed architect I.M. Pei designed the World Trade Center, which has an ideal harborside location. A public observation level on the 27th floor of this five-sided building provides a sweeping view of the Inner Harbor. Photo by Lonnie Timmons III

Following page: The houses along Stirling Street in East Baltimore date back to the 1830s. Like much of the housing stock in the inner city, they fell into disrepair in the mid-twentieth century. Today, these same homes look as good as new thanks to the 1973 homesteading program which offered dilapidated houses to enterprising buyers for one dollar. Photo by Greg Pease

of Architects called "one of the supreme achievements of large-scale urban design and development in U.S. history . . . a masterpiece of planning and execution that took a ramshackle, rat-infested, crumbling old dock and transformed it into one of the most beautiful, humane, diverse center-city places in the world." In August 1979 the new Baltimore Convention Center opened, with 110,000 square feet of exhibition space and 45,000 square feet of meeting room space. In 1980 the 13-story, 500-room Hyatt Regency Hotel opened, achieving an incredible 92.3 percent occupancy rate in its first year, the second-highest in the Hyatt company's worldwide chain. Within the next decade nearly a dozen new hotels would open in and around downtown, from the Stouffer, Sheraton, and Harbor Court hotels

Schaefer was elected governor of Maryland in 1986, and Baltimore—a majority-black city since 1970—got its first black mayor when city council president Clarence "Du" Burns succeeded him. It was an appropriate achievement for the dedicated, longtime toiler in the city's political vineyards who had risen to such prominence from a post, held years earlier, as a locker-room attendant at Dunbar High School. In the 1987 Democratic primary Burns ran a close race against State's Attorney Kurt L. Schmoke, an Ivy League-educated Rhodes scholar who eked out a narrow primary victory and went on to become Baltimore's first elected black mayor.

Mayor Schmoke and the city's business leaders are determined to continue Baltimore's forward movement, not just in the downtown area but throughout the city and the metropolitan region. Robert Keller, executive director of the Greater Baltimore Committee, has said that the city is in "a different ball game now . . . In the same way our predecessors invested in the downtown, we have to invest in the area's infrastructure." The GBC, now comprised of 2,000 member firms, has redirected much of its promotional efforts toward solving local problems, as well as touting the Baltimore metropolitan area nationally. The GBC sees Baltimore's renaissance serving as "the cornerstone for continued growth, not only in Baltimore City but also in the five surrounding counties," according to a committee official.

"Commerce," a Baltimorean of 1820 wrote, "is the mainspring of this city," but as a civic leader of 1904 observed: ". . . a city will be great or small in direct ratio to the greatness or smallness . . . of its people." Since its people remain great, Baltimore remains, as historian Sherry Olson wrote, "a model of political economy and a mirror of the human condition."

A TOUR OF THE TOWN

▪ ▪ ▪

Proudly illuminated at night, the Washington Monument serves as a
beacon in Mount Vernon Square. Completed in 1829, this marble
column topped by a statue of the father of our country has long
been one of the city's identifying landmarks. Photo by Greg Pease

n 1893 a reporter for the London *Daily Chronicle* wrote of his visit to Baltimore's placid, already venerable Mount Vernon Square neighborhood: "You feel that it is always afternoon here, and are grateful that so quiet a city is to be found in the same country which contains New York and Chicago."

What this English visitor of nearly a century ago sensed about one Baltimore neighborhood is an atmosphere the city still radiates and relishes: a compactness, a village-like congeniality that prompted a writer for *National Geographic* to observe early in 1989, "Baltimore has . . . the appeal of *Our Town* in a big city."

Just as *Our Town* had its individual streets and houses, Baltimore has its distinct neighborhoods, each proud of the special qualities that give it spice and add to the flavorfulness of the city at large. Some retain the ambience of their colonial beginnings; others have the aspect of quaint rural villages or elegant suburbs; still others reflect the grittiness—and enduring toughness—of the inner city.

Many of the city's neighborhoods feature the long, undulating rows of brick townhouses with their ubiquitous white marble steps, which enthralled even so finicky a travel writer as Mrs. Frances Trollope, mother of the famed Victorian novelist. She wrote of her 1828 visit to Baltimore: ". . . even the private dwelling houses have a look of magnificence from the abundance of white marble with which many of them are adorned." And within those homes, another travel writer wrote nearly 150 years later, can be found the "dialects and customs, names and faces of Italy, Russia, Greece, Poland . . ., the food of Germany, the wit of Ireland, the vitality of Africa." Each summer more than a dozen ethnic festivals celebrate the city's diversity; not just its Italians, Greeks, Poles, Jewish-Americans, Irish, and African-Americans, but its Lithuanians, Hispanics, Ukranians, Koreans, Caribbean and West Indian natives, emigrants from India, and American Indians.

In December 1980 a city hall exhibition of artwork from various communities was titled "A Patchwork Quilt of Neighborhoods." The metaphor remains appropriate: a patchwork quilt of colorful residential areas providing warmth and friendliness to their inhabitants. "One of the most appealing aspects of living in Baltimore is that neighborhoods matter to people here," wrote Rob Kasper, a native of Dodge City, Kansas, who now is *The Sun*'s witty and piquant food writer. "When you meet at social gatherings in other cities, the first thing they want to know is what you do for a living. In Baltimore, people want to know where you live. And if your answer is 'in the neighborhood,' a bond is formed . . ."

In the names of Baltimore's neighborhoods echo the titles of vanished colonial estates, a roll call of long-dead city fathers, a barbecue held more than two centuries ago, and, in one case, a gentle, devout woman who became the first American-born saint.

As Baltimore grew, communities sprouted whose names were often the creation of real estate developers. They plumbed the depths of an area's history in order to find an appellation with a suitably obscure lineage likely to appeal to Baltimore's taste for anything new that bears a

touch of the old. To the residents of specific areas 25 or 30 years ago, these neighborhood names may have been familiar; to Baltimoreans from other parts of the city, however, they often were arcane. John Goodspeed, a veteran Baltimore newspaperman and critic, once confessed in an article for *Baltimore Magazine* that a recent list of more than 800 metropolitan neighborhoods left him baffled—and astonished. As an *Evening Sun* reporter and columnist for 18 years, he regularly patrolled the city, but this new list contained more than 100 neighborhoods he couldn't recall and at least 20 he had never heard of.

That is because in the "pre-renaissance" days when Goodspeed was a streetwise reporter, he and the police and cab drivers who knew the city intimately and made their living traveling its byways were prone, with two dozen or so exceptions, to apply simple geographic designations to its neighborhoods. An area was either in East Baltimore, South Baltimore, or West Baltimore—or situated near a major thoroughfare—Broadway, Pennsylvania Avenue, Mount Royal, Park Heights, or whatever.

Now such geographic and street-based nomenclature, while still accurate (if occasionally imprecise), is insufficiently specific for a city that prizes more than ever the bright patches in its quilt. This has become especially so since Baltimore's renaissance flowered and pride-of-place blossomed as never before. The city's department of planning currently recognizes more than 270 organized neighborhood associations.

Baltimore began, as did the United States, in what is now its south and east. In the south, at the foot of the harbor, the mill owners, merchants, shipbuilders, and sailors settled in colonial times; later, to the east, new European immigrants sought refuge. "They came from the old world seeking the promise of the new one," writes Dan Rodricks, an *Evening Sun* columnist and feature reporter for WBAL-TV. "They turned from poverty and persecution, hoping to find a better life. Jews, Italians and blacks from America's rural South, they came to East Baltimore, settled in neighborhoods near the city's harbor; they hoped for answers to their prayers; they dared America to live up to its promise."

In 1730, the year after Baltimore's founding, William Fell, an immigrant from Lancashire, England, built a small shipyard in the southeastern corner of Baltimore's harbor, taking advantage of the deeper channel there. In 1773 his son, Edward Fell, laid out the town of Fells Point (sometimes spelled "Fell's Point," with an appropriately possessive apostrophe). Fells Point soon became a major shipbuilding center. It was the birthplace of the legendary Baltimore clippers and the first two ships in the U.S. Navy, the *Hornet* and the *Wasp*. Prosperous shipowners and captains built themselves two-and-one-half-story brick rowhouses in Fells Point, and to serve their needs, the Fells Point (now Broadway) Market was built on land donated by another William Fell, grandson of the neighborhood's founder. It was the first of the network of city neighborhood markets, all redolent with the feel and taste of Baltimore.

The most successful privateering ships of the war of 1812 were built in Fells Point, but the area's first boom ended once the guns of war went silent and yellow fever, inflation, and a glut of clipper ships spelled depression for the neighborhood. Nearly 20 years went by before good times returned to Fells Point. Prosperity was heralded in 1833 with the launching of the *Ann McKim*, prototype of a new generation of larger clipper ships that won international fame for America's merchant marine.

When steam-powered vessels supplanted sailing ships toward the end of the nineteenth century, the shipyards in Fells Point faded away with the wind. Lumberyards and canning and packaging firms took their place. Fells Point became an industrial center and its residential character declined as the twentieth century progressed. By mid-century the area was bereft of its historic name, just a dingy derelict with Lower Broadway simply an East Baltimore skid row, ripe for the steamroller of "urban renewal" and obliteration by highway planners. In

1960 they proposed routing the city's east-west expressway along the south waterfront—right through Fells Point.

City preservationists sounded a battle cry against the highway proponents. Community meetings, hearings, lawsuits, and countersuits dragged on for 18 years before a way was found to save Fells Point, which became Maryland's first National Register Historic District in 1969. Today it is a municipal showpiece, with dozens of its 350 late eighteenth-century and early nineteenth-century buildings meticulously restored. Restaurants, pubs with live music, shops, a quaint hotel, two community theaters, and one dinner theater draw and delight visitors. Shipping activities still are carried on there, and the Broadway Market, recently refurbished and surrounded by a handsome brick promenade, continues serving the neighborhood's residents as it has for more than 200 years.

Facing Fells Point on the opposite bank of the Patapsco River is Federal Hill. Known as "Baltimore's best show window," Federal Hill has always afforded an unsurpassed view of the city. Some of the earliest photographs of Baltimore were taken from Federal Hill, and its commanding view of the city made it a natural site for a military fortress—and for its occupation by Union troops shortly after the Civil War broke out.

The military fortifications remained on Federal Hill until 1880, when it was declared a public park.

Above: This bright red sign for Bertha's restaurant/bar signals to Baltimoreans that this is the place to indulge in mussels, a regional delicacy. Touted on innumerable promotional bumper stickers, Bertha's is just one of many restaurants in the old waterfront community of Fells Point. Photo by Walter Calahan/Folio

Facing: The flavor of maritime Baltimore is alive and well in the waterside neighborhood of Fells Point. Photo by Alan Bolesta/Third Coast Stock Source

The neighborhood beneath the hill contains homes both huge and petite. As were their late eighteenth- and early nineteenth-century-rowhouse counterparts in Fells Point, these homes were saved from the expressway juggernaut by the stubborn resistance of the Society for the Preservation of Federal Hill and Fells Point. Restoration of these residences and revitalization of the neighborhood has made it another Baltimore showpiece.

Perhaps even better known among urban planners worldwide is the south-central Baltimore neighborhood called Otterbein, named after the Reverend Phillip William Otterbein. In 1774 he became pastor of a church in the area, and in 1785 another church was built there and given his name. It was on Otterbein's teachings that the Church of the United Brethren in Christ was based.

The original Otterbein neighborhood residences dating from the late eighteenth and early nineteenth centuries—the so-called federal period—were joined around 1840 by the modest homes of the workers employed in nearby shipping businesses. Fortuitously spared during the Great Fire of 1904, Otterbein became home to succeeding generations of immigrants, then deteriorated into a festering slum following the Depression and World War II. The Otterbein neighborhood was slated for demolition, but in 1975 the Urban Homesteading Program proved its salvation and reclamation. It became the largest "one-dollar" house homesteading project in the United States, with 110 homes—located just two blocks from the Inner Harbor—vibrantly brought back to life by enthusiastic, enterprising urban "pioneers" whose faith in city living never flagged. And now the old homes have new townhouses, condominiums, and apartments as neighbors.

Another late eighteenth-century community with a religious connection is nearby Seton Hill, named after a former resident, Mother Elizabeth Ann Seton, the first American-born saint. The French-based Sulpician Order of Priests first settled the neighborhood in 1791. There they founded Saint Mary's Seminary, the first Catholic seminary in the U.S. In 1807 Elizabeth Seton, a widowed mother from New York, came to Baltimore and opened a school for girls on Paca Street, next to the Sulpicians' Chapel of Our Lady of the Presentation, now the oldest example of Gothic Revival architecture in the country. In 1809 she took her vows in the chapel and later founded her religious order, the Daughters of Charity.

Many of Seton Hill's homes are tiny, narrow rowhouses, squeezed into streets that are equally narrow and tiny. The neighborhood declined as did others during the period when all roads seemed to lead out of the city, but in the late 1960s the trend began to reverse. It was named a Historic Preservation District, and in the years since, the neighborhood has been restored block by block, house by house.

In 1902 Henry James, the American-born Victorian novelist who preferred living in London, visited Baltimore, took a carriage ride around the city, and proclaimed Bolton Hill "the gem of the town." Its substantial, stately nineteenth-century townhouses, tree-lined streets, and elegant vest-pocket parks grace a 20-block area on two gently sloping rises above the downtown.

At the time James bestowed his encomium on the neighborhood, Bolton Hill was in what was generally known as the Mount Royal area. It was home to many of the city's intellectual and professional elite—the sort who would take in stride a visit and compliment from the likes of Henry James. The "Mount Royal" and "Bolton" names memorialize two late eighteenth-century manors built on the hill by prosperous entrepreneurs who felt (correctly) that the air there was

healthier than the then-potentially noxious breezes beside the harbor.

In the late nineteenth and early twentieth centuries, the roster of the neighborhood's residents was awash with the names of notables. Among those who lived there prior to World War I were Daniel Coit Gilman, the first president of The Johns Hopkins University and Hospital; Ottmar Mergenthaler, inventor of the Linotype; Dr. Jesse Lazear, who sacrificed his life by allowing himself to be bitten by a yellow-fever mosquito during Walter Reed's experiments to conquer the disease; onetime Hopkins medical student, later writer and art patron Gertrude Stein; Dr. Claribel Cone and her sister Etta, friends of Stein who followed her example and amassed one of the greatest private collections of modern art; Woodrow Wilson, the future president who lived on Eutaw Place while studying history and government at Hop-

Facing: Like Federal Hill, Otterbein is also a neighborhood of late eighteenth- and early nineteenth-century rowhouses that have been lovingly restored in recent years. From their upper story windows, residents can look towards the Inner Harbor skyline. Photo by Greg Pease

Below: This quiet little residential street in Federal Hill seems so secluded that it's hard to believe the bustle of the Inner Harbor is just a few blocks away. Photo by Greg Pease

kins (and two decades later was nominated for president at the Fifth Regiment Armory); and historian Edith Hamilton, author of the classic *The Greek Way*. After World War I the neighborhood's residents included essayist Christopher Morley; novelist F. Scott Fitzgerald and his wife Zelda; Alger Hiss, the former State Department official at the center of a controversial, early 1950s espionage and perjury case; and Garry Moore, subsequently a star of radio and TV.

Rather than being revived, Bolton Hill has survived; it withstood the post-World War II suburban exodus and foreshadowed the renaissance of other Baltimore neighborhoods. In 1955 residents of the area set up a private rehabilitation company, Bolton Hill, Inc., which paid $75,000 for 15 homes that then were refurbished and sold; they won *Look* magazine's Community Home Achievement Award in 1959. With pride, they invited—and still invite—tourists from other neighborhoods and cities to visit their red-brick and white-marble Victorian aerie, inspect their homes and gardens, and savor the neighborhood's serenity.

Also a survivor—and a neighborhood whose identification predates the name-coining renaissance—is Little Italy. A tiny, 12-square-block area of rowhouses, restaurants, and shops in Southeast Baltimore, it is the city's premier ethnic enclave and the favorite of the nonresidents who gorge in its wonderful eateries and revel in its annual festivals. For the families who live there—in some cases, three generations in the same rowhouse—it instills a devotion that persists even

for those who move away. It is said that no one who was born or raised there ever really leaves Little Italy.

According to Gilbert Sandler, an *Evening Sun* columnist, Baltimore folklore specialist, and chronicler of Little Italy, Italians had been immigrating to Baltimore since the early nineteenth century, but it was the California Gold Rush of 1849 that ironically gave birth to the neighborhood. Many adventuresome Genoese intended to make Baltimore just their first port of call on the way to California's gold fields, earning traveling money on the waterfront where they landed. They got jobs working for the railroad, hotels, restaurants, and construction projects. Lulled by the pleasantness of the community, they "ran out of time, or money, or dreams or perhaps all three," Sandler has written, and decided to exchange "the will-of-the-wisp of gold and riches for the mundane rewards of a day's wages . . ." Joined by immigrants from Naples, Sicily, and the province of Abruzzi, they brought the institutions and atmosphere of their native villages to every house on every street that became Little Italy.

In 1880, at the corner of Stiles and Exeter streets, the cornerstone was laid for Saint Leo's Church, the centerpiece and soul of Little Italy. For more than a century it has been the place where the neighborhood has baptized its babies, married its youth, and buried its dead. In Saint Leo's assembly hall, Little Italy's great spaghetti and ravioli suppers are held, and from its sanctuary emerge the processions celebrating Saint Anthony in June and Saint Gabriel in late August—Saint Gabriel because he was the patron saint of Abruzzi, and Saint Anthony because it was to him that Little Italy prayed as the Great Fire of 1904 raged, begging to be spared from the flames, which it was.

In many ways Little Italy is, as Gilbert Sandler has observed, the "prototype of Baltimore's neighborhoods." It is easy to become sentimental about Little Italy—easy, and essential—for sentiment and faith are what have kept Little Italy alive when other ethnic neighborhoods have faded. And while the neighborhood's commercial life, its restaurants, is vibrant, its life as a residential neighborhood is precarious. Yet Sandler sees a glimmer of hope in the remaining residents' "spiritual belief in the staying power of their neighborhood." Yes, some of the younger generation is moving away, but the warmth, the security, the appeal of Little Italy remain—and some of those who left have moved back. Of Little Italy's future, Sandler writes, "you can only feel optimistic . . ."

In part of polyglot Southeast and East Baltimore, where ethnicity is supreme, stands a public housing project called Flag House Court, just across Pratt Street from Little Italy but in many respects a world away; and farther to the east is the German, Polish, and Greek community of Highlandtown.

The blacks who live in Flag House Court, built right after World War II on the site of a Jewish bakery and other businesses, hope that it will be for them what Little Italy and its Jewish counterpart were for the residents at those places: a pathway to better times. As one young black mother told Dan Rodricks: "We're all struggling for something better. I have the same desires, the same heart, the same mind, the same soul, as everyone else."

Highlandtown's residents have had their dreams, too, and one of its daughters, Barbara Mikulski, now embodies those dreams by serving as one of Maryland's U.S. senators.

Highlandtown (pronounced "Hollandtown" in "Baltimorese") began its existence as Snake Hill, site of Fort Marshall, a federal barracks abandoned in 1866 when Union troops left Baltimore. Three brothers—George, William, and Conrad Schluderberg—soon established a butcher shop in the neighborhood, laying the foundation for the Schluderberg-Kurdle meat-processing firm best known to Baltimoreans as "Esskay," a producer of local bacon, hams, hot dogs, and cold cuts.

Within a few years, residents of the area began objecting to its unpleasant designation as "Snake Hill," so in 1870 a group of community leaders met at a neighborhood beer garden and selected Highland Town as the neighborhood name, since from the heights of its center one could see miles of the surrounding countryside. When Baltimore City annexed it in 1918, the community's name was telescoped to "Highlandtown" —although for many years, proud, longtime

land from Howard and combined it with more acreage from another plantation, called Brotherly Love, then dubbed the entire estate Ridgely's Delight.

A combination of two-and-a-half-story federal-period rowhouses and large Italianate homes of the Victorian era, Ridgely's Delight once was a community of physicians and dentists. It suffered the gradual deterioration experienced by so many inner-city areas following the Depression and World War II. Baltimore's Urban Homesteading Program began working its wonders on Ridgely's Delight in the early 1970s, and private real estate speculators—a number of them from Washington—have found it a wise place in which to invest money and, in some cases, live themselves.

To the south of the elegantly named Ridgely's Delight stands Pigtown, a neighborhood proud of its working-class heritage; proud of the legend of the pigs that were herded through its streets on the way to their reward at the Union Stockyards (hence the area's name); proud of its glorious contribution to baseball, Babe Ruth. Although Ruth spent only a few years in his Emory Street birthplace and had only vague recollection of his time in Pigtown, the neighborhood has never forgotten him. And with the completion of the new Camden Yards baseball stadium nearby in 1992, the national pastime may have an even bigger impact on Pigtown (which some now prefer to call "Washington Village").

Many West Baltimore natives have refused to leave it. Mencken spent all but a few of his 75 years in the same Hollins Street rowhouse overlooking Union Square, a Victorian vest-pocket park and neighborhood with a cast-iron fountain at its center. The original fountain, sacrificed to a World War II scrap-metal drive, was restored by a neighborhood organization dedicated to reviving Union Square's charm. Now designated as an historic district, Union Square and its neighborhood victualer, Hollins Market (opened in 1835), represent perhaps the major theme of all of Baltimore's renaissance: renewal, not restoration.

Edmondson Village, a conglomeration of communities that sprouted west of the central city after World War I and grew even more following World War II, became and long remained the main home of Schaefer, who continued to spend more of his time in the two-story Edgewood Street rowhouse his parents purchased in the 1920s than in

residents of the neighborhood continued to disparage the rest of the city by referring to it as "West Highlandtown."

In addition to its meat-processing plants, Highlandtown developed into a major commercial center. In its midst, affording a verdant refuge not just for Highlandtowners but all the residents of East and Southeast Baltimore's neighborhoods—Canton, Butcher's Hill, Oldtown, Jonestown, Locust Point—lies Patterson Park, a five-acre oasis in which stands a curious, faintly exotic, 60-foot-tall pagoda, built in 1891 at the height of a craze for things Oriental.

The western side of the city, its north, south, and center, also has its share of colonial-era neighborhoods, Victorian outposts, and ethnic strongholds. Some of the city's most celebrated native sons, including H.L. Mencken, Babe Ruth, and Maryland's redoubtable governor (and the city's former mayor) William Donald Schaefer, have also emerged from this area. In this section of the city, each spring witnesses Baltimore's greatest sports event, the Preakness at Pimlico. This area also once served as the "black capital of Maryland," with black churches, the *Afro-American* newspaper, leading black educational institutions, and the entertainment and jazz mecca along Pennsylvania Avenue.

Northbound travelers from Washington often first encounter Baltimore at Ridgely's Delight, a neighborhood whose name was derived from the plantation owned by Charles Ridgely, the son-in-law of Revolutionary War hero John Eager Howard, who bestowed the land as part of the dowry of his daughter, Rebecca. In 1732 Ridgely took the

the gubernatorial mansion in Annapolis that is his constitutionally mandated "official" residence. (In late 1989 the governor bought a townhouse in Anne Arundel County—but did not sell his boyhood home.) Shortly after World War II the Edmondson Village Shopping Center, an 11-acre commercial complex that became the first "regional" retail district in the nation, served as a model for all subsequent collections of suburban outlets for downtown retailers.

From the 1920s through the mid-1950s, when the city remained essentially a segregated Southern town, the West Baltimore neighborhood centered on Pennsylvania Avenue served as the heart of Baltimore's growing black community, "the quintessential black neighborhood," according to one local historian. From North Avenue at "the top" to "the bottom" by Preston Street, all the key black institutions of the city—its major churches, savings and loan associations, social clubs, hotels, and entertainment centers—could be found along what was simply called "the Avenue."

The nightclubs featuring live entertainment, the Ritz, the Casino, the Comedy Club, Kelly's Wonderland, and the Plantation Club, thrived, but king of "the Avenue" was the appropriately named Royal Theater. It opened in 1921 and became part of a deluxe circuit of

Above: Italian food and festivals can be found in the compact neighborhood of Little Italy. Many descendants of the original Italian immigrants still make their home in Little Italy. Shown here is Chiapparelli's restaurant. Photo by Alan Bolesta/Third Coast Stock Source

Facing: Haussner's restaurant is as renowned for the art on its walls as for the German food on its tables. This culinary landmark epitomizes the ethnic pride of the various nationalities that have established themselves in the working class neighborhood of Highlandtown. Photo by Greg Pease

black theaters, including the Apollo in New York, the Lincoln in Philadelphia, the Howard in Washington, and the Regal in Chicago, where top black performers appeared regularly. The theater managed to survive into the mid-1960s, with appearances by such performers as the Supremes and Smokey Robinson, but in 1965 inroads made by television, competition from the larger Civic Center downtown, and an increase in crime on "the Avenue" forced a final curtain call at the Royal. It was torn down in 1971 as part of what was called the Uptown Renewal Project, an effort initiated by the Uptown Planning Community Inc., a neighborhood association that was founded in 1967 and helped coordinate the continuing drive to revive the area.

The development of Baltimore's tree-lined, outlying neighborhoods to the north predated World War I. As far back as 1859 the city's leaders devised a plan for creating and maintaining municipal parks by taxing the local transit companies—which then operated horse-drawn trolleys—and funneling the proceeds into a city parks system, of which the 693-acre Druid Hill Park in the northwest and Clifton Park in the northeast are among its jewels. The electrification of these park-producing transit lines in the 1890s led enterprising real estate speculators to envision communities of commuters beyond what then were the northern boundaries of the city, close by the elegant "country" houses of Baltimore's old-line elite. Once the land on which these neighborhoods had grown was annexed by Baltimore in 1918, they became virtual suburbs within the city.

In 1891, a year after Baltimore's electric streetcars were inaugurated, the outlines for Roland Park, the city's first planned suburb, were drawn up. William Edmunds, owner of 550 acres of hilly woodland north of the city line, joined forces with Charles Grasty, the editor of the *Baltimore News* (and later editor of *The Sun*), and Edward Bouton, a developer from Kansas, to found the Roland Park Company. They were bankrolled by the Lands Trust Company of England, which pro-

posed that the new development be named for Roland Thornberry, an Englishman who also owned a lot of land in the area.

The company's original topographical and landscape engineer was George E. Kessler, who laid out the streets for the community's first 100 acres. Later the developers hired Frederick Law Olmsted, the celebrated landscape architect from Boston, whose designs for additional sections of the suburb sought to follow the natural topography of the property and leave undisturbed, save for enhancement, its hills and valleys and trees.

The company's organizers initially conceived of their project only as a land development and sales firm, but to give a boost to lagging public interest, they decided to build some houses on the property and managed to sell them. Perhaps reflecting Bouton's Kansas upbringing, among the early house styles was a clapboard-and-shingle Midwest bungalow in the Victorian mode, with an encircling porch. Later houses were larger and constructed more of stucco and brick. Olmsted's plans mandated strict design standards and also included a country club and a grouping of retail establishments, considered by some the first (or surely one of the first) community shopping centers in the country. Its Tudor-style shops, designed by local architects J.B. Noel Wyatt and William G. Nolting, are designated genuine landmarks and

Patterson Park is a green oasis in the middle of the tightly packed rowhouses of Highlandtown and Butcher's Hill. The Patterson Park Observatory, popularly known as The Pagoda, is an eight-sided tower built in 1891 with all the Victorian love of exotic oriental design. Photo by Greg Pease

help account for Roland Park's placement on the U.S. Department of Interior's National Register of Historic Places.

In the neighborhood's early years Roland Park's developers attached restrictive covenants to its properties, barring their sale to Jews or blacks. The U.S. Supreme Court struck down such convenants in 1948, but some time elapsed before Roland Park became the integrated community it is now.

Something about the air of Roland Park, now celebrating its centennial, apparently nurtures creativity. Two Pulitzer Prize-winners are linked to it: novelist Anne Tyler (who lives in adjacent Homeland) uses Roland Park as the setting for many of her books, and critic Jonathan Yardley writes many of his reviews and columns for *The Washington Post* in his 13-room, Victorian home there. The neighborhood also retains an atmosphere of suburban placidity combined with a small town's feistiness, perhaps best exemplified by a popular local grocery's meat counter sign: "Our beef is aged; our fish is fresh; our butchers are both."

With Roland Park successfully launched, the company that funded it looked for another area to develop and settled on the wooded acreage that once comprised the estate of A.S. Abell, founder of *The Sun*. He christened his Italianate mansion "Guilford," so that is what

the Roland Park Company called its new community, in which lots were first offered for sale in 1913.

From its inception Guilford was promoted as a community for Baltimore's well-to-do—which it remains to this day, with nearly 700 single-family houses, ranging in style from Tudor to Georgian to Mediterranean. It is home to physicians, attorneys, and academicians, a number of whom work at The Johns Hopkins University and Loyola College, which skirt its borders.

Guilford's planners pioneered special zoning procedures years before Baltimore itself had a zoning board, and its design included several parks that serve as entrances to the community. A neighborhood landmark is the nine-acre Sherwood Gardens, six acres of which were once the private, backyard preserve of a single family. Now it is a community enterprise and source of pride, lauded as one of the finest floral displays on the East Coast. Its tens of thousands of tulip, pansy, and azalea blossoms, as well as flowering trees, attract visitors from every section of the city—and from around the world. It is owned by the Guilford Association and is perhaps the largest privately owned garden in the East open free to the public.

Of far older origin than either Roland Park or Guilford, but developed after both of them, is the North Baltimore neighborhood of Homeland, yet another suburb-in-the-city project on which the Roland Park Company and the Olmsted firm of Boston collaborated. Originally a 391-acre plantation called "Homeland" that could trace its lineage to the late seventeenth century, it once was considered by the city as a potential park prior to its purchase by the Roland Park-Homeland Company in 1924 "for a consideration of not less than $1 million."

The developer wisely left intact six ornamental "lakes," actually ponds, dug at the behest of the plantation owners in 1843, and its original pathways became some of the neighborhood's main roads. As with its older siblings, Homeland has a wide variety of architectural styles reflected in its houses, although the designs for all of them originally had to survive the strict scrutiny of the developers' planning committee. Georgian, colonial-style homes, Tudor manors, and French country houses abut each other with easy elegance.

Northwest of Homeland, clustered on the 300 acres of wooded hills surrounding the onetime site of the Washington Cotton Manufacturing Company, the homes that comprise the neighborhood of Mount Washington can be found. Similar to Roland Park and Homeland in its suburban-like atmosphere, Mount Washington is unlike them (and Guilford) in that its development was unplanned and did not spring from a real estate firm's blueprints.

A small village, Washingtonville, sprouted around the Washington Cotton Manufacturing Company, founded in 1810. The Baltimore and Susquehanna Railroad extended its tracks through the community in 1830, and in 1897 the Baltimore and Northern Railroad Company began additional service between the area and downtown Baltimore. The advent of the automobile—and the roads built to accommodate it before and after World War II—made Mount Washington an even more accessible community.

The Mount Washington Improvement Association, founded in 1949, won a nationally famous, landmark case for neighborhood groups when it successfully fought to have the area's zoning upgraded to limit development density to six families per acre. The new limit has helped preserve the neighborhood's village-like character: homes range from Victorian-era residences to the ranch-style split levels built during the 1950s, 1960s, and 1970s. One local chronicler described the community as "a true hodgepodge of people, homes and neighborhoods," with several distinct subsections recognized by the residents. One such subsection is "Pill Hill," identified as such because many physicians built modern homes on it in the mid-1950s. And not to be outdone by its neighbors, Roland Park and Homeland, Mount Washington also has its own Pulitzer Prize-winner in residence: historian Taylor Branch, a longtime Washingtonian who succumbed to Baltimore's ambience, affordable housing, and Orioles and moved here in 1986.

Of comparable vintage to these various suburbs-within-the-city, but possessed of more recently minted cachet, are several neighborhoods that have been around a long time but took on an enhanced patina as a new generation of residents began occupying them and Baltimore's renaissance spurred neighborhood pride.

The quaintest of these is Dickeyville, a petite, picket-fenced New England-style town that seems frozen in time beside the Gwynns Falls in Northwest Baltimore. The oldest of the neighborhood's 138 stone and clapboard homes were built to house the workers in several mills erected in the eighteenth century by members of the Gwynn family, for whom the stream that powered the mills is named; the Tschudi family, later mill-owners; and the Wethered family, a Quaker clan who succeeded the Tschudis and whose name

These enterprising Roland Park residents show an entrepreneurial spirit. The same entrepreneurial spirit led to the carefully planned development of this leafy and wealthy North Baltimore neighborhood at the turn of the twentieth century. Photo by Rich Riggins

gave the community its original designation, Wetheredsville.

John Wethered became a member of Congress, and in 1844 his wife, Mary, was the recipient of the nation's second telegraph message. After Samuel F.B. Morse tapped out his epochal inquiry, "What Hath God Wrought?" he dutifully transmitted a greeting from former first lady Dolley Madison to her friend, Congressman Wethered's wife.

William J. Dickey, an Irish-born woolgatherer, bought the mills and the town for $71,250 in 1872, built more homes for the workers, and saw to it that the area prospered until his death in 1896. The community then experienced a slow decline along with diminished work in the mills, one of which burned to the ground in 1934. The year 1934 also marked the beginning of Dickeyville's revival, with its sale to a development firm for just $42,000. Then, bit by bit, house by house, the former mill town became a residential village. Yarn continued being spun at one of its mills as recently as 1967, but by 1975 the remaining mill had become a center for local crafts and other businesses. The village and its mill have been entered on the National Register of Historic Places, and tiny, once-derelict Dickeyville now thrives as a separate, unique, picturesque yet integral part of Baltimore.

Slightly north and east of Dickeyville is Ashburton, an area that experienced changes that often spelled decline for similar urban neighborhoods, but by the determined efforts of its residents, it avoided that fate.

Named for the manor house and farm of a prominent landowner (who had sought to honor Great Britain's Lord Ashburton by giving the estate his name), the property was sold to a developer in the early part of

Above: Flying an American flag on the front porch is a common sight in Hampden—and not just on Memorial Day or the Fourth of July. Photo by Greg Pease

Left: Hampden is a North Baltimore neighborhood that is stable and seemingly unchanging, as though the march of time was frozen here in the 1950s. Photo by Roger Miller

The expansive residential properties of Guilford are enhanced by the blooming wonderland of azaleas and tulips in the nine-acre Sherwood Gardens. Photo by Greg Pease

this century. It became an exclusive preserve of the city's white, Christian elite in the 1920s, but the reversal of fortunes brought about by the Great Depression compelled many of Ashburton's original residents to abandon their restrictive covenants and accept the purchase of homes there by Jews. By the 1940s the neighborhood was about half Jewish.

In 1956, according to one local historian, a city high school principal who happened to be black bought a home in Ashburton, and within three years 110 black families had moved there. In time it became known as the city's black "Gold Coast," home to many prosperous black professionals, including Mayor Kurt L. Schmoke. The existing white population, seeking to prevent the blockbusting tactics that had damaged other neighborhoods, established an integrated community organization that won praise from *The New York Times* and other publications for its progressive activities.

Ashburton's black population continued to grow, and pride in the neighborhood and its amenities grew with it. The Ashburton Area Association has kept the neighborhood elegant, with its large, one-family houses and bucolic streets.

With the origin of many Baltimore neighborhood names owing so much to the original estates of wealthy land-barons, the businesses of early entrepreneurs, or the fancies of turn-of-the-century developers—all male—most of the communities can be said to have had "founding fathers." Charles Village owes its identity to a "founding mother," Grace Darin, an *Evening Sun* copy editor and writer who coined the name for her community newsletter in 1967 and single-handedly promoted it as a way to ignite neighborhood pride and enhance area real estate values.

Jacques Kelly, an *Evening Sun* columnist, local historian, and lifelong Charles Villager, has written that the developers who launched the neighborhood in 1879 actually dubbed it "Peabody Heights." They were trying to graft the distinguished name of philanthropist George Peabody's conservatory, which is about a mile downhill of the neighborhood's borders, with the new location's elevation, deemed to be healthier in summer and attractively situated near the "country seats of our most prominent and cultivated citizens," as the development's promotional literature declared. Among these celebrated "country seats" were the once-grand but now-demolished Wyman Villa, the Italianate mansion of financier William Wyman, set on expansive grounds that eventually became a park and the campus of The Johns Hopkins University; and Homewood House, a federal-period Georgian masterpiece built by Charles Carroll, Jr. (with $40,000 of his father's money). Now a museum, it also became part of the Hopkins campus.

The original Peabody Heights development was slow getting off the ground, but as the twentieth century dawned, each new year produced a new crop of rowhouses, many of them featuring oak doors and woodwork, parquet floors, stained-glass windows, ornamented plaster ceilings, mahogany trimming, and other embellishments.

The families of professional people, merchants, and bankers were the rowhouses' first residents, and with the arrival in 1915 of Hopkins from its original downtown site, a contingent of academics joined the mix. Mammoth apartment houses went up in the 1920s.

The more prosperous of the neighborhood's early residents gradually began moving farther north, and many of the original three-story rowhouses were converted into multifamily apartments. The chronic

housing crunch caused by the city's growth during World War II accelerated this subdivision of the neighborhood's dwellings, and the 1950s and 1960s saw a further erosion of the area's "Peabody Heights" identity and ethos.

Enter Grace Darin, then a resident of a 26th Street block of colorfully painted houses called Pastel Row, as christener of "Charles Village." The neighborhood's boundaries are imprecise, generally stretching from 33rd Street on the north to 23rd Street on the south; Guilford Avenue on the east and Howard Street on the west. A new generation of residents, imbued with the enthusiasm and perseverance required for

renovation, have restored many of the neighborhood's rowhouses. Now, as Jacques Kelly has put it, "having passed its years of uncertainty . . . the Village ranks high on the list of Baltimore's success stories."

All of these neighborhoods—as well as equally appealing areas in surrounding Baltimore, Howard, Anne Arundel, Harford, and Carroll counties—reflect a sense of the character and commitment encapsulated in a comment made to *Baltimore Magazine* by one proud city dweller in 1976: "There's a difference between living in a place and belonging to it." Baltimoreans belong to their neighborhoods just as surely as their neighborhoods belong to them.

A LOVE OF THE ARTS

The creation of *Red Buoyant* marked the beginning of Inner Harbor redevelopment. This distinctive landmark, located in front of the IBM building, was created by Baltimore-based sculptor Mary Ann Mears. Photo by Greg Pease

Baltimore's devotion to museums and the arts—decorative, fine, and theatrical—is as old as the city itself. In the past two decades, however, the city has experienced a revitalization on all its cultural fronts that is as extraordinary and striking as its urban rejuvenation.

A new, multimillion-dollar wing and two sculpture gardens have been added to the Baltimore Museum of Art; a new wing and an exquisite $6-million renovation now grace the Walters Art Gallery; a new $23-million concert hall has been built for the Baltimore Symphony; while the orchestra's former home, the venerable Lyric, has been renovated and rechristened the Lyric Opera House, home to the Baltimore Opera Company and touring Broadway musicals. The Morris A. Mechanic Theater has become one of the premier pre-Broadway tryout houses in the country, as well as a coveted stop on the route of touring plays. The city's community theaters are thriving; its art galleries are multiplying; it is becoming a popular location for making motion pictures; and some of its oldest buildings have become its newest museums.

On the literary front, the works of three Maryland writers (two from Baltimore) hit the best-seller lists in 1988, and during one springtime week in 1989, four Baltimore-based, -born or -educated artists—including two of those bestselling authors—received the nation's top prizes in writing and filmmaking: the Pulitzer and the Oscar. Such a shower of encomiums for Baltimore-nurtured talent prompted two reporters for *The Sun* (one of them a Pulitzer Prize-winner herself) to wonder in print, "Is culture replacing crab cakes as this city's chief export?"

Hardly. But for a city not generally associated in the public mind with cultural accomplishments, Baltimore's recent achievements seem all the more stunning.

Baltimore's oldest museum, the Peale, is also the oldest in the nation—the first building in this country designed and erected specifically to serve as a public showplace of art, scientific exhibits, and oddities. Conceived by painter and scientist Rembrandt Peale in 1813, it was designed by Robert Cary Long and opened in August 1814.

Originally touted as "an elegant rendezvous for taste, curiosity and leisure," Peale's Baltimore Museum and Gallery of Fine Arts failed to become profitable, despite its enticing attractions. The museum became Baltimore's city hall in 1830 and served in that capacity until 1875. It then became a public school for black children and finally returned to its original role as a museum in 1931. Recently renovated and restored, it features a fascinating collection of "Baltimoreana," as well as a collection of splendid paintings by the multitalented Peale family, which included Rembrandt Peale's brother Rubens and sister Sarah.

The Peale now is one of a sextet of buildings collectively called the Baltimore City Life Museums. These include nearby Carroll Mansion, the East Lombard Street home built in 1812 for the son-in-law of Charles Carroll of Carrollton. It became the winter home of the aged Founding Father, who died there in 1836 at the age of 95. The starkly furnished ground floor served as Carroll's business office, but the house's elegantly appointed second and third floors show how a wealthy Baltimorean of that day lived. The lives of the city's non-elite a century-and-a-half ago are chronicled in two adjacent City Life Museums that form a "Museum Row," the Center for Urban Archaeology and the 1840 House, a rebuilt nineteenth-century rowhouse where actors portray the residents of such a home in that era and participatory programs engage visitors in a lively re-creation of the period.

Also operated under the aegis of the City Life Museums are the H.L. Mencken house at 1524 Hollins Street and the B&O Railroad Museum at 901 West Pratt Street. Opened as a museum in 1984, the Mencken House has been filled with original furnishings and features an audio-visual show on Mencken's life and ideas. He did much of his writing in the second-floor study overlooking Union Square. The B&O Railroad Museum contains the country's finest collection of vintage locomotives, including "Tom Thumb," the first. Luxurious parlor cars from railroading's golden age, artifacts, and model trains are all housed in a reproduction of the nation's first passenger and freight station, built in 1830, adjoining the B&O's 1883 passenger carbarn, with its original rails still in place.

Not part of the City Life Museums but included on "Museum Row" is the Flag House at 844 East Pratt Street, the small home in which Mary Pickersgill, a young widow, made the original 30- by 42-foot Star-Spangled Banner that flew over Fort McHenry, itself a historical shrine. Additional treasure troves of Baltimore-related artwork, colonial- and federal-era furniture, silverware, nautical gear, clothing, library materials dating to the state's founding in 1634, and the original manuscript of "The Star-Spangled Banner" can be found at the Maryland Historical Society at 201 West Monument Street, part of which is the nineteenth-century home of merchant banker and philanthropist Enoch Pratt. Homewood House, on the campus of Johns Hopkins, is the only surviving federal-period villa in the city. Built between 1800 and 1810 by Charles Carroll, Jr., it is among the finest and best-preserved Georgian buildings in the country. It underwent a meticulous, five-year restoration and was opened as a museum in 1987.

Farther north on Charles Street is another extraordinarily elegant old home, Evergreen House, reopened in September 1990 after a three-year, $4.3-million restoration. A 48-room, mid-nineteenth-century classic revival mansion, Evergreen was the residence of the Garrett family, among the founders of the B&O Railroad. Bequeathed to Johns Hopkins in 1942 by John Work Garrett, a diplomat as well as an art connoisseur and bibliophile, Evergreen has thousands of rare books, maps, manuscripts, Oriental art treasures, Tiffany glass, a small private theater with the only surviving stage sets and decorations designed by Léon Bakst, once the renowned designer of sets for the legendary Ballets Russes, and lovely formal gardens on 26 landscaped acres.

The city's two greatest repositories of art and artifacts are the Baltimore Museum of Art (BMA) and the Walters Art Gallery, both of

which benefitted immensely from the canny eyes and near-incalculable generosity of local connoisseurs who collected with care and bequeathed with aplomb.

William T. Walters (1819-1894) and his son, Henry (1848-1931), were hard-nosed railroad builders and bankers whose skill at business was balanced by an equally remarkable sensitivity to artwork. Together they amassed a private collection of ancient Greek, Roman, and Egyptian art; medieval armor; paintings from the Renaissance through the nineteenth century; rare jewelry from ancient to modern times; Oriental, Viennese, French, and English porcelain, as well as Italian glazed pottery and glass; sculpture in ivory, wood, marble, and bronze; and medieval manuscripts. The Walters is, as *The Washington Post* put it, "one of the world's great treasure houses of art from ancient to *nouveau*."

Between 1904 and 1908 Henry Walters built a seventeenth-century-style Italian palazzo on Mount Vernon Place to house his burgeoning collection, which he bequeathed to the city along with his house in 1931. The museum was opened to the public full-time in 1934, and in 1974 an adjacent, four-story addition was completed. In 1988 a three-year, $6.1-million restoration and modernization of the original building revived—and enhanced—its turn-of-the-century magnificence while expanding its exhibition space. The Walters' restoration "is nothing short of miraculous," wrote *The Sun*'s architectural critic, Edward Gunts. "People say they don't build the way they used to, but at the Walters they still do—and then some." Next on their agenda is the conversion of a large nineteenth-century Mount Vernon Place mansion known as the Hackerman House into a new

gallery for the Walters' collection of Asian art.

While the Walters Art Gallery in a sense sprang full-grown from the brows of its father-and-son founders, the Baltimore Museum of Art had a rockier beginning. Full of honorable intentions but lacking much else, a group of city leaders incorporated the museum in November 1914. It "had no museum to put a collection in, and no collection to put in a museum," as *The Sun*'s art critic, John Dorsey, observed when the Museum—grown to a world-class institution of considerable substance—celebrated its 75th anniversary in 1989.

The BMA initially set up shop in the Mount Vernon Place home of the Garrett family, relying on the items assembled by local collectors for the artworks it exhibited. In 1924 Henry Walters himself led the campaign for a referendum authorizing a one-million-dollar city loan for the construction of a suitable museum building. Erected on a six-acre park site beside The Johns Hopkins University, which had donated the land, the museum's neoclassic building opened in 1929.

Just as the Walters had drawn on the beneficence of its founders, the BMA began and remains a "collection of collections," renowned for "the grandeur of its inheritance from early Baltimore collector-patrons," as the BMA's director, Arnold L. Lehman, has written of the museum's original benefactors and their modern-day successors. Among the former were Jacob Epstein, a discount clothing magnate, who lent (and later bequeathed) his exquisite collection of European Old Masters paintings, and the redoubtable Cone sisters, assemblers of an incomparable collection of French impressionist and post-impressionist paintings.

The Cone sisters, who began their collection in the late nineteenth century, were a fascinating and formidable duo: Dr. Claribel, a physically imposing medical doctor who studied at Johns Hopkins, among other schools, and Etta, a self-effacing but strong-willed art fancier. They became friends of Gertrude Stein, a onetime Hopkins medical student, nascent author, and budding art patron. Making use of their modest, inherited fortune, the Cones took Stein's lead in collecting the works of the masters of late nineteenth-century and early twentieth-century art: Matisse (who affectionately called the Cones "my two Baltimore ladies"), Cezanne, Picasso, Gauguin, van Gogh, Renoir, and others. The Cone sisters also purchased important works of American artists, European prints and drawings, textiles, jewelry, decorative arts, antique ivories and bronzes, African art, and Japanese prints.

While the Cone Collection may be the BMA's crown jewel, the museum has some 130,000 additional items that glitter, including an acclaimed collection of antique silver, much of it made in Maryland; colonial- and federal-era furniture, again much of it Maryland-made; one of the largest and best collections of prints in the world, representing more than five centuries of printers' art; artworks of the Americas, Oceania, and Africa; three lush acres of sculpture gardens donated by the late Alan and Janet Wurtzburger and Robert and Ryda Levi; and the newly acquired Dalsheimer collection of twentieth-century photographs. A new wing, planned for the west side of the museum, soon will add 30,000 square feet of exhibition space.

The visual arts in Baltimore are by no means confined to the BMA and the Walters. The city has a large and active artistic community, one that is instructed at the Maryland Institute College of Art (founded in 1826) and exhibited in an expanding variety of galleries. These range from the long-established Bendann and Katzenstein galleries to the more than half-dozen new showplaces that have sprung up along North Charles Street, making it the city's "art neighborhood." Other exhibition outlets include Maryland Art Place, a private, nonprofit center on Saratoga Street that has offered hundreds of Maryland artists a venue in which to show their work, and School 33, a city-sponsored visual arts center on Light Street with three gallery spaces.

Given Baltimore's rich religious heritage, industrial history, and the legacies of literature, sports, and science it has fostered, it is not surprising that special museums and showplaces celebrate these vibrant themes in the city's life.

Above: The Walters Art Gallery holds the treasures amassed by the father-and-son collecting team of William and Henry Walters. Open as a public museum since 1934, the Walters has exceptional holdings that range from ancient sculpture to art nouveau jewelry. Photo by Alan Bolesta/Third Coast Stock Source

Top: Visitors to the Baltimore Museum of Art flock to the galleries containing its famed Cone Collection. Works by Matisse, Picasso, van Gogh, and other masters of late nineteenth- and early twentieth-century art are on display for everyone's appreciation. Photo by Roger Miller

Facing: The B&O Railroad Museum has the best collection of vintage locomotives in the country. Serving as the main museum building is a 22-sided passenger carbarn, called a "roundhouse," which was erected in 1883. Photo by Jed Kirschbaum

In addition to the Basilica of the Assumption and the Lovely Lane Methodist Church, among the significant religious sites is the Jewish Heritage Center and Museum at 15 Lloyd Street, parts of which are the Lloyd Street Synagogue and B'nai Israel Synagogue.

Surely the greatest sports figure in Baltimore's history—indeed, in the history of the national pastime —is commemorated at the Babe Ruth Birthplace Museum at 216 Emory Street. It is the rowhouse in which the Sultan of Swat, George Herman Ruth, was born in 1895. Reconstructed and opened as a museum in 1970, then expanded in 1983, it now is the country's second-largest baseball museum (after the Hall of Fame in Cooperstown, NY) and home of the Maryland Baseball Hall of Fame. It features films, 26 exhibits on Ruth, Oriole memorabilia, and items associated with famous Maryland-born baseball players.

The beginning of modern mass transportation in Baltimore is represented by more than just the B&O Museum. The Baltimore Streetcar Museum at 1901 Falls Road features old trolleys that can

Above: The Babe Ruth Birthplace Museum preserves the rowhouse home of the baseball immortal who won tremendous fame and fortune with the New York Yankees, but got his start in Baltimore. The museum is also home of the Maryland Baseball Hall of Fame. Photo by Alan Bolesta/Third Coast Stock Source

Facing: The architectural ideals expressed in the Cathedral of Mary Our Queen date back to the Middle Ages, but the building itself only dates back to 1959. The cathedral's modernistic streamlining of Gothic design includes some Art Deco motifs. Photo by Roger Miller

the U.S. and now, at 134 years of age, one of Baltimore's oldest arts institutions. Built along with Mr. Peabody's conservatory was his library, one of the country's greatest collections of rare books in perhaps the grandest of Baltimore's interior spaces.

The conservatory building, opened in 1866, wowed Russian composer Peter Ilyich Tchaikovsky when he visited it in 1891. He praised the "enormous building, marvelously arranged classrooms, music library . . . and faculty." The conservatory's faculty remains renowned. "What Peabody is all about are the teachers," said one conservatory graduate in 1989. And the students taught by those teachers come from all around the U.S. and overseas.

Although petite by comparison to other major American conservatories, the Peabody produces graduates who perform in top symphony orchestras throughout the country and direct some of the most prestigious ones. Peabody graduates and faculty members who have won international acclaim as individual perfomers include pianists Leon Fleisher and

be ridden up and down a one-mile track. Baltimore's central role in the advancement of science is reflected in the Maryland Science Center and Davis Planetarium at 601 Light Street and the National Aquarium on Pier 3, 501 East Pratt Street. Industry and the nuts and bolts of urban life, are the subjects of two special museums: the Baltimore Museum of Industry at 1415 Key Highway, which re-creates a South Baltimore cannery of 1865 and provides demonstrations on steel-making, shop-building, and other industrial endeavors, and the Public Works Museum and Streetscape at 701 Eastern Avenue, which provides a fascinating view of what goes on under the streets of a modern city and shows how cities are built.

It takes more to move a great city forward, however, than trains, trolleys, and avenues of commerce, as George Peabody recognized. These mechanisms and byways give a city muscle, Peabody knew, but other sources must provide succor for its mind and heart. This he sought to supply with his conservatory of music, the first established in

Andre Watts, Metropolitan Opera tenor Richard Cassilly, bass James Morris, soprano Phyllis Bryn-Julson, bandleader Tommy Newsom, and the late Virgil Fox, organist extraordinaire.

George Peabody's vision for his institute included an extensive library of rare books. Opened in 1878, the multitiered book repository with its ornate, cast-iron balconies now houses an estimated 280,000 volumes. Despite the sale in recent years of some extremely valuable books in order to raise endowment funds, the library remains an incredible scholarly resource—in part because it or other branches of the Johns Hopkins library system have duplicates of the items sold, including a rare, complete "Elephant Folio" of the bird paintings of John James Audubon.

Just as the Peabody was the first established music conservatory in the country, the Baltimore Symphony Orchestra (BSO) was the first orchestra in the U.S. to be supported by public funds. Founded in 1915, it began as a municipal agency with a city Board of Estimates

Above: To think only about fish when contemplating the National Aquarium is to take in less than the complete picture. Through audiovisual presentations, simulated ecosystems, and other means, the Aquarium is able to show the natural interrelationships earth dwellers must work to maintain. Photo by Skip Brown/Folio

Facing: Baltimore's central role in the advancement of science is reflected in the exhibits at the National Aquarium. Photo by Edwin H. Remsberg

grant of just $6,000. Its first season in 1916 consisted of only three concerts under the baton of Gustav Strube, a Peabody Conservatory faculty member who had been conductor of the famous Boston Pops prior to moving to Baltimore and leaving the Pops in the capable hands of a young violinist named Arthur Fiedler.

From these modest beginnings the Baltimore Symphony has grown into a world-class orchestra, showered with accolades from New York to Moscow. Although conductor Reginald Stewart, who directed the BSO from 1942 to 1952, was the first to take it on tour and turn it into a fully professional orchestra, it was the appointment of maestro Sergiu Comissiona as conductor in 1968 that heralded a turning point for the

symphony. Under his baton the BSO began receiving rave reviews in New York's Carnegie Hall and Washington's Kennedy Center, going on more extended tours, including trips overseas, and making records for several major companies.

In 1976 the BSO launched a massive fund-raising drive in an effort to raise $3.4 million to lift the orchestra over the "threshold of greatness." Successfully completed in three years, the fund-raising campaign provided the impetus for the symphony's supreme undertaking: construction of a new symphony hall. Ground was broken in the Mount Royal area for the new concert hall in March 1978, with the state ultimately allocating $10.5 million for the symphony's new home while BSO president Joseph Meyerhoff donated $10.5 million of his own to ensure completion of the hall—which was named for him when it opened in 1982. In 1984 Comissiona announced his plans to leave the BSO, and David Zinman took up where Comissiona had left off, moving the symphony toward the greatness it seeks to achieve.

During a 21-month period beginning in 1986, the BSO raised $40 million to make its endowment financially secure. Then in May 1987 the BSO made a triumphant tour of Europe and became the first American orchestra in more than a decade to perform in the Soviet Union. But the echoes of the cheers it received in Moscow and elsewhere overseas had faded by the time lengthy negotiations between the orchestra's management and the symphony's 96 musicians broke down in September 1988, and the longest strike ever by a major American orchestra began. It lasted 22 weeks and wiped out 84 concerts of the 1988-89 season. At last a four-year agreement was hammered out, and the BSO not only returned but rebounded with panache, appearing soon thereafer in Carnegie Hall to the hosannas of one *New York Times* critic, who called the orchestra a "brightly polished, finely tuned engine" that the New York audience "loved." In 1990 Zinman and the BSO won a Grammy in the classical music category with cellist Yo-Yo Ma, and Zinman picked up a share of two more Grammys for work he did with other orchestras.

Before the Meyerhoff Symphony Hall was built, the BSO performed in the age-encrusted, almost hallowed Lyric Theater, Baltimore's grand dame of playhouses. Opened in 1894, the Lyric possesses acoustical attributes that have been celebrated by musicians from around the world. On its stage have appeared a galaxy of the twentieth century's greatest orchestras and musical performers, from Nellie Melba and Enrico Caruso to Beverly Sills, from Jascha Heifetz to Isaac Stern, and from Yul Brynner to Carol Channing. The Lyric also was a favorite meeting hall for major political speeches and popular lectures. Speakers ranging from Theodore Roosevelt, William Jennings Bryan, and Woodrow Wilson to Clarence Darrow, Charles A. Lindbergh, and Will Rogers have been just a few of the public figures to declaim from its stage.

During the 1930s and 1940s, New York's Metropolitan Opera Company regularly appeared at the Lyric with its top stars, and the

This contemporary sculpture by Kenneth Snelson seems to float in the air in front of the Maryland Science Center. A major Inner Harbor attraction, the science center has hands-on educational exhibits that kids love, including a planetarium and an IMAX theater. Photo by Lonnie Timmons III

major ballet companies—the old Ballet Russe de Monte Carlo, the Ballet Theater, the New York City, London Festival, and Sadler Wells/Royal Ballet—all appeared there.

Many major out-of-town ballet companies now bypass Baltimore in order to appear at Washington's Kennedy Center, but the Washington Ballet Company reverses that migration and travels to Baltimore a half-dozen times a year to perform. Baltimore's hometown ballet company, the Maryland Ballet, is a fledgling troupe still working on establishing itself. More solidly grounded here are several modern dance companies—such as the Path Dance Company headed by Kathy Wildberger and the Forrest Collection directed by Juliet Forrest—that perform at Goucher College, the Theatre Project, the Baltimore Museum's auditorium, and elsewhere. And beginning in late 1990, the world-famous Alvin Ailey American Dance Theater established a residency program in Baltimore, using the city as a base from which to mount performances and educational efforts throughout the state and overseas.

Among the opera stars who performed at the Lyric was the great Metropolitan soprano Rosa Ponselle, who later married the son of a Baltimore mayor and settled down on a country estate north of the city. Although her marriage did not last, Ponselle's devotion to Baltimore did. She became one of the moving forces behind the creation of the Baltimore Opera Company in 1950. Originally known as the Baltimore Civic Opera, it performed three productions a year at the Lyric under Ponselle's artistic direction.

During the 1968-69 season the Baltimore Civic Opera Guild was formed to expand fund-raising, and in 1970 the organization changed its name to the Baltimore Opera Company. A nonprofit operation, it now produces up to four operas a season, as many as three of them entirely new productions. All are performed in the refurbished and rechristened Lyric Opera House, which underwent a $14-million facelift between 1979 and 1981.

The symphony and opera represent only a portion of Baltimore's musical world. The city's instrument has many strings. Among these are the Baltimore Chamber Orchestra, Baltimore String Quartet, Res MusicAmerica Inc., the Baltimore Choral Arts Society, Concert Artists of Baltimore, and the Baltimore Consort, each providing music lovers—and performers—with opportunities to hear and play a wide variety of musical compositions and disciplines.

The strains—and beats—of music other than classical has entranced Baltimoreans. For the inimitable James Hubert "Eubie" Blake, a son of ex-slaves, born in Baltimore in 1883, the classics were his first musical lessons, but ragtime proved a far more powerful allure.

"It just swung and made me feel good," he explained decades later. "It was my baby. Goodbye Beethoven." Blake would win fame as the composer of "The Charleston Rag" and Broadway musicals that contained such songs as "I'm Just Wild About Harry" and "Love Will Find a Way." He lived to be 100 and was among the first of the "generation of blacks who revolutionized American music," as historian Robert J. Brugger has written.

Other Baltimoreans—Cab Calloway, Billie Holiday, Chick Webb, Larry Adler—made jazz history in the 1920s, 1930s, and 1940s, and showplaces such as the Royal Theater on Pennsylvania Avenue were entertainment meccas where out-of-town stars such as Ethel Waters, Ella Fitzgerald, Earl "Fatha" Hines, Nat King Cole, and Pearl Bailey performed. For the past decade the city has sponsored a summer festival known as Artscape, a three-day weekend celebration of jazz and the visual and performing arts that takes place in July.

The history of theater in Baltimore can be traced to a hazy beginning, sometime between 1751 and 1763, when plays may have been performed in a market-house-turned-ramshackle-theater at Baltimore and Gay streets. As Jacques Kelly has observed, Baltimore may not have been a great theater town in years past, but all the great performers played here. In 1848 the greatest Shakespearean performers of the age—Englishman William Macready and American Edwin Forrest—appeared in rival productions of *Macbeth* at the same time, with Forrest at the Holliday Street Theater and Macready at the Front Street Theater. In 1850 Jenny Lind, the "Swedish Nightingale," was brought to Baltimore by her American impresario, P.T. Barnum, and later that decade Baltimore-born producer and theater-owner John T. Ford began his career in town. He later expanded his operations to Washington and built the Ford's Theater where President Abraham Lincoln was assassinated in April 1865. In 1871 Ford opened a new theater on Fayette Street in Baltimore, and in an effort to avoid association with the assassination site in Washington, he dubbed his new building Ford's Grand Opera House—although grand opera was rarely performed there.

Instead, what Baltimoreans chose to call simply "Ford's" became a legendary theater where virtually every renowned performer of the

Above: Music director David Zinman conducts the Baltimore Symphony Orchestra in a concert at the Joseph Meyerhoff Symphony Hall. The national reputation of the orchestra has risen as a result of its tours and recordings and Zinman's leadership. Photo by Greg Pease

Facing: Perhaps the finest interior in the city, the library of the Peabody Institute was opened in 1878. It is notable for the cast-iron balconies on which are shelved some 280,000 volumes. Photo by Greg Pease

next 93 years appeared. To the boards at Ford's came Victorian beauty Lily Langtry; Edwin Booth, the great tragedian whose brother, John Wilkes Booth, murdered Lincoln; Buffalo Bill and his Wild West Show; magicians such as Harry Houdini, Howard Thurston, and Alexander Herrmann; all of the Barrymores; Katharine Cornell; Fred and Adele Astaire; and Alfred Lunt and Lynn Fontanne. Not far from Ford's, at the northwest corner of Howard and Franklin streets, what might have been called the city's theater district developed at the beginning of the twentieth century with construction of the Maryland Theater, a legitimate vaudeville house, and the Auditorium Theater (now the shuttered Mayfair movie house) near the Academy of Music, which had opened in 1875. Musicals featuring stars such as Al Jolson played at the Auditorium, while top vaudeville acts played at the Maryland. In 1914 the Hippodrome opened on Howard Street, featuring major vaudeville acts and first-run movies. Burlesque houses, where many famous comedians got their start, were a fixture on Baltimore Street and elsewhere downtown.

With four legitimate theaters—Ford's, the Auditorium, the Academy, and the Maryland—Baltimore was a major pre-Broadway tryout town for plays and musicals in the 1920s, 1930s, and 1940s.

By the early 1950s, however, the curtain on Baltimore's theater scene began a slow descent. One by one the legitimate theaters folded, the victims first of the movies and then of television. In January 1964 the lone survivor, Ford's, doused its footlights after the cast of *A Funny Thing Happened on the Way to the Forum* sang "Auld Lang Syne" with the closing night's audience.

When Ford's fell to make way for a parking lot, it looked like professional theater was dead in Baltimore. Within a few years, however, the man who had sold Ford's—former theater-owner Morris A. Mechanic—agreed to build a new legitimate theater as the centerpiece of the Charles Center renewal project. Mechanic died in July 1966, just as construction of the theater was getting under way, and it was named for him when it opened in January 1967.

The Mechanic Theater had a rough first decade. In a last-ditch effort to save it as a legitimate theater, the city agreed to do something no other city had done: take over the theater and run it as a nonprofit, municipal entity. First under the direction of Broadway and television producer Alexander Cohen, then under Hope Quackenbush, a former public relations consultant, the Mechanic has become "one of the best houses to play in the country and . . . one of the most successful legitimate theaters in America," wrote Elaine F. Weiss in *Warfield's* magazine, the Baltimore business monthly. "It may sound like the punch line from a soggy vaudeville routine, but Broadway is dying to play Baltimore. Honest."

With an 82-percent re-subscription rate, among the highest of any theater in the country, the 1,600-seat Mechanic is one of the best-attended theaters beyond the Great White Way. The New York Theatre Guild's Philip Langner, who used to be the Mechanic's booking agent in Manhattan, told *Warfield's* that "Baltimore has become *the* leading tryout place."

While the Mechanic was undergoing the metamorphosis from an ugly duckling to a swan of pre- and post-Broadway road theaters, Baltimore's Center Stage was transforming itself into one of the top 10 resident professional theaters in the nation. From its shaky 1963 debut in a remodeled gymnasium that was almost shut down on opening night because it lacked a proper emergency exit, to a home in a converted cafeteria that burned out in 1974, Center Stage experienced a series of trials by fire that might have extinguished a less-resilient regional theater.

Baltimore rallied to the support of Center Stage following its devastating 1974 fire. The vacant, century-old Loyola College building at Calvert and Monument streets was bought by the city from its Jesuit owners for $200,000, which the Jesuits donated to Center Stage; the city in turn sold the building to the theater company for a token five dollars. Local banks, private contributors, and grants from the Ford Foundation and the National Endowment for the Arts provided the $1.8 million needed to turn the former school into a theater that won an American Institute of Architects national award for the exceptional adaptive reuse of an old building. And even more gratifying than the recognition its physical facility received from architects was the reception the reborn Center Stage got from its audiences. When it reopened in December 1975, it had 11,500 subscribers, more than double the number it had prior to the fire. By 1990 Center Stage had 13,000 subscribers and entertained audiences totaling 111,000 each year, and its Young People's Theatre tours elementary schools throughout the city and the state, providing plays especially designed to challenge the imaginations of young students.

Late in 1989 Center Stage announced plans to launch a $4.8-million project to renovate and expand its theater while raising $13 million to allow more innovation and artistic advancement for the company.

The activities of Baltimore's amateur and community theaters have been just as extensive and lively as those on its legitimate stage. From the "little theater" movement prior to the First World War to the din-

ner theaters of today, Baltimoreans have never been at a loss for theatrical entertainment.

In November 1916 Baltimore's initial "little theater" company—the Vagabonds—held its first performance. Today the Vagabonds proudly claim to be the nation's oldest "little theater" troupe still in operation. The second-oldest "little theater" group in Baltimore is Theatre Hopkins, founded on the Johns Hopkins campus in 1921 as the Homewood Playshop. Housed since 1942 in the converted barn (circa 1803) of Homewood House, Theatre Hopkins hires professional directors to guide the efforts of a dedicated group of experienced, nonprofessional actors. Its productions, amazingly diverse and skillful despite its tiny stage, receive respectful scrutiny by the press and praise from its audiences. Similarly constrained in size but not ambition is the Spotlighters Theater, a fixture on Saint Paul Street since 1962. A direct descendant of the Stagecrafters troupe founded in

Left: The Joseph Meyerhoff Symphony Hall opened in 1982 as a new home for the Baltimore Symphony Orchestra. Acclaimed for its acoustics, it enables Baltimore audiences to hear the BSO at its very best. Photo by Jed Kirschbaum

Below: French horns beckon a symphonic audience at the Meyerhoff Symphony Hall. Photo by David S. Lavine

1944, the Spotlighters put on a different play each month.

Other notable semiprofessional and amateur theatrical companies in town include the nearly century-old Paint and Powder Club, founded in 1893, which puts on annual satiric reviews to raise funds for charities and nonprofit groups such as the Baltimore Opera Company; the Fells Point Corner Theater; the Theater Project; the Dundalk Community Theatre; the "Cockpit in Court" summer theater at Essex Community College; and the Young Victorian Theatre Company, imaginative yet faithful summertime performers of the Gilbert and Sullivan canon since 1971. And virtually every night of the week, Baltimoreans can select from a smorgasbord of dinner theater productions put on by up to 10 different companies in the metropolitan area.

Baltimore was the birthplace of a few of the silver screen's early stars—most notably Francis X. Bushman, one of the first "matinee idols," and comedian Charley Chase, a contemporary, friend, and often colleague of comics such as Charlie Chaplin and Laurel and Hardy. Only in recent years, however, has the city itself become a star in the movies. What's more, during the 1970s and 1980s, a surprising number of Baltimore-born, -based, or -educated filmmakers began weaving a cinematic thread in the city's artistic tapestry, establishing a name and presence for Baltimore in an industry where it previously had gone unheralded. With movie companies now looking far beyond Southern California for authentic locations and reduced production costs, Baltimore has earned a reputation as one of the most versatile—and cooperative—cities available to moviemakers on the prowl for interesting backdrops and experienced yet economical support personnel. With Baltimore as its chief resource, Maryland has become one of the top 10 states in U.S. filmmaking.

Every creative process requires a period of gestation, and the seeds of Baltimore's role in the motion picture business were planted in the 1960s. It was then that an unusual group of Johns Hopkins students—Walter Murch, Matt Robbins, and Caleb Deschanel—began

experimenting with the medium in which they would later excel; that Barry Levinson, as a student at what is now The New Community College of Baltimore, began focusing on film as a possible career, one in which he would later celebrate Baltimore in a series of critically acclaimed movies and win the Academy Award for best director; and that John Waters, the iconoclastic, self-proclaimed master of avant-garde movies, shot his first films—and got arrested for photographing a would-be movie star cavorting naked in public.

Despite a shoestring budget for Hopkins film studies, the university spawned a remarkable set of cinematically talented alumni in the 1960s: Robbins, who graduated in 1965, won the top award at the Cannes Film Festival 10 years later for his screenplay for *Sugarland Express*; Deschanel, who graduated in 1966, won instant acclaim as the cinematographer of *The Black Stallion* and was nominated for Academy Awards for cinematography on *The Right Stuff* and *The Natural*. He also was the cinematographer on *Being There* and directed *The Escape Artist* and *Crusoe*. Murch, a friend of Robbins and Deschanel who graduated from Hopkins in 1965, shared the 1980 Academy Award for sound work on *Apocalypse Now*, having earlier done the sound editing on *Godfather I* and *II*, among other films, and later directed *Return to Oz* for Walt Disney Studios.

Levinson, an admittedly indifferent student at the city's Forest Park High School, credits a two-year program at what was then the Baltimore Junior College with providing him the direction he needed to embark first on a career as a writer and then as a filmmaker in Hol-

lywood. He has returned to Baltimore to direct *Diner*, *Tin Men*, and *Avalon*, three films, which he wrote, about the people and atmosphere in Baltimore between 1914 and 1968. Although Levinson won the Academy Award for best director for his 1988 film, *Rain Man*, his "Baltimore films" are more personal epics, depicting the travails and triumphs of his friends and family. *Avalon* is largely based on the story of how Levinson's immigrant grandparents came to Baltimore just before World War I and saw their offspring and grandchildren gradually become assimilated into American society.

A filmmaker who almost always uses Baltimore as his location—and inspiration—is John Waters, who won a devoted following with

Above: An annual three-day celebration of the arts, Artscape is an important part of the summer festival lineup in Baltimore. Jazz and other musical entertainment, visual arts exhibits, and children's activities are among the Artscape attractions that draw thousands of visitors to the Mount Royal cultural corridor each July. Photo by Greg Pease

such oddball epics as *Pink Flamingos* and *Female Trouble* in the 1970s, then earned mainstream critical praise with *Hairspray* (1988) and *Cry-Baby* (1990).

In addition to these indigenous filmmakers, Baltimore and Maryland have entered the big time as a location for moviemaking. Since its founding in 1979, the Maryland Film Commission has smoothed the way for Warner Brothers, MGM, Columbia Pictures, Twentieth Century Fox, and others to film more than 25 major motion pictures in the state; television programs and commercials also are made here often. In 1988 alone, motion picture and television production pumped approximately $45 million into Maryland's economy. One local developer has plans in the works to build a $45-million film production studio complex on a 17.8-acre site in the North Point section of Baltimore County, in order to bring more filmmakers to the area.

And for nearly 25 years the Baltimore Film Forum, a group of

cinematic connoisseurs, has annually sponsored a month-long Baltimore Film Festival featuring between 25 and 30 foreign and independent films.

Although Baltimore's place in the film world is relatively new, its role as a literary city has been long-lasting, diverse, and distinguished.

The city's first burst of belles lettres began shortly after the War of 1812 with the founding of the Delphian Club, a social and literary group, in 1816. Among the Delphians were the writers of three of the nation's most popular—and enduring—songs: Francis Scott Key of "The Star-Spangled Banner"; Samuel Woodworth, who wrote "The Old Oaken Bucket"; and John Howard Payne, an actor who penned "Home Sweet Home."

Not long after the Delphian Club folded its tent, Baltimore became the home of a struggling young writer named Edgar Allan Poe. He had moved here from Richmond to live with relatives in Baltimore, one of whom, his teenage cousin Virginia Clemm, became his wife. He lived with the Clemms in their tiny home at 203 N. Amity Street from 1832 to 1835. The house is now preserved as a Poe memorial to which visitors from all over the world pay their respects. While there, Poe received his first public recognition as a writer, winning a $50 prize awarded by the *Baltimore Saturday Visitor*, a weekly magazine, for "Ms. Found in a Bottle." It was published in the magazine's edition of October 19, 1833. One of the judges for the magazine's contest was

Baltimore attorney John Pendleton Kennedy, who befriended Poe and helped advance his career by introducing him to the editor of the *Southern Literary Messenger,* a magazine to which Poe became a regular contributor and ultimately its editor. Poe left Baltimore in 1835 but made a last, fatal visit to the city in September 1849. He was waylaid by political thugs, plied with drink, used as a multiple voter in a local election, and left to die. He, his wife, and mother-in-law are buried in the city's Westminster Churchyard at Fayette and Greene streets, another shrine to which the world's many Poe admirers pay homage.

Except for the works produced in the late nineteenth century and early twentieth century by poets Sidney Lanier and Lizette Woodworth Reese, both once acclaimed but now obscure, Baltimore's literary field lay fallow until the 1920s. Then the colorful fulminations of H.L. Mencken, which had been gaining in notoriety for a decade, exploded upon the national consciousness. His biting observations in *The Evening Sun,* in books, and in popular magazines made an indeli-

Native son Barry Levinson has become one of Hollywood's leading directors, but he often returns to Baltimore to make some of his finest movies such as *Diner, Tin Men,* and *Avalon,* which celebrate the city in which they were shot. This street scene from *Avalon* captures the vitality of Baltimore's streets in the immigrant era. Photo by Greg Pease

ble mark not only on the 1920s but on American literature. His scholarly masterpiece, *The American Language,* remains the definitive lexicon of our native idiom, and even 33 years after his death in 1956, Mencken's writings still could stir up controversy. Publication of his long-secret diary in 1989 caused a major literary ruckus, and the unsealing of seven additional volumes of autobiography in 1991 probably will add fuel to the fire—just as Mencken expected (and no doubt wished) when he ordered that the volumes be sealed for 35 years after his death.

Mencken was not the only nationally famous writer working in Baltimore during the 1920s—he was simply the best known. With his encouragement other local authors began making names for themselves. Dashiell Hammett, then a real-life detective in the Baltimore office of the Pinkerton agency, began submitting detective stories to the *Black Mask,* a 20-cent fiction magazine edited by Mencken and George Jean Nathan. Within 10 years Hammett would write *The Thin Man* and *The Maltese Falcon,* among other classic tales. James M. Cain, a reporter on Mencken's paper, *The Evening Sun,* later wrote *The Postman Always Rings Twice, Double Indemnity, Mildred Pierce,* and a dozen other novels. Gerald W. Johnson and R.P. Harriss, friends and colleagues of Mencken on *The Evening Sun*'s editorial page, became best-selling authors; Fulton Oursler, a reporter on the old Baltimore *American* during the 1920s, later wrote the religious epic *The Greatest*

Above: Movie director John Waters has built a career capturing life's oddities on film, and he finds plenty of material right in his home town. After making a series of campy gross-out pictures for the midnight circuit, he started to gain mainstream acceptance. In such recent movies as *Hairspray* and *Cry-Baby* he toned down some of the excesses, but Waters is still as irreverent as ever in directing movies he insists could only be made in Baltimore. Photo by Edwin H. Remsberg

Story Ever Told; and the impish poet Ogden Nash, who settled in town with his Baltimore-born wife, caught the nation's fancy with his witty—and sometimes incisive—rhymes.

In the 1930s F. Scott Fitzgerald, down on his luck, moved to Baltimore with his emotionally unstable wife, Zelda, who sought treatment at the Sheppard-Pratt Hospital. Fitzgerald had ancestral ties to the city; his full name was Francis Scott Key Fitzgerald, in honor of his great-uncle. Here he worked fitfully on *Tender Is the Night,* drank heavily, and mused melancholically: "Baltimore . . . is so rich with memories . . . I belong here, where everything is civilized and gay and rotted and polite." He, Zelda, and their daughter Scottie now rest in Saint Mary's Cemetery in Rockville.

In the late 1940s and early 1950s, The Johns Hopkins University graduated Russell Baker and John Barth, both of whom became masterful writers. William Manchester, a transplanted New Englander, began his writing career as a reporter on *The Evening Sun* and protégé of the aging Mencken at the same time Russell Baker was on its morning sibling, *The Sun,* earning the writing spurs that would later win

Below: Traci Lords is among the oddball casting choices Baltimore movie director John Waters loves to make. Here, Lords is shown with her husband, Brook Yeaton, at the local premiere of Waters' *Cry-Baby* in 1990. Photo by Edwin H. Remsberg

him a column at *The New York Times* and two Pulitzer Prizes. In the late 1950s J. Anthony Lukas, a Baltimore native, became a reporter for *The Sun*, beginning a career that also would lead to *The New York Times* and a pair of Pulitzers.

Today Baltimore's newspaper and literary scene is as laden with talent as at any time in the city's history. When the Pulitzer Prize committee devised several new journalistic categories in the 1970s and 1980s, it seemed as if *The Evening Sun's* Jon Franklin was always the first to win: In 1979 he won the first Pulitzer awarded for feature writing; in 1985 he won the first Pulitzer for scientific writing. Earlier, with colleague Alan Doelp, he wrote the national bestseller *Shocktrauma*, about the pioneering emergency treatment center at the University of Maryland Hospital. Also in 1985, *The Sun's* Alice Steinbach won the Pulitzer for feature writing; the year before, *Evening Sun* columnist Dan Rodricks won the American Newspaper Guild's Heywood Broun Award, considered by many journalists the equivalent of a Pulitzer.

The Evening Sun's political cartoonist, Mike Lane, has won the prestigious Sigma Delta Chi Award from that national journalists' society; the top award of the International Salon of Cartoonists in Quebec; the Fischetti Award bestowed by his fellow cartoonists; and the National Headliners Award, among other honors. *The Sun's* cartoonist, Kevin Kallaugher, has won a special award at an international cartoon festival in Budapest, Hungary, as well as encomiums elsewhere. Two Headliner Awards in a row were given to columnist Roger Simon, a native Chicagoan, after he joined *The Sun* in 1985. He also has won two top awards in a row from the American Society of Newspaper Editors, a group that also has honored *The Evening Sun's* Carl Schoettler, an uncommonly skillful and sensitive feature writer. And somehow or other *The Sun's* prolific movie critic, Stephen Hunter, manages to produce a best-selling thriller novel every few years. A film version is being made of his latest, *The Day Before Midnight*.

Baltimore's newspapers are far from its only font of literary achievements today. Poet, playwright, and essayist Daniel Mark Epstein, one of the city's most versatile writing talents, has five volumes of poetry, four prose works, two plays and the prestigious Prix de Rome to his credit; poet and short story writer Josephine Jacobsen has served a term as the poet in residence at the Library of Congress; Clarinda Harriss Raymond, a professor at Towson State University, edits the New Poets series, a local press that publishes the works of aspiring poets. *The Washington Post's* Pulitzer Prize-winning book critic, Jonathan Yardley, also writes books in his Roland Park home, while the *Post's* Baltimore correspondent, Paul Valentine, produces critically praised mystery books in his Homeland residence. Other local writers whose work receives national exposure and approbation include Christopher Corbett, a comic novelist; Madison Smartt Bell, a novelist who writes grimmer tales; his wife, poet Elizabeth Spires; and short story writer Steve Dixon.

Above: Edgar Allan Poe, who died in Baltimore in 1849, is the most famous literary figure associated with the city. His tomb in a downtown graveyard attracts many visitors. Photo by Greg Pease

Facing: The celebrated journalist and literary critic H.L. Mencken lived in this house on Union Square in West Baltimore for all but a few years of his life. It is now a museum. Photo by Alan Bolesta/Third Coast Stock Source

The committees, peers, and public who reward literacy excellence with citations—and sales—have amply recognized it in the recent works of Baltimore artists. Novelist Anne Tyler's 11th book, *Breathing Lessons*, and historian Taylor Branch's *Parting the Waters*, a history of the civil rights movement, joined Marylander Tom Clancy's *The Cardinal of the Kremlin* on the 1988 best-seller lists; and both Tyler and Branch won 1989 Pulitzer Prizes for their books, as did Johns Hopkins alumnus James M. McPherson for his history *The Battle Cry of Freedom: The Civil War Era*. The same week the Pulitzers were handed out to Tyler, Branch, and McPherson, the Academy of Motion Picture Arts and Sciences gave Barry Levinson the Oscar for best director—and two Oscars were awarded to the film adaptation of Tyler's 10th novel, *The Accidental Tourist*.

"Baltimore is *real* America," filmmaker John Waters told *The Sun* in the wake of the latest triumphs of the city's artistic community. "It's a great place to create whatever you create, good or bad, because it's away from New York and Los Angeles." Barry Levinson said of Baltimore at the 1987 premiere of *Tin Men*, "It's a great colorful city with great colorful characters. It's a rich and fertile place . . ." John Barth has echoed that sentiment: "Baltimore . . . is a place that continues to charge my batteries," just as it charges the batteries of so many artists and writers who draw inspiration from it.

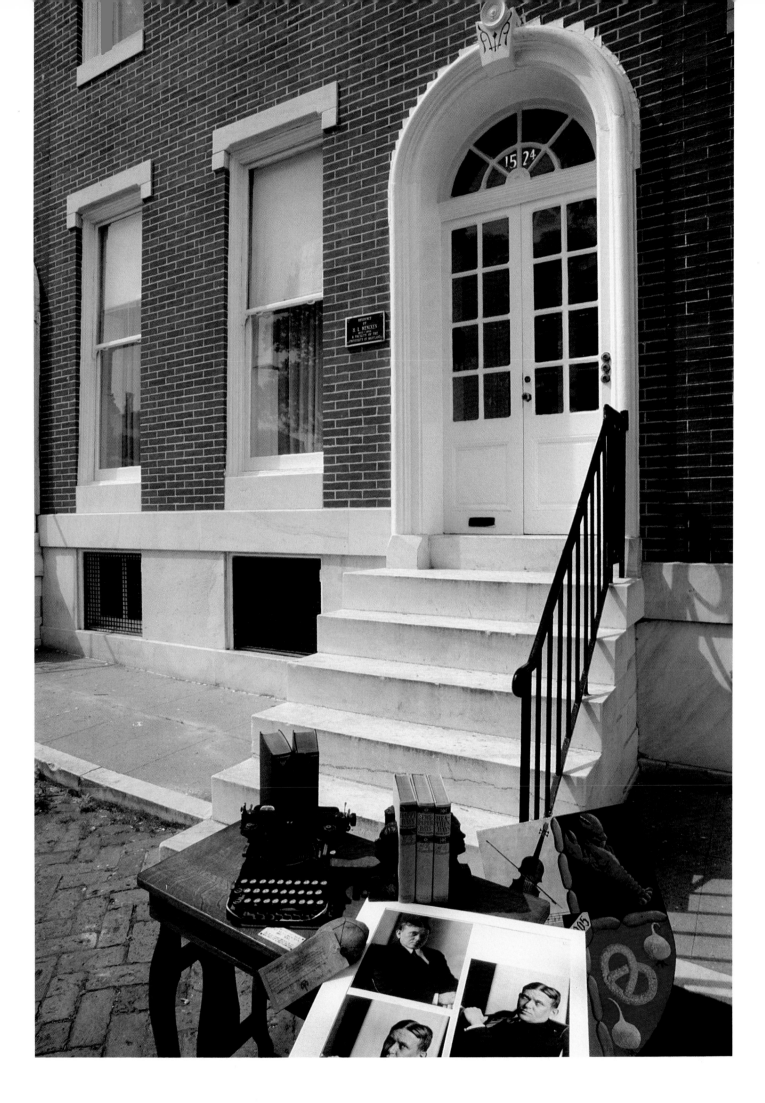

4

A City That Teaches— And Cares

. . .

The sound of music making fills the classrooms and corridors of
the Peabody Conservatory of Music. A landmark presence on
Mount Vernon Place, the Peabody is an integral part of the city's
cultural history. Photo by Roger Miller

As it was a century ago—as it has been for several centuries—Baltimore remains a center of broad educational initiatives and opportunities, as well as some of the finest health care available anywhere in the world.

"Baltimore as we know it is a city of schools, libraries, lecture courses, university advantages, and all that can conspire to the cultivation of intellect," wrote Jacob Frey in 1893. Home of America's first true university and preeminent medical school; birthplace of the nation's parochial school system; in the forefront of scientific and technological advances; Baltimore continues its "cultivation of intellect" as it prepares its citizens for the challenges of the next decade and century.

Even more important than its rich educational and medical heritage and current resources is Baltimore's recognition that more—much more—needs to be done to enhance and expand its centers of learning and research in order to ensure the economic vitality of the city and state.

Maryland boasts more than 300 colleges, universities, and trade and technical schools. It is an educational establishment well equipped, as *The Sun* has observed, to assure businesses "a work force that's ready to take on any job." And it offers ample outlets for those who seek the entrepreneurial innovations, career advancement, and sheer intellectual challenges that a thriving educational community can provide.

In 1792, four years before Baltimore Town was transformed by incorporation into a city, Bishop John Carroll—a member of the Baltimore Society for the Promotion of Useful Knowledge—presided over the founding of Saint Mary's Seminary for the training of priests. In 1805 the Maryland General Assembly chartered it as a university, and soon it became an important promulgator of education as it made Baltimore the center of Catholic publishing in the country. Three years later, in 1808, Mother Elizabeth Seton began the system of parochial schooling in America when she opened an academy in a building on Paca Street adjacent to Saint Mary's College.

Other religious denominations also sought to foster education. The Quakers began supporting a school in Baltimore as early as 1784; the Zion Lutheran Church and the German Reformed Congregation each opened schools to teach German-speaking students; the Methodists and the Episcopalians operated tuition-free schools for youngsters; and Hebrew schools were opened by the synagogues.

Baltimore's role in improving both medical education and health care can be traced to the efforts of sectarian academicians, led by Dr. John Beale Davidge, a native of Annapolis, to persuade the General Assembly in 1807 to incorporate what would become one of the state's most prestigious educational institutions, the University of Maryland School of Medicine in Baltimore. Ironically, on the very day that Davidge and several associates arranged for the introduction of the bill to create the then-College of Medicine of Maryland, a furious mob practically demolished it. Outraged by tales of doctors turning grave robbers in order to acquire bodies for dissection, the mob stormed the college's laboratory and anatomical theater, destroying everything inside the building.

The pioneering educators soon found other temporary quarters, and in 1812 they opened a new building of their own at Lombard and Greene streets. A round, dome-topped structure based on the Pantheon in Rome, now called Davidge Hall, it was the sixth medical school in the country and the first south of Pennsylvania. Today Davidge Hall is the oldest medical education building in the nation still in continuous use, and the University of Maryland that sprang from it now comprises 11 campuses around the state; at the University of Maryland at Baltimore campus, schools teaching medicine, law, dentistry (the oldest dental school in the country), pharmacy, social work, and community planning can be found.

The largest University of Maryland campus, the 1,510-acre complex in College Park, near Washington, is the seventh-largest academic institution in the country, with 235 major buildings and 38,000 students. In the past decade it has experienced triumphs and tragedies—tragedy in the drug-related death of basketball star Len Bias; triumphs in the strengthening of its research and graduate programs, enhancement of its partnerships with business and science groups, and embarkation on an ambitious, multimillion-dollar drive to establish itself as one of the nation's leading research institutions. Improvements in its basic arts and sciences curriculum will accompany efforts to build on the university's already strong programs in such high-technology fields as computer science, physics, and engineering, while it also aims to strengthen its molecular and cellular biology faculties and research facilities.

These initiatives represent a "remarkable public policy change," according to the chairman of the university's board of regents. Acknowledging the need to make Maryland's system of higher education among the best in the country, the General Assembly allocated some $200 million for public universities in fiscal 1989 and 1990.

Increased support from alumni is also being sought. In one spectacular instance, even a College Park dropout has shown extraordinary interest—$2 million worth—in the school he loved but felt compelled to leave because of a drive he now promotes in others: entrepreneurship.

Michael D. Dingman, president of Allied-Signal Corporation, dropped out of College Park in the late 1950s after having "too good a time" there. Now he has donated not only his money but an unlimited amount of his time and energy to found the Dingman Center for Entrepreneurship at the university's college of business and management. It is set to make Maryland a prime location for new venture management enterprises and aspiring entrepreneurs.

The center is open to undergraduate and graduate students, offering five core courses as well as independent study and research projects. The core courses cover venture creation and management, new venture financing, uncovering venture opportunities, entrepreneurship case studies, and strategies for emerging businesses.

As proof of College Park's move toward placement in the top ranks of research institutions, nothing could be more persuasive than the decision of the National Archives to put more than half of its incomparable collection of historical records in a new $205-million research building now under construction on a 33-acre site on the College Park campus.

The 1.7-million-square-foot archives annex—to be known officially as Archives II—is scheduled to open in 1993 and will house such priceless historic items as Mathew Brady's Civil War photographs and the documents of World War II, the assassination of John F. Kennedy, the Vietnam War, and the Challenger space shuttle explosion, among hundreds of other events. The university's president, William K. Kirwan, was engaging in no hyperbole when he observed: "The university will have access to resources in history, political science, international relations, and other similar fields that is unrivaled by any other in the nation."

Hyperbole also is unnecessary in describing the health-care achievements and impact of the Maryland Institute for Emergency

Below: The University of Maryland at Baltimore includes a hospital and a nationally renowned Shock Trauma Center among its medical facilities. Photo by Roger Miller

Bottom: Davidge Hall, which was constructed in 1812, is the oldest medical school bulding in the country that is still in continuous use. In addition to a medical school, the University of Maryland at Baltimore now has a number of other professional schools at its downtown campus. Photo by Roger Miller

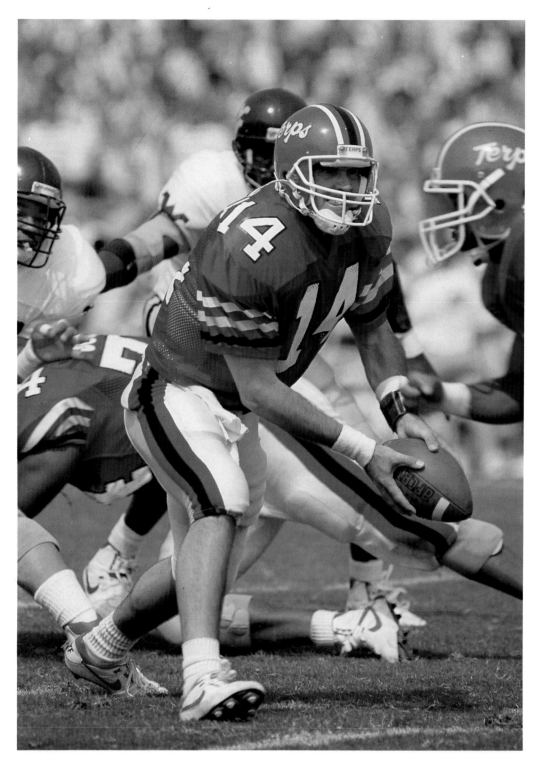

Medical Services and its Shock Trauma Center at the University of Maryland Hospital in Baltimore.

Brainchild of the abrasive yet compassionate Dr. R Adams Cowley, the Shock Trauma Center was founded in 1961 and has established procedures and techniques for treating the critically injured that have been adopted throughout the world, saving countless lives.

Dr. Cowley, a heart surgeon, possesses what *The Evening Sun* called "the unique ability to confront an old problem and ask new questions," an attribute essential to all great pioneers. He was distressed to realize that little more than 40 percent of critically injured people—the victims of car crashes, boating accidents, shootings—rushed to Maryland hospital emergency rooms survived. He wanted to know why. Following meticulous research, he detailed extraordinary new procedures for employing massive treatment to injuries during what he termed the "golden hour" following the trauma that caused them. Cowley's techniques more than doubled the survival rate, which now is about 90 percent. From the two-bed "laboratory" he established 30 years ago, the Shock Trauma Center has grown to a $44-million, 138-bed high-tech center that is the hub of a statewide emergency medical system—housed, appropriately enough, in the eight-story R Adams Cowley Shock Trauma Center building, opened in January 1989 beside University Hospital, itself a major research and treatment facility in downtown Baltimore.

The University of Maryland's College Park and Baltimore campuses are not the only expanding divisions within its system. Major improvements have been made at the university's campus on the Eastern Shore, a traditionally black campus, and the Catonsville campus of the University of Maryland at Baltimore County (UMBC) is becoming a leader in the biotechnology field. Along with Johns Hopkins and the University of Maryland at College Park, UMBC is among the top 100 universities nationwide in spending funds on research and development.

University of Maryland football teams are among the sporting organizations on the school's College Park campus. Photo by Rich Riggins

In 1989 UMBC's Center for Structural Biochemistry installed a custom-built, 12.6-ton tandem mass spectrometer, a $1.4-million instrument that is only one of five of its kind in the world. Along with a gas chromatograph-mass spectrometer and other instruments already at the center, UMBC now is equipped to become a national and international research center for chemists, physicists, biologists, and engineers, jointly funded by the National Science Foundation, the Maryland Biotechnology Institute, and the university.

Baltimore has been a medical mecca since colonial times, with

renowned physicians such as Dr. Charles Frederich Wiesenthal, once doctor to Frederick the Great of Prussia, calling it home and becoming president of the state's first medical society in 1788.

Yet as *The Evening Sun* observed on the occasion of the centennial of the Johns Hopkins Hospital in 1989, "it is no exaggeration to say that modern medical education and medical practice throughout the world owe more to Johns Hopkins than to any other single establishment," and Baltimore itself "can reasonably claim that Johns Hopkins Hospital and university [are] the institutions that, above all others, mark this as a unique city."

Other educational institutions in the United States had called themselves universities prior to the founding of Johns Hopkins in 1876, but even the redoubtable Charles Eliot, longtime president of Harvard, acknowledged that Hopkins was "America's first true university," created in the image of the great research and postgraduate institutions of Europe. It was to these universities in Great Britain, Germany, and elsewhere on the continent that American scholars had been required to go if they wanted the kind of advanced scholarship and research that Hopkins offered from its inception. Today Hopkins has the largest university research program in the country, with a budget of more than a half-billion dollars devoted to such fields as medicine, public health, biotechnology, and biomedical engineering.

It is doubtful that Johns Hopkins (the "Johns" was his mother's maiden name) could have foreseen the international impact his university, medical school, and hospital would have. Considerable doubt even exists over whether Hopkins—a flinty, aggressive, and hard-nosed businessman whose own education had ended when he was 12—knew what he was creating when he decreed in his will that a "university" and hospital bearing his name be founded, and that the medical school of the university be associated with the hospital. Such a link between a university, medical school, and a working hospital was unprecedented.

The founding faculty at Hopkins changed the face of American higher education. Hopkins and its medical school have an impressive list of historic firsts to their credit,

a roster of prestigious faculty members and alumni whose contributions to American scholarship and society are widespread and pervasive, and a commitment to innovation and excellence that remains undiminished despite severe recent budget deficits in the arts and sciences division that have required a rigorous financial belt-tightening.

Research at the faculty, graduate, and undergraduate levels has always been the hallmark of education at Hopkins, both in medicine and other academic fields. Medical students were first taught in a working hospital at Hopkins, and residency training was begun there. The first school of hygiene and public health was founded at Hopkins; its school of continuing studies, founded as an evening college to provide university education for adults, is the oldest in the nation; the Johns Hopkins University Press was the first of its kind in the country; and the first American journals devoted to scholarly research, part of the handiwork of the original Hopkins faculty, were among the JHU Press' first publications. The Hopkins' Paul H. Nitze School of Advanced International Studies, headquartered in Washington, D.C., maintains the only American graduate school in Europe at its Western European Center in Bologna, Italy, and Hopkins broke additional academic ground internationally in 1986 when it opened a joint graduate center in China with Nanjing University. The Space Telescope Science Institute located on Hopkins' Baltimore campus (and operated by a consortium of 17 institutions, including Hopkins) is the nerve center for the data received from the Hubble Space Telescope, which still uncovers important astronomical information despite flaws in its main mirrors discovered after its launch. Another shuttle mission in 1993 may be able to fix some of the Hubble's worst glitches, which have never prevented it from producing unprecedented scientific work.

For relatively small institutions, the Johns Hopkins Hospital and its medical school have nurtured and produced an astonishingly disproportionate number of outstanding scholars and physicians. In almost every realm of medicine, Hopkins' influence has been so great that Hopkins alumni who obtained their degrees in other fields continually find themselves emphasizing

Facing: Ronald G. Michels, M.D., a professor of opthamology, stands in front of the world-famous Johns Hopkins Hospital. Photo by Alan Bolesta/Third Coast Stock Source

Below: The Applied Physics Lab is one reason why The Johns Hopkins University receives more in federal research grants than any other university in the country. Photo by Greg Pease

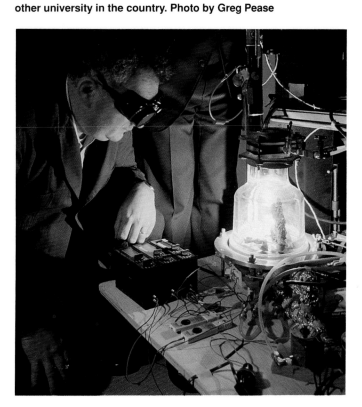

Left: Johns Hopkins Hospital, which opened in 1889, has a world-wide reputation. Thousands of patients from around the globe have come here for treatment, and many of the medical professionals who trained at Hopkins have taken their expertise to distant places. Photo by Greg Pease

Facing: Shriver Hall, on the Homewood campus of The Johns Hopkins University, has been the site for many a distinguished lecture and concert over the years. Photo by Greg Pease

Below: Hopkins' Applied Physics Lab developed the nonreusable syringe in 1989. Photo by Edwin H. Remsberg

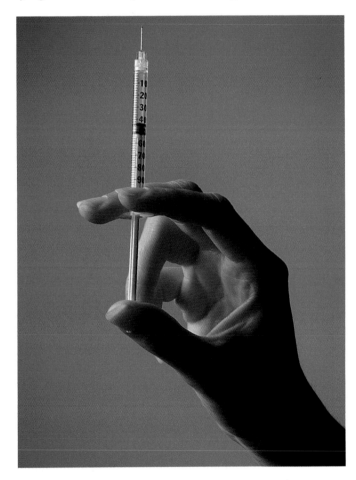

the fact that they are not medical doctors.

The Hopkins School of Medicine was the first to make a college degree a requirement for admission, the first to admit women on an equal basis with men, and the first to establish the standard four-year curriculum for medical education—two years of classroom and laboratory science followed by two years of clinical education in the hospital.

When the Hopkins Hospital opened in 1889, *The Sun* presciently hailed the event as "the beginning of the career of an institution the prospective usefulness of which to the world it would be difficult to over estimate." As Hopkins Hospital celebrated its centennial in 1989, the *New England Journal of Medicine* stated: "Medical education in this country has been shaped by many institutions and personalities, but a century ago none were more influential than The Johns Hopkins University and the men who conceived and directed its new hospital and medical school . . . Today, Hopkins remains one of our most distinguished centers of medical care and scholarship, still vital and innovative after an illustrious century of service . . ."

Although Hopkins is synonymous with unexcelled medical research and treatment, and the University of Maryland's Shock Trauma Center, research, and general quality of care are known worldwide, they are by no means the only first-class medical facilities in the Baltimore region. There are 28 hospitals in the Baltimore metropolitan area, many of them acute-care general hospitals with specialized as well as basic services. Among these are the Baltimore Regional Burn Center at the Francis Scott Key Medical Center; Children's Hospital's Center for Reconstructive Surgery; Church Hospital's hospice program; Union Memorial Hospital's hand surgery and sports medicine clinics; the renowned Wilmer Eye Clinic at Hopkins; and the Sheppard and Enoch Pratt psychiatric hospital.

Hopkins' economic impact on Baltimore and Maryland is as great as its educational influence nationally and internationally. It is one of the largest employers in the state, has satellite campuses in Montgomery and Howard counties, receives more in federal research grants than any other university in the country, and in fiscal 1990 adopted its first billion-dollar budget. With the creation in 1984 of the Dome Corporation, a unique for-profit joint venture by the university and the Johns Hopkins Health Care System, Hopkins is poised to increase its economic impact in Baltimore and the state.

Dome, created with investments of $800,000 each by the university and the hospital, is an enterprise involved in property development and management, creation of service ventures, and identification and pursuit of ways to benefit financially from the research and intellectual properties at both institutions.

So far Dome has embarked on a wide variety of commercial enterprises, from real estate planning and development to hotel management, personnel training, stress-management seminars—even the management of parking lots. To date, Dome's most ambitious project involves its plan to develop a $500-million biomedical research park on the 130 acres that surround Francis Scott Key Medical Center, the former City Hospitals long owned by Baltimore City but taken over by Hopkins—at the city's behest—in 1982. The research park, The Johns Hopkins Bayview Research Campus, will be one of the largest real estate projects in Baltimore's history. Its price tag will equal the combined costs of Harborplace, the Maryland Science Center, the World Trade Center, the Equitable Bank Center, the USF&G and IBM buildings, and the Hyatt Regency Hotel. It is expected to generate 5,000 to 8,000 jobs, providing the city with as much as $3 million in annual taxes, and have a profound impact on the development of East Baltimore. Dome's ultimate aim, according to its president and chief executive officer, James D.M. McComas, is to keep Hopkins—and Baltimore—"on the leading edge of technology development into the twenty-first century."

That the twenty-first century should dawn without the Peabody Conservatory of Music is an unthinkable prospect to Baltimore's educational and cultural communities. Plagued by annual multimillion-dollar deficits for more than a decade, Peabody was absorbed by

Hopkins in 1977. For a dozen years Hopkins covered the conservatory's deficits to the tune of $22 million, but the university's own financial plight compelled it to announce in 1988 that it would have to reduce its yearly support of Peabody to $500,000. The Maryland General Assembly extended a $3.2-million lifeline to Peabody in 1989, and a special task force under Lieutenant Governor Melvin A. Steinberg immediately undertook the job of devising a rescue plan with determination—and realism. After an intense five-month fund-raising drive between April and September 1990, Peabody raised $15 million in order to qualify for a matching grant from the state that will increase its endowment fund to between $40 million and $50 million by 1996. In the 1990s a second fund-raising campaign will endeavor to boost the endowment to about $80 million, ensuring the conservatory's financial stability.

Peabody's artistic standing is equal to that of the Juilliard School in New York, the Curtis Institute in Philadelphia, and the Eastman School of Music in Rochester, but its endowment pockets are far shallower. A musical education is extremely costly because it requires one-on-one instruction between student and teacher. And with a diminishing

Above: One of the more recent additions to the Homewood campus of The Johns Hopkins University, the Space Telescope Science Institute is a nerve center for analyzing data from space telescopes. Photo by Greg Pease

Facing: John Singer Sargent's famous painting *The Four Doctors* honors a quartet of physicians who helped make the Johns Hopkins Hospital a great institution. Depicted from left to right are William H. Welch, William S. Halsted, William Osler, and Howard A. Kelly. The painting hangs in the Welch medical library. Photo by Greg Pease

pool of talented students seeking placement in prestigious conservatories, Peabody has had to discount its tuition while increasing faculty salaries in order to attract students and retain the high-caliber musicians to teach them.

But the determined effort to keep Peabody open—and first-class—appears to have succeeded. "We don't want to *save* Peabody," Lieutenant Governor Steinberg said, "we just want to maintain an institution that is vital and precious to this state."

Despite its financial exigencies, Peabody has in no way diminished its commitment to superiority—and innovation—in musical education. In 1984 it created a recording arts program, combining highly technical training in sound engineering with the conservatory's traditional courses in musical performance. It is the only program of its

kind in the country based at a conservatory. Select students work on obtaining a Peabody diploma in their chosen musical instrument while also taking engineering courses at Hopkins and earning a second degree at Peabody's recording studio. They are specially trained in the art of recording classical music ensembles—and are almost immediately employable upon graduation.

The practical application of an artistic training is also a goal at the Maryland Institute College of Art, the oldest college in the city and one of its liveliest. Under the leadership of Fred Lazarus IV, who became director in 1978, the institute's budget has tripled to $12 million, its endowment has jumped from $1,250,000 to $5 million, annual giving has grown from $150,000 to $575,000, and its philosophy of art education has evolved toward a more liberal arts approach with an emphasis on how to prepare students for life after art school. In the process the institute, founded in 1826, has become recognized as one of the five top independent art colleges in the nation, with a small (800-plus) student body now drawn from 35 states and 30 foreign countries.

There has been no lessening in the institute's commitment to traditional art school training—requiring, for example, that students take 12 credits in drawing regardless of their specific art major. But a broad program of business internships, courses in professional skills, and workshops on such subjects as business for artists, taxes for artists, marketing and promotion, finding art jobs with the federal government, and "grantsmanship" prepare students for the hard realities beyond the

institute's splendid artistic enclave on Mount Royal Avenue. It is a curriculum, Lazarus has written, that is "surprisingly entrepreneurial" and encourages students "to work in or start small firms." Today, Lazarus notes, graphic-design firms founded by or employing Maryland Institute alumni stretch from one end of Charles Street to the other. They have had a considerable impact on the printing industry, the sixth-largest in Maryland. At the same time, a growth in the number of downtown art galleries, many of which display the works of Maryland Institute faculty and alumni, has brought Baltimore the attention of the national arts community. Art and commerce, the institute has shown, need not be incompatible.

Artistry in the kitchen also is addressed—and served up with style—at the Baltimore International Culinary Arts Institute, founded in 1972 as part of the then-Community College of Baltimore. Now it is a private, nonprofit corporation that is one of the few cooking schools in the U.S. offering an associate degree in restaurant management and cooking.

The institute's 350 culinary arts students put in intensive, eight-hour days in the school's downtown classrooms and kitchens, as well as its adjacent restaurant, L'Ecole. There they offer an exotic bill of fare including everything from Coquilles Saint Jacques (scallops and shrimp in a white wine sauce) to alligator schnitzel, as well as wait on tables, tend bar, and wash dishes, too.

Employers from around the country recruit the institute's graduates, and more than 80 percent of the seniors are hired before they graduate. The school itself recruits students from around the country and the world, with recent graduates coming from as far away as Great Britain, Guam, Saudi Arabia, and Peru. The "international" in the institute's name also reflects more than just the origins of its student body; it refers to the unusual overseas branch the school maintains at the 55-room, lakefront Park Hotel, located on a

50-acre site in County Cavan, Ireland. Plans now are under way to expand the institute's Baltimore operation by converting a vacant, 80-year-old elementary school near Little Italy into an academic center that will accommodate twice the number of students now enrolled at the college.

The institute's president, Roger Chylinski, emphasizes that the school does not graduate "chefs." It graduates "cooks." Becoming a chef requires the practical experience learned in the heat of a professional kitchen. And in fact some of the institute's graduates don't even end up cooking. A school brochure boasts that one alumnus became a "food stylist" who has served as a consultant to Burger King, Hardee's, Jell-O, Bacardi, Pillsbury, and other food and beverage corporations. He comes up with ways to make Burger King Whoppers or Bacardi daiquiris look terrific in print and television advertisements. Among his accomplishments has been the discovery of how to guarantee that strawberries plop into a bowl of cereal with an extra-special, eye-catching splash: Use Elmer's Glue instead of milk.

Around most of the U.S.—and overseas, for that matter—the

Left: Founded in 1845, the United States Naval Academy is ranked among the top educational institutions in the country. Of its annual 15,000 applicants, only 1,300 are accepted. Photo by Greg Pease

Below: The training program at the Naval Academy in Annapolis is extremely rigorous. During graduation jubilant young men and women toss their caps into the air, in keeping with Academy tradition. Photo by Roger Miller

name "Annapolis" does not evoke the image of Maryland's capital but rather the United States Naval Academy, the undergraduate college of the U.S. Navy, which was founded there in 1845.

Covering 338 beautifully landscaped acres along the Severn River, the Naval Academy is ranked among the top educational institutions in the country. A 600-member faculty that is equally divided between military officers and civilian professors teaches some 4,500 midshipmen a broad curriculum that offers more than 500 courses and 18 academic majors. All midshipmen, even those majoring in such subjects

as English or economics, must take enough required technical courses to qualify for a bachelor of science degree, which they receive along with their commissions as Navy ensigns or Marine Corps second lieutenants.

Professional military training begins on day one at the Naval Academy. Midshipmen are given instruction and training in navigation, seamanship and tactics, naval engineering, naval weapons, military law, and leadership. All midshipmen must also meet minimum requirements in various strength tests, including swimming, running, and certain gymnastics. In addition every midshipman must participate in a sport either at the varsity or intramural level, with 37 intramural sports to choose from—including everything from basketball and boxing to water polo and wrestling. The annual Army-Navy football classic was first played in 1890—with Navy the winner—and the academy's sailing team (at 225 members, the school's largest varsity team) won intercollegiate sailing's top prize, the Leonard Fowle

Trophy, for an unprecedented seven years in a row, 1977 to 1983.

The Naval Academy receives applications from more than 15,000 young men and women each year. About 1,300 of them are accepted. In 1975 federal legislation was enacted authorizing the admission of women to the nation's service academies. The first female midshipman, Elizabeth Anne Belzer of Freeman's Trace Tabb, Virginia, entered Annapolis in 1976 and graduated 29th in her class in 1980.

The Naval Academy's mission has remained the same throughout its long history: to prepare midshipmen for leadership roles in the Navy, Marine Corps, and elsewhere. Among its distinguished graduates have been Alfred Thayer Mahan, class of 1859, who became an esteemed historian, naval strategist, and biographer; Albert A. Michelson, class of 1873, who was the first American to receive the Nobel Prize for physics; Chester Nimitz, class of 1905, who commanded the U.S. Pacific Fleet during World War II and later served as chief of naval operations; and Jimmy Carter, class of 1946, who became the 39th president of the United States.

Also among the more than 20 higher educational institutions in the Greater Baltimore area are Loyola College and the University of Baltimore, which along with the University of Maryland have earned the rare honor of receiving accreditation for their business programs at both the undergraduate and graduate levels; Morgan State University, Coppin State College, and Bowie State College, all distinguished, historically black institutions that are establishing new directions in such important fields as teacher education, urban affairs, business, and engineering; Goucher College; the College of Notre Dame of Maryland,

the first Catholic women's college in the country; Villa Julie; and Western Maryland College. All provide depth in the liberal arts. Towson State University, the second-largest campus in the state university system, is nationally recognized among large East Coast schools and is expanding its research and community service programs in a wide variety of ways. Among these is its opening of what is believed to be the first university study center for suburban and regional problems.

The Greater Baltimore area has seven community colleges—The

New Community College of Baltimore, Catonsville Community College, Dundalk Community College, Essex Community College, Harford Community College, Howard Community College, and Anne Arundel Community College—offering two-year programs that prepare students to transfer to four-year colleges and universities or go right into the job market with advanced training.

The Harbor Campus of The New Community College of Baltimore—whose complex consists of two bright red buildings on East Lombard Street, within view of the Inner Harbor—has become the college's business and industry center. There students are not trained in history or literature (which are taught at the college's other campus on Liberty Heights Avenue) but in how to operate computers, function in a biotech laboratory, and manage personnel. The college's former president, Joseph T. Durham, explained the reasoning behind the school's philosophy:

Because of the tremendous amount of reshuffling and change that's been going on in American industry, there is a growing number of jobs that require strong technological literacy and problem-solving skills . . .

Somebody needs to help train those workers so they can function in those jobs. Here . . . we've got the know-how, we've got the equipment and we've got the location . . .

The other community colleges recognize a similar mission. The Greater Baltimore area has more than 1,000 public, private, and parochial schools, an educational system of great accomplishments, facing great challenges. The region's private schools are among the finest in the country, as are many of its public schools. Within Baltimore City proper, however, the problems that are familiar to public school systems in many major cities have not been avoided—and are now being addressed. To admit that many of the city's public schools have troubles is not a failing but a strength; an acknowledgment that the only way to correct the difficulties is to meet them head-on.

That has been the approach—and commitment—of Mayor Kurt L. Schmoke, himself a product of the public school system who went on to become a Rhodes Scholar. He made improvement of the public schools a major campaign pledge when he first ran for mayor in 1987, and he devotes an enormous amount of his time and energy to fulfilling that promise. State officials also are determined to improve public education in the city—and throughout Maryland. New performance standards, set to take effect in 1992, will make local school districts accountable for achieving higher test scores, ensuring better student attendance, and reducing the number of high school dropouts. Most school systems are already striving to meet the new standards, and some are achieving several of the goals.

Among the community initiatives undertaken in Baltimore in recent years is the Commonwealth program, a project created in 1984 by

Above: Loyola College is one of the small private colleges in the Baltimore area. Students hard at work in a laboratory classroom will soon be taking their places in the local work force. Photo by Roger Miller

Facing: United States Naval Academy plebes participate in the annual competition to climb the Herndan Monument. It is no easy task because the monument has been greased. Many plebes fall in frustration before one determined sailor-in-the-making, standing on the shoulders of his buddies, is hoisted to the top. Photos by Edwin H. Remsberg

a church-based organization, BUILD (Baltimoreans United in Leadership Development); the Greater Baltimore Committee; the city's Office of Employment Development; and the school system. The project, funded by a broad array of local businesses, guarantees college aid or job interviews for every city high school senior who has maintained a record of 95-percent attendance. Its ultimate goal is to help all public school students find employment or a way to attend college.

Within the city's system of 182 public schools, which provides instruction to more than 100,000 students, the most heartening success stories remain the special selective schools that have long attracted students with outstanding potential. Applicants to these schools can come from any city neighborhood but need to have qualifying grades and test scores.

The oldest selective school, Baltimore City College, was founded in 1839 and is the third-oldest public high school in the U.S. After occupying a number of locations downtown, it moved in 1928 to a massive, "collegian Gothic" building on an elevated site at 33rd Street and the Alameda, an edifice that soon was dubbed "the Castle on the Hill." It was integrated in 1954 and began accepting female students in 1977.

Applicants for admission to Baltimore City College must maintain an 80-percent average, have a good attendance record, and perform above their grade level. All 1,400 students at "City" must take at least one year of Latin, as well as a "Man and His Culture" course that

weaves together history, literature, and the arts. Some 20 percent of the students belong to an honors program that consists of a demanding curriculum featuring two years of classical studies, with a concentration on philosophy. Not suprisingly, about 85 percent of City College graduates go on to college.

Among City's distinguished—and devoted—alumni are Mayor Schmoke, Governor William Donald Schaefer, Lieutenant Governor Melvin Steinberg, novelist Leon Uris (who flunked English but later wrote *Exodus*), and *New York Times* columnist Russell Baker. Baker once devoted a column to the school he "still remembered lovingly." He reported attending a special assembly with other City College graduates being honored for their achievements and finding it a place, he was proud to recount, where "they now say the Pledge of Allegiance in Latin." It is also a place, Baker wrote, that "was not the all-white, all-male school we had known in another life, but an elite place made possible by the conviction of a few old-timers that one nation, undivided, could be more than a hollow phrase for political rogues to abuse at election time."

Other selective schools include the Polytechnic Institute, where a

Towson State University, recognized as one of the finer large East Coast institutions, is expanding its research and community service programs, which will include a university study center for suburban and regional problems. Photo by Roger Miller

special curriculum of science, math, and engineering is taught along with standard offerings, and Western High School, an all-female institution.

The Polytechnic Institute—"Poly" to all Baltimoreans—was founded in 1883 as an engineering school. Today it offers two special programs: Course A, in which students complete a four-year, college preparatory course in three years and then begin college-level work in the fourth year; and Course B, which is a regular, four-year college preparatory course. Like its main rival, City College, it inspires fierce loyalty. Poly's students have a 96-percent attendance record (the highest in the city), attain the highest scores on college admissions tests, and send 90 percent of each class to college. It was the first city high school to integrate and to have its own student government. In 1967 Poly moved to a complex on Falls Road that it shares with Western

High School, but it remained an all-male school until 1974. Now about a third of the student body is female.

Poly, like City, has its own roster of famous alumni: H.L. Mencken, who of course pursued a literary rather than a technical career; Alonzo Decker, Jr., former head of Black and Decker, the giant power tool firm; Bradford Butler, former chief executive officer of Proctor and Gamble; Willard Hackerman, head of Whiting-Turner, the huge contracting company that has been instrumental in the rebuilding of Baltimore; and George McGowan, president of the Baltimore Gas and Electric Company.

Although not strictly classified as one of the city's select schools, Dunbar High School, a nearly all-black institution, has established a unique partnership with The Johns Hopkins University, which provides Dunbar students with special training in health-care fields. While it is nationally renowned for its basketball team, Dunbar is equally proud of the 85 percent of each graduating class that goes on to college.

The newest selective school in the city is the Baltimore School for the Arts. Opened in 1980, it offers a full academic curriculum as well as arts courses in music, dance, theater, drawing, painting, sculpture, photography, ceramics, design, and mixed media. The students, who come from the entire metropolitan area and are selected at annual auditions, put in a grueling day: after four one-hour periods for academic studies, the students devote four one-hour periods to the arts. The extra pressure of combining an academic and artistic education evidently pays off. Ninety percent of the school's graduates go on to a liberal arts college, conservatory, or art school.

High school football rivalries can be intense, as seen in this Overlea vs. Franklin game. Photo by Joe Giza

Governor Schaefer, who was mayor of Baltimore when the School for the Arts was founded, now wants to create a public math-science boarding school for special students from throughout Maryland. At the University of Maryland at Baltimore County, a summertime Academy for Mathematics, Science and Technology already has been established as a school for a select group of elementary and secondary school-teachers, readying them to prepare their students even better for future training and careers in technological jobs.

Private elementary and secondary schools in the Baltimore area are among the best in the country. Calvert School, a small private elementary school in Roland Park, has long been renowned worldwide for its home-teaching curriculum, as well as for the quality of courses at the school itself. The Gilman School, with classes ranging from first to 12th grade, has been named one of 60 exemplary schools by the Council on American Private Education. Its graduates traditionally head to Hopkins, Princeton, Yale, Duke, and the University of Maryland at College Park. Saint Paul's School (one for boys and one for girls); McDonogh School; Boys' Latin; Friends School; Oldfields (where the Duchess of Windsor went as a girl); the Park School—all are among the dozens of private schools offering college preparatory and advanced placement courses in academic settings characterized by small classes, close teacher-to-child interaction, and a sense of community that enhances the learning environment.

Just as education, in its truest sense, is never completed, neither is the quest for its improvement in the Baltimore area. Polls taken in recent years by *The Sun* and *The Evening Sun* reveal that Baltimore residents are growing increasingly frustrated by the lack of apparent improvement in the city's schools, even though they give Mayor Schmoke high marks for making education a top priority.

At the collegiate level, a special report prepared for the Greater Baltimore Committee by SRI International, a California-based consulting firm, had hard words but a hopeful outlook for higher education in the Greater Baltimore area. Despite acknowledging Baltimore's "technological leadership in such fields as biotechnology and biomedicine," its "nationally recognized physical revitalization program . . . , lower development costs than other Eastern Seaboard cities, and massive federal spending and spillover activities from Washington, D.C.," the report criticized the area's higher education system for "acting as a silent bystander in the region's economic development

when it should be playing an active leadership role in building Balti-more's economic future."

"Fortunately," the report's authors wrote, "the emerging recognition of an economic role at many institutions, the new appreciation for higher education in Annapolis, and the newly developed interest in the business community all suggest the potential for making historic changes in the way higher education serves the region's economic future."

Since the release of the SRI report in 1988, the main Baltimore-area business schools—the University of Maryland, University of Baltimore, Loyola College, Towson State, and Morgan State—have risen to the challenge and made significant strides toward improving their programs to meet the "regional needs" of the business community. "The SRI report was like a two-by-four on the side of the head. It got our attention," Dean C. Robert Margenthaler of Loyola's Joseph J. Sellinger School of Business and Management told *The Sun*'s Cindy Harper-Evans.

"Indeed, the now-legendary SRI report may well be the best thing that ever happened to all of the area's business schools—and an important contribution to the long-term health of the regional economy," Harper-Evans wrote.

Tom Chmura, project director for the SRI report, said that there "is growing evidence of higher education's willingness to collaborate with the business community . . ."

"We're moving in the right direction, and the early signs are positive," said Chmura, who demonstrated his faith in Baltimore's future by leaving SRI to become head of economic development for—guess what?—The Greater Baltimore Committee.

Above: This wall mural at Mount Washington Elementary School, painted by students and parents, helps brighten the day for students—and teachers, too. Photo by Jed Kirschbaum

Right: Considered one of Baltimore's finest private schools, the Gilman School has students from the first through 12th grades. Many of Baltimore's business and community leaders have benefited from their educations at such schools. Photo by Greg Pease

5

A City at Play

There are plenty of ways to see the splendors of a state often
referred to as "America in Miniature," as this ultra-light flying over
Baltimore County demonstrates. Photo by Jed Kirschbaum

As its *official* state sport, duly codified by legislative act and gubernatorial approval, Maryland honors an athletic pursuit with origins that are remote even by European standards: jousting. A medieval pastime featuring lance-bearing riders endeavoring to spear a tiny ring while galloping by it on horseback, jousting gained popularity among Marylanders just prior to the Civil War, when romantic notions of the age of chivalry captured the fancy of the state's landed gentry. Its small but sturdy cadre of latter-day adherents succeeded in having it designated the official state sport in 1962.

Although subsequent efforts to give lacrosse, America's oldest sport and one of Maryland's favorites, the state's imprimatur have met with fierce resistance by jousters (who have shown up at the state legislature in full medieval regalia, lances at the ready), ask the average Baltimorean what the official state sport should be and the answers would reflect the diversity of the city's sport scene and the devotion of its fans.

Several especially devout horse-racing fans have had their ashes scattered over the finish line at Pimlico Race Track, and when the U.S. Postal Service issued a stamp honoring Maryland, it depicted a skipjack sailing serenely past the State House in Annapolis. During the depths of the Baltimore Orioles' horrifying 1988 season, which began with an appalling 0-21 record, the turnstiles at Memorial Stadium still twirled at a unprecedented pace. And despite the shameful, middle-of-the-night decampment of the once-proud Baltimore Colts to Indianapolis in 1984, the Colts Marching Band of amateur musicians still meets, rehearses, and performs publicly, faithfully awaiting the resurrection of NFL football in Baltimore. Hockey, soccer, basketball—all beckon Baltimoreans.

The recreational opportunities available to Baltimore residents are equally rich. More than 30 years ago *National Geographic* hailed Maryland as "America in Miniature," offering as it does the mountains to the west, the beaches and bay to the east, the attractions of a major city, and the ambience of small towns.

While sailing and horse racing in Maryland can trace their origins to the colonial era, and lacrosse literally goes back to the Indians (albeit New York and Canadian Indians, whose sport was transplanted in Maryland late in the nineteenth century), major-league, professional sports in Baltimore began with the Birds—the legendary Orioles of the 1890s.

Baseball in Baltimore actually preceded the Orioles by nearly 25 years. Its birth "can be dated, placed and named," according to James H. Bready, an Oriole historian and former *Evening Sun* editorial writer. On July 12, 1859, at a site known as Flat Rocks (which now rests beneath the waters of Druid Lake), an amateur Baltimore team called the Excelsiors held an inner-squad exhibition game duly reported in a front-page notice in the Baltimore *American*. A year later, on June 6, 1860, the Excelsiors met the Washington Potomacs on what is now the Ellipse south of the White House and whipped them 40 to 24. It was—outside of the New York area, where most early baseball clubs began—the first intercity, nine-inning baseball game in U.S. history,

and it "originated the tradition that Baltimore plays winning baseball," Bready noted in his Orioles history, *The Home Team*. (Alas, a month after that Washington triumph, the Baltimore Excelsiors played the Brooklyn, NY, Excelsiors and were drubbed 51 to 6.)

The first professional, major-league baseball franchise in Baltimore belonged to the Lord Baltimores, launched in 1872 and called "the Lords" by locals when they won, "the Mosquitoes" when they lost. They were members of the National Association of Professional Base Ball Players, founded in 1871. When the National League absorbed the National Association in 1875, Baltimore lost its franchise. In 1882 a rival American Association was founded and nicknamed the "Beer and Whiskey League" because it allowed the sale of spiritous liquors at games, something the then-abstemious National League banned.

Baltimore got a slot in the new league, and in 1883 a local brewing family, the Von der Horsts, bought the team and built a field. For reasons now lost to posterity, they named it Oriole Park. It was at what is now Greenmount Avenue and 25th Street, and despite the dismal play of the newly named team, it thrived. Harry Von der Horst, co-owner of the brewery and team, supposedly found the action on the diamond no cause for concern, given the sales in the stands. "Vell, ve don't vin many games, but ve sell lots of beer," he is alleged to have said.

By 1894 the Orioles had joined the National League (which then had no rival) and had developed a fearsome roster of now-legendary players who won three championships in a row. Manager Ned Hanlon, employing "scientific" or "inside" baseball and the skills of such greats as John J. McGraw, William "Wee Willie" Keeler, Hugh Jennings, Dennis "Dan" Brouthers, Jack Doyle, Joseph Kelley, Walter "Steve" Brodie, Henry P. "Heinie" Reitz, and Wilbert Robinson captured the league pennant in 1894, '95 and '96.

During these "golden years," the Orioles stymied opponents with a masterful blend of hit-and-run strategy, cagey defense, and outright intimidation—grimly and silently sharpening their spikes before a game in full view of the opposing team. They even made base-running a daunting gauntlet for their foes, as Honus Wagner, the great shortstop, recalled: "Jack Doyle gave me the hip at first, Heinie Reitz almost killed me when I rounded second, Hughey Jennings tripped me at shortstop, and when I finally limped into third John McGraw was waiting for me with a shotgun."

From these heights, Baltimore's major-league star went into a rapid but long-lasting eclipse. League consolidation in 1899 left the city without a team; in 1901 the new American League granted Baltimore a franchise, but in 1902 it was transferred to New York, leaving the city in the minor leagues for the next 51 years.

The minor league Orioles had a "silver age" of which the city need feel no shame. Baltimore teenager Babe Ruth began his professional baseball career in an Oriole uniform during the 1914 season, only to have the financially shaky Orioles sell him to the Red Sox for ready cash; and from 1919 through 1925 the minor International League Orioles won seven consecutive pennants, the only team to achieve

such a succession of titles in the history of the professional leagues. And prior to the integration of baseball, Baltimore's all-black teams, the Black Sox and the Elite Giants, boasted championship seasons and soon-to-be-famous players, including Leroy "Satchel" Paige, Roy Campanella, Junior Gilliam, Joe Black, and Leroy Ferrell.

Major-league baseball was reborn in Baltimore in September 1953 when the American League franchise of the struggling Saint Louis Browns was transferred to the city. The resurrected Birds took to the field the following spring, heralded by an Ogden Nash poem titled: "You Can't Kill an Oriole":

Wee Willie Keeler / Runs through the town,
All along Charles Street / In his nightgown,
Belling like a hound dog / Gathering the pack:
Hey, Wilbert Robinson, / The Orioles are back!
Hey, Hughie Jennings! / Hey, John McGraw!
I got fire in my eye / And tobacco in my jaw!
Hughie, hold my halo, / I'm sick of being a saint;
Got to teach the youngsters / To hit 'em where they ain't.

In time the Orioles became one of the most successful teams in major-league baseball, winning the 1966 World Series in four straight games against the mighty Los Angeles Dodgers, then going on to appear in six playoffs and four World Series since 1967, winning the Series in 1970 and 1983. The '83 Birds also scored big at the ticket office, drawing more than 2 million fans for the first time.

Within five years, however, the Orioles hit bottom on the field. Experiencing their year of woe in 1988, they lost a gruesome 107. But

their fans remained faithful. During the Orioles' 21-game losing streak, a local disc jockey vowed to stay on the air until they won—and ultimately spent 258 hours fulfilling his pledge. And during that season more than 1.6 million fans still went to Memorial Stadium despite the likelihood that the Birds would lose.

The Orioles' name became "a synonym for futility," said ABC-TV's Ray Gandolf, and *The Washington Post*'s Tom Boswell smugly advised O's fans before the 1989 season began that they had better "realize that . . . [1989] could be even more amazingly bad than 1988."

The 1989 season proved to be amazing, but not as Boswell had predicted. By early June the Orioles were in first place in the American League East by five games; by mid-July, they were 7-1/2 games ahead. A horrendous 1-13 road trip still left them in first place. Now the youngest team in the major leagues, they had done more than turn themselves around and go "from worst to first," as the sportswriters put it; they had regained their self-respect. And Oriole fans responded in record fashion, too, setting an unprecedented 2.5-million attendance mark at Memorial Stadium.

The 1989 Orioles logged 87 wins and 75 losses (compared to the 1988 record of 54 and 107). They spent 116 days in first place, 98 of

Above: Baseball has been a passion of Baltimoreans since 1859 when an amateur team known as the Excelsiors played its first game. Photo by Walter Larrimore

Right: Orioles shortstop Cal Ripken, Jr., virtually never misses a game or makes an error. He's pretty steady with the bat, too. Photo by Rich Riggins

Top: Long one of the dominant teams in baseball, the Orioles have had some rough seasons of late. However, attendance at the ball-park remains high, and fans are always eager for an autograph. Photo by Rich Riggins

Above: Now a Hall of Famer and a broadcaster, retired pitcher Jim Palmer ranks with the all-time great Baltimore Orioles. Photo by Jed Kirschbaum

Left: Baltimore Orioles pitcher Ben McDonald winds up. Whether the team wins or loses, Orioles fans have been turning out in record numbers in recent seasons. Photo by Rich Riggins

them in a row, the most ever by a team coming off a last-place finish the year before and the most impressive one-season turnaround in 43 years. They "surpassed every hope, challenged every assumption and stretched the envelope of disbelief as few baseball accomplishments this century have done," a humbled and awed Boswell wrote after the Birds fell just two one-run victories shy of capturing the American League East title. In the process, *The New York Times* reflected editorially, the '89 Orioles "earned the affection of millions," not just in Baltimore but across the country. And their record earned Orioles skipper Frank Robinson manager-of-the-year honors from the Baseball Writers Association of America and the national wire services, while relief pitcher Gregg Olson won rookie-of-the-year from the Baseball Writers Association. (In the final week of the 1990 regular season, precisely one year after the Toronto Blue Jays beat the Orioles for the 1989 American League East title, the O's had a measure of revenge by winning two out of three games against the Blue Jays, effectively ending their bid to snatch the division flag from the Boston Red Sox.)

Recognizing the economic importance of the Orioles, the state and the city both have gone to bat for construction of a new $105.4-million, 45,000-seat downtown stadium, set to open in 1992 on the site of the old Camden Yards railroad warehouse and industrial area adjacent to the Inner Harbor. It will host major-league baseball's All-Star Game in 1993. The new stadium will be the first landmark visitors will see when entering Baltimore along Russell Street, and its design, which *The New York Times* called "the best plan for a major-league baseball park in more than a generation," aims at artfully blending the best of early as well as late twentieth-century ballparks. Its stepped-back, indented roof will echo the stadiums of an earlier era; its high-tech "focused beam" lighting won't cast wayward rays into the surrounding neighborhood. A video board will flash replays high above center field, but the scoreboard itself will be anchored at field level in right field. Herbert J. Belgrad, chairman of the Maryland Stadium Authority, has said that this combination of old and new seeks "to carry out the theme of a redeveloped Baltimore." To Jim Bready, the site of the new ballpark "is testimonial to the rising importance attached to this game in Baltimore." Memorial Stadium, set in the midst of a North Baltimore neighborhood, "was invisible, you had to go out of your way to see it," said Bready. "Now, you will have a couple of hundred thousand people see it every day . . . The importance of this business-disguised-as-recreation has risen beyond where it ever was. Baseball has become more than a game to go to, it's a feature of the landscape."

In 1987, when the Maryland legislature authorized the issuance of bonds and the use of statewide sports lotteries to build the new baseball stadium, it also set aside bonding authority for construction of an adjacent football stadium as part of a $264-million complex of stadia—provided Baltimore is granted a new National Football League (NFL) franchise. The ignominious departure of the Colts remains a painful memory, casting a pall on what had been a glorious football history in Baltimore.

The saga of the Colts began on December 28, 1946, when Baltimore was granted the All-American Football Conference franchise of the bankrupt Miami Seahawks. A local contest was held to name the new team and "Colts" won. That early team lasted only five years and folded in 1951. Late the following year NFL commissioner Bert Bell issued a challenge to the city: Sell 15,000 season tickets in six weeks and Baltimore can re-enter the NFL. The tickets were sold in four weeks, and Baltimore was back in the game—in a big way. At the September 1953 NFL opening game, the Colts upset the mighty Chicago Bears, 13-9, at Memorial Stadium, soon to be dubbed "the world's greatest outdoor insane asylum" in tribute to the Colts' exuberant, raucous fans.

The Colts of the 1950s included such legendary, future Hall of Fame players as quarterback Johnny Unitas, tackle Art Donovan, end Gino Marchetti, linebacker Bill Pellington, running back Lenny Moore, end Raymond Berry, and offensive tackle Jim Parker, all coached by Weeb Ewbank, a Hall of Famer, too. On December 28, 1958, in Yankee Stadium, they won the world championship by

defeating the New York Giants, 23-17, in pro football's first overtime, "sudden death" championship contest, ever since proclaimed "The Greatest Game Ever Played."

Season tickets to Colts games became precious family heirlooms, actually bequeathed in wills to lucky legatees. Weddings were delayed if the date happened to coincide with a Colts game, and divorce settlements were known to include the rights to tickets. In Barry Levinson's film, *Diner*, a character won't marry his girlfriend until she passes a quiz on the Colts. Elsewhere in America, audiences laughed, *Sun* columnist Michael Olesker wrote, but not in Baltimore. "It seemed perfectly reasonable. Who could marry somebody who didn't know John Unitas' jersey number?"

After the team's 1958 triumph the Colts managed to win three Western Division titles despite the inroads of injuries and age. In 1964 they had another great season, soured only by a 27-0 defeat by the Cleveland Browns in the championship game. In 1969 they were the favorites to win Super Bowl III but lost, 16-7, to "Broadway Joe" Namath and the New York Jets. (That fall the Orioles lost the World

Series to the "amazin" New York Mets, a defeat so improbable that years later it inspired a memorable line in the movie *Oh, God*. George Burns, as the Deity, says he doesn't do miracles much anymore: "The last miracle I performed was the '69 Mets.")

The Colts rebounded in 1970, winning the American Football Conference championship, and then on January 17, 1971, they won the first American Football Conference/National Football Conference Super Bowl, 16-13, over Dallas, on a 32-yard field goal by Jim O'Brien with just five seconds to go in the game.

The beginning of the end of the Baltimore Colts can be pinpointed precisely: Longtime owner Carroll Rosenbloom, enamored of Los Angeles, worked out a deal with Rams owner Robert Irsay to swap teams in 1972. Irsay—volatile, unpredictable—eventually ran the Colts into the ground, repeatedly shopped the team around to other cities, then moved it to Indianapolis in a demeaning, unannounced, middle-of-the-night departure on March 29, 1984.

Five years after the Colts left, the pain lingered in Baltimore, and the city's yearning for an NFL franchise remained. Although an *Evening Sun* poll in March 1989 showed that a majority of Baltimore-area residents didn't think the loss of the team adversely affected the region, Baltimore's business community wants its share of the football buck again. It lobbies for a new franchise whenever the NFL decides to expand. With Baltimore and Maryland both pledging to build a new, $150-million football-only stadium, it is hoped that Baltimore—given its great football heritage—will receive a nod from the league soon, perhaps by 1993.

The Colts' departure has not left Baltimore entirely bereft of football's glories. The University of Maryland and Penn State played in Memorial Stadium before 61,000 fans in November 1989; many Baltimoreans now follow the fortunes of the Washington Redskins, and the great rivalry between the Baltimore City College and Baltimore Polytechnic Institute football teams—the second-oldest public school series in the country—remains an attention-grabbing Thanksgiving classic after more than a century. To George Young, the coach at City from 1959 to 1967, his team's 30-26 triumph over Poly in 1960 was a greater thrill than the Super Bowl victory of the New York Giants team he later built; to Mayor Kurt L. Schmoke, quarterback of the City teams of 1965 and 1966, the City-Poly series is what helped his high school alma mater survive a period of serious decline in the 1970s. "Had the game ended, there was a sense that this was the final chapter of City College," said Schmoke in 1988, the centennial year of the rivalry. "If we could keep the game alive, there would be hope for the school." The game survived, and City College was revitalized.

If football heralds the arrival of fall all over the United States, springtime in Baltimore means lacrosse—and because of lacrosse, spring comes early to the city.

According to the United States Weather Service, spring arrives on March 20th each year. Baltimoreans are sophisticated enough, however, not to be bamboozled by such an insignificant astronomical occurence as the advent of the vernal equinox. They know that spring arrives when lacrosse sticks begin to sprout, and that occurs early in February.

That is when students at local high schools and colleges begin to whip the still-frigid air with their lacrosse sticks. They are engaged in a time-honored seasonal rite that inspires the presentation of tiny lacrosse sticks to newborn Baltimore babes.

Although a Major Indoor Lacrosse League was founded in the mid-1980s and boasts six teams, including the Baltimore Thunder, outdoor lacrosse remains a resolutely amateur sport. Why that's so is something of a mystery, for lacrosse is fast-paced, graceful, exciting, and as American as baseball, basketball, or the Super Bowl—as well as a lot older than any of them. It was, after all, invented by the Indians.

French settlers gave the game its name, likening the distinctive, net-topped sticks with which the Indians tossed a ball around to the crosier—or *la crosse*—carried by a bishop. The first reference to the game can be found in a 1636 report written by a Jesuit missionary who saw Indians playing lacrosse near Thunder Bay, Ontario, and wrote about it to his superior.

Intimidated by the fierce, proficient play of the Indians, European settlers shied away from lacrosse for two centuries. Finally, in 1834, a group of Montreal pioneers played an exhibition game against some Caughnawaga Indians—and lost, of course. It wasn't until 1851 that a non-Indian team at last tasted victory, according to Robert H. Scott,

Johns Hopkins' athletic director and a veteran lacrosse coach.

Intercollegiate lacrosse began in 1877, with New York University and Manhattan College battling one day until the sun went down. Two years later members of the Baltimore Athletic Club visited a sports carnival in Newport, Rhode Island, were entranced by a lacrosse game they saw there, and returned to Maryland laden with lacrosse equipment. By the turn of the century, collegiate lacrosse was dominated by teams from Maryland—Johns Hopkins, Navy, Maryland, and Saint John's. All but Saint John's (which abandoned most athletics during the Depression) remain lacrosse powers, with Loyola College and Towson State now moving into the top ranks.

Hopkins, however, has by far the most consistent, enduring record of excellence in the sport. It has won or shared more national lacrosse championships—42 so far—than any other university in any other sport; won more than 87 percent of its games in a century of play; placed 149 players on the first-team All America roster since it first was compiled in 1922; had 46 former players named to the Lacrosse Hall of Fame (which is located on the Hopkins campus); represented the United States in the 1928 and 1932 Olympics; and served as the site of the 1982 World Lacrosse Games, a quadrennial tournament featuring national teams representing the U.S., Canada, Great Britain, and Australia. When an Australian player attending the 1982 World Games was asked if he had ever heard of Hopkins' Homewood Field, he gazed at it with awe and said: "Why, it's Mecca, isn't it?" Hopkins alumni (and other Maryland-born players) were key members of the U.S.A. lacrosse team that won the 1990 World Lacrosse Games in

Right: Johns Hopkins and Towson State universities fight it out in the time-honored fashion: with a lacrosse game. Hopkins holds a number of records in the sport. Photo by Rich Riggins

Facing: Though unknown or little known in most parts of the country, lacrosse is very popular in the Baltimore area. The competition is aggressive during this Baltimore County high school all-star game. Photo by Rich Riggins

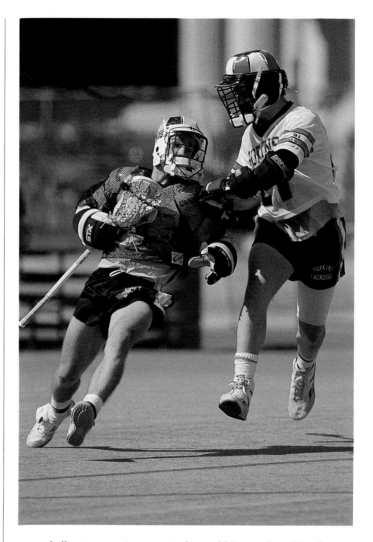

Perth, Australia, and the athletic staff at Hopkins has taken the lead in spreading the lacrosse gospel to Japan, which will send a team to the 1994 World Games in Manchester, England.

Lacrosse may be the oldest game played in the Baltimore area, but two other sports have a far older claim on the region's heart: horse racing and boating. Both have been passionately pursued pastimes in Maryland since colonial days, and both now are experiencing an extraordinary growth—with an accompanying economic impact—that is nothing less than mind-boggling.

Maryland has been a mecca for horse-racing fans ever since the days when George Washington visited Annapolis annually to bet on the ponies and keep careful records of his winnings—and losses—at the track.

Now the state is a major producer of thoroughbred and standardbred racehorses, second only to Kentucky as the birthplace of horses per acre and sixth overall in the production of thoroughbreds alone. In 1987 the crop of thoroughbred foals (baby horses) was the largest in Maryland's history, with 2,020 newborns registered. According to Richard W. Wilcke, executive vice president of the Maryland Horse Breeders Association, Maryland's horse industry is estimated to contribute $400 million annually to the state's economy. That figure includes the yearly expenditures owners make to buy and maintain their horses, the revenues and taxes generated by the state's five racetracks, prize money paid to owners, and related expenditures. It does not include the appreciation each year of farmland and other horse-related investments, which can bring the industry's value to the state up to approximately one billion dollars.

More than 20,000 jobs can be linked to horse racing in Maryland. Equipment and feed suppliers, trainers, grooms, jockeys, exercise personnel, blacksmiths—all earn a living from horses, as do the employees of Baltimore's Pimlico Race Track and the Laurel Race Course in Anne Arundel County, Timonium Race Course in Baltimore County, Rosecroft Raceway in Prince George's County, and Delmarva Downs near Ocean City on the Eastern Shore. Fans attend thoroughbred races at Pimlico, Laurel, and Timonium; harness-racing aficionados go to Rosecroft and Delmarva Downs.

Four times each year the attention of the entire equine world is focused on Maryland: for the Hunt Cup, the Preakness, the International, and the Maryland Million.

On the last Saturday in April, the green and yellow flag of the four-mile Maryland Hunt Cup Steeplechase signals the start of one of the most challenging jumping races in the world. Located just 19 miles northwest of Baltimore City in Baltimore County's lush Worthington Valley, the Hunt Cup has been held every year since 1894, with the exception of a three-year lapse during World War II. Often compared to Great Britain's Grand National Steeplechase at Aintree, the Hunt Cup is run on a rectangular course of meadowland containing 22 chestnut-rail and oak-plank fences over which the horses must jump at a grueling pace. One of the few sports events in the U.S. still open solely to amateur athletes, the Hunt Cup offers its champions just a small purse and a one-foot-high silver tankard bearing the Maryland coat of arms.

And in Fair Hill, on Maryland's Eastern Shore, the only pari-mutuel steeplechase course in the country hosted the Breeders Cup Steeplechase, the richest steeplechase race in the world, in 1986, 1987, and 1988. Fair Hill is scheduled to host the race again in 1991.

Within a few weeks of the Hunt Cup, on the third Saturday each May, all eyes turn to Baltimore's Pimlico Race Track where the Preakness, middle jewel of thoroughbred racing's Triple Crown, is run. The city's 10-day Preakness Celebration, featuring dozens of events and festivities, alone generates an estimated $20 million for Baltimore. As impressive as such a figure may be, an incalculable prestige is attached to

Above: For the Preakness it's standing room only at the infield of the Pimlico Race Track. Photo by Edwin H. Remsberg

Right: Pimlico Race Track is among the most hallowed sites in the horse-racing industry. It is here that one leg of the Triple Crown—the Preakness—is run every year. Photo by Greg Pease

Top: Races at Pimlico are not just a matter of placing a bet and hoping for the best. There are racing rites like this one to remind spectators of the sport's glorious heritage. Photo by Greg Pease

Previous page: This horse farm is one of the beautiful reasons why Maryland is a leading producer of racehorses. More than 20,000 jobs can be tied to horse racing in the state. Photo by Greg Pease
Inset: Even as the Baltimore metropolitan region has grown, there is still fox hunting in the area. Following the hounds is a beloved tradition among a select group of Marylanders. Photo by Roger Miller

These skipjacks elegantly glide by the Chesapeake Bay Bridge. Fewer and fewer of these unique sailboats remain on the bay, but efforts have been made to maintain this sailing fleet. Photo by Greg Pease

the Preakness, which follows the Kentucky Derby in Louisville and precedes the Belmont Stakes in New York. Only the best thoroughbreds qualify to race in it; only the best win it and the most valuable trophy in sports, the million-dollar Woodlawn Vase, and the sounds and sights of the race are broadcast to an estimated 19 million viewers in 15 countries. The crowd at Pimlico itself has grown astronomically in recent years, with a staggering 90,145 in attendance at the memorable 114th running of the Preakness Stakes in 1989, when Sunday Silence won a breathtaking photo finish against Easy Goer. (In 1990 a slightly smaller crowd—86,531—came to Pimlico to see Summer Squall upset Unbridled, the Derby-winner, by 2-1/2 lengths.)

Among that expanding Preakness crowd is a growing contingent of Maryland's corporate community. At the infield of Pimlico, once the exclusive preserve of the beer, barbecue, and sunbathing bunch, a separate village of hospitality tents, costing $17,500 apiece, has sprung up in recent years, with many of the region's major companies hosting their clients with cloth-covered tables of fine food and roving entertainers. The firms are recognizing—as *The Sun* put it in a 1989 editorial—that Preakness Week and the Preakness itself are "a sound investment that benefits the economy of most of Metropolitan Baltimore."

Six months after the Preakness, on the first Saturday in November, thoroughbreds from all over the globe travel to Laurel Race Course near Washington to compete in the International, a race that has been instrumental in the development of a worldwide thoroughbred market, according to Lucy Acton, an editor of *The Maryland Horse*, an award-winning magazine published by the Maryland Horse Breeders Association. And since 1986 another major equestrian event has been run each fall, the "Maryland Million," the richest one-day, nine-race stakes program. It also has served as "a model for the industry," Acton said. Conceived by Marylander Jim McKay, the ABC-TV sportscaster, the Maryland Million is patterned on the Breeder's Cup. A total of one million dollars in purses is offered in a single day to horses sired by Maryland stallions.

Under the leadership of the late Frank DeFrancis and brothers Bob and Tom Manfuso, co-owners of Pimlico and Laurel, both tracks underwent extensive refurbishment. Multimillion-dollar "sports palaces" featuring giant television screens, computer-assisted handicapping and plush accoutrements have made Pimlico and Laurel the fastest-growing racetracks in the country, recognized nationally as leaders in marketing pizzazz. The remarkable revitalization of racing in Maryland during the 1980s has added new luster to one of the state's oldest industries, no doubt helped persuade the National Steeplechase and Hunt Association to move its headquarters to Cecil County's Fair Hill in 1988, and convinced the prestigious Thoroughbred Racing Association (TRA) of North America to

move its national headquarters from Long Island to Fair Hill in 1990. Joining the TRA in a new $1.3-million building will be its subsidiary, the Thoroughbred Racing Protective Bureau, which enforces the sport's code of conduct.

Maryland and Baltimore host a wide variety of races and recreational activities on the surf as well as the turf. Given the 6,000 miles of Chesapeake Bay shoreline within easy reach of the city, and the 120,000 acres of public land providing hunting and camping opportunities, that should not be surprising. Maryland's Department of Natural Resources issued 168,763 registrations for power and sailboats in 1988, and 907,486 applications were filed for fishing and hunting licenses and stamps.

Chesapeake Appreciation Day, the oldest annual conservation event in the United States, is sponsored each fall by Chesapeake Appreciation, Inc., a nonprofit, Annapolis-based organization that is dedicated to preserving Maryland's invaluable waterways and unique skipjacks, a dwindling flotilla of aging sailboats that is the last commercial sailing fleet in North American waters. With raking, rough-hewn masts and leg-of-mutton sails, they ply the bay and dredge its bottom for oysters, a task reserved for them by state conservation laws that restrict oyster dredging by power boats. Since 1964 a race

Above: Riding bicycles on the boardwalk in Ocean City is a great way to appreciate the sand, sea, sun, and commerce that turn this Atlantic Ocean resort town into the temporary home for an average of 250,000 tourists on summer weekends. Photo by Greg Pease

Top: Deep-sea marlin fishing off of Ocean City gives anglers a chance to go for the big ones. Photo by Greg Pease

featuring skipjacks has been held off Sandy Point State Park near Annapolis on the last Saturday before the oyster season begins.

The race itself used to begin at the Annapolis City Dock, surrounded by the thousands of pleasure boats berthed there. Annapolis is synonymous with sailing. It is a major port of call for recreational sailors up and down the East Coast, and its yachting clubs host several renowned, highly competitive regattas, including the Annapolis-to-Newport and Annapolis-to-Bermuda races that are held in alternating years.

Closer to home, Baltimore has 15 marinas in the Patapsco area with nearly 2,000 slips (another 2,000 slips are now on the developers' drawing boards), and the city hosts a world-class yachting competition itself, the annual Columbus Cup, held in advance of the 1992 celebration of the 500th anniversary of Christopher Columbus' voyage to the New World. Olympic and America's Cup sailors from the U.S., Australia, Denmark, Japan, New Zealand, Spain, and the Soviet Union competed in Baltimore's Inner Harbor and the Northern Chesapeake in October 1989 and October 1990 as part of the World Match Racing Championship. Fittingly, the 1989 race began within sight of the *Pride of Baltimore II*, the $4.5-million floating ambassador for Maryland that replaced the original *Pride of Baltimore* clipper ship, which was tragically lost during a storm in the Caribbean in 1986.

For thousands of Baltimoreans summer would be incomplete without a trip "down the ocean," where the beaches and boardwalk at Ocean City beguile visitors to the Eastern Shore. Each weekend an average of 250,000 vacationers converge on Ocean City, which ends up hosting from 8 million to 9 million visitors each year. They fill some

Above: Recreational opportunities for Baltimoreans stretch all the way to Western Maryland, where open fields and rolling hills give a taste of Appalachian life. Photo by Greg Pease

Facing: This team from the U.S.A. heads through some really wild waters on the appropriately named Savage River during the 1989 World Whitewater Canoe and Kayak Championships. This competition, which was brought off by an impressive collaboration between public and private sources, brought much-needed tourist dollars to the economy of Western Maryland. Photo by Edwin H. Remsberg

35,000 hotel, motel, and rented condominium units, spending an estimated $750 million during the summer alone.

Aquatic and other recreational activities available to Baltimoreans are by no means limited to the immediate area or the Eastern Shore. To the west lie the mountains, lakes, rivers, and streams that have enthralled visitors from President Grover Cleveland, who honeymooned at Garrett County's Deer Park, to modern-day skiers, boaters, and campers. (And modern-day presidents, too: George Bush rests at the retreat in Frederick County's Catoctin Mountains that Franklin Roosevelt called "Shangri La" and Dwight Eisenhower dubbed Camp David.)

Western Maryland also has been host to its own world-class sports competition: the 1989 World Whitewater Canoe and Kayak Championships that drew 301 athletes from 25 nations to the swirling, turbulent currents of the appropriately named Savage River. The whitewater championships gave a much-needed boost to Western

In 1988 Baltimore hosted one of golf's most prestigious tournaments—the U.S. Women's Open. Jan Stephenson is seen here teeing off at the Baltimore Country Club Five Farms. Photo by Rich Riggins

Maryland, long beset by economic doldrums. The contests were the result of an imaginative partnership between private enterprise and government that augurs well for the area. The Chesapeake and Potomac Telephone Company, Potomac Edison, Mid-Atlantic Coca-Cola, and Westvaco were among the companies that contributed equipment, money, and manpower to the project, which also engaged the energies of such state agencies as the Maryland National Guard, Frostburg State University, and the State Railroad Administration, as well as the U.S. Army Corps of Engineers. Their combined efforts turned the river's banks into a whitewater amphitheater capable of handling the competition's estimated 20,000 spectators. The bulk of the money for the championships themselves came from the Marriott Corporation, one of the state's major corporate entities, and from Pepsi-Cola.

The lures of nature are not limited to the rural spots surrounding Baltimore, and neither are the area's professional sports attractions limited to the Orioles.

Golf aficionados follow the performances of the sport's top stars at

the Kemper Open, a Professional Golfers' Association tournament with a one-million-dollar purse, held in the Maryland suburbs of Washington two weeks before the U.S. Open each spring. Maryland has some 140 golf courses, with 14 private clubs and 12 popular (and crowded) links in the Baltimore metropolitan area. Construction of new private golf clubs is moving forward rapidly, reflecting a tremendous boom in the sport. Caves Valley, a 7,020-yard, par-72, world-class course being built in Baltimore County, is scheduled to open in May 1991. Beaverbrook Golf and Country Club, a mile northeast of Caves Valley, is being designed by Ben Crenshaw and Bill Coore and is set to open in 1992. Also due to open in 1992 will be Greystone, a club on 319 lush acres in northern Baltimore County.

Birdies of a different sort can be found in the splendid animal sanctuary that is the Baltimore Zoo, located in the middle of Druid Hill Park—at 600 acres the city's largest arboreal oasis; and pro hockey, soccer, and basketball can be seen at the downtown Baltimore Arena or nearby Capital Centre in Largo, Maryland.

The Baltimore Zoo was created by the Maryland legislature in 1876 and officially opened in 1881, although the year before it already had 298 animals on display, including 215 deer, 15 China geese, 13 monkeys, 2 bears, one tiger, and a three-legged duck.

Now home to 1,200 mammals, birds, and reptiles, the privately operated, nonprofit zoo has undergone its own $23-million renaissance in recent years. It has been installing innovative exhibits annually and attracting larger and larger crowds each year—more than 380,000 in 1989.

In a determined effort to do away with traditional cages and bring visitors closer to the animals, the Baltimore Zoo has created habitats, not holding areas, for its permanent residents; improved landscaping; and designed imaginative, plaudit-winning attractions. These include a children's zoo, centered on a small barnyard filled with cows, goats, chickens, and ponies, all eager to be petted; a $5.7-million Maryland wilderness exhibit, with a hand-carved cave featuring owls, bats, salamanders, and fiberglass stalactites and lichens cast from actual Western Maryland cave formations; giant latex birds' nests big enough for visitors to sit in; and a freshwater pond in which a huge acrylic tube enables the inquisitive to walk through an underwater beaver dam and look the beavers and otters in the eye. A tree exhibit shows how a tree grows from its roots up and what kind of creatures live in one, and a meadow exhibit features underground tunnels and pop-up domes. "Steel cages don't teach you anything about wildlife," stated zoo director Brian Rutledge. "A habitat invites humans to become a part of the animal's environment."

While the new downtown stadium will soon be the natural habitat of the Orioles, other locations in and near the city echo with the cheers of sports fans. At the Arena, the Skipjacks hockey team and Blast soccer team regularly thrill their followers, and the erstwhile Baltimore Bullets basketball team, since 1973 the Washington Bullets based down the highway at the "Cap Center," return every so often for

a game. At their home in Largo, the Bullets routinely rack up an average attendance of 2.6 million, drawing on the basketball fans from both Baltimore and Washington.

The Skipjacks, earlier known as the Clippers, were the American Hockey League farm team for the Pittsburgh Penguins until May 1987; they became the top farm team for the Washington Capitals in May 1988. Between February 23 and March 23, 1985, the Skipjacks set an all-time pro-hockey record with a 16-game winning streak, and the team won six championships between 1968 and 1988. The Baltimore Blast of the Major Soccer League (MSL) won the MSL championship in 1985 and picked up the MSL's Eastern Division championship in 1990. Outdoor soccer has long been popular in the city, particularly in East Baltimore, and the Maryland Bays (earlier known as the Baltimore Bays and Baltimore Comets) won the American Professional Soccer League championship in 1990. (The Bays plan to merge with the Washington Stars in 1991 and play their games in Columbia's Cedar Lane Park, while aiming for a new stadium in Howard County in 1992.)

The Arena, christened the Civic Center when it opened in 1962, then refurbished and renamed 25 years later, has been home to more than just basketball, hockey, and soccer. During its quarter-century, it has hosted international ice-skating competitions; wrestling; indoor lacrosse; tennis; track meets; horse shows; tractor pulls; roller games; circuses; conventions; revival meetings; and rock concerts. In a way it has been and remains a microcosm of the variety of sports and recreation available to Baltimoreans: diverse and first-class all the way.

Above: Wild rides down snow-covered slopes are among the many wintertime recreational opportunities available to kids all over Baltimore County. Photo by Rich Riggins

Top: The Baltimore Zoo, which was created in 1876, is now home to 1,200 mammals, birds, and reptiles. The zoo has long been one of the principal attractions of Druid Hill Park, a huge green oasis in a densely populated part of the city. Photo by Greg Pease

111

6

A STRONG FOUNDATION

■ ■ ■

Black & Decker Corporation, the world's best-known power tool
company, has its headquarters in Baltimore. It sells some 40
percent of the power tools marketed in this country. Photo by
Greg Pease

With business and home-buying alike, the validity of the cliche is unassailable: The three most important points to remember are "location, location, and location."

For more than two centuries Baltimore's business and industry have been powered in part by an inexhaustible resource, its geographic location as the farthest inland East Coast port, some 200 miles closer to the great industrial and agricultural centers of the Midwest than Boston, New York, or Philadelphia. Today, goods shipped from Baltimore by either truck or rail can reach more than a third of the U.S. population within 24 hours. Businesses of every sort in Baltimore are at the center of the Boston to Atlanta megalopolis. Baltimore is just a 2-1/2-hour train trip from the financial centers of New York and only an hour's drive from the nation's capital in Washington, D.C.

The industrial, business, and political leaders of the Greater Baltimore metropolitan area are fully aware, however, that neither the city nor the state can afford to rest on the laurel of location. Baltimore City and Anne Arundel, Baltimore, Carroll, Harford, and Howard counties have united in the successful—and continuing—transformation of the region from its role as a hub of heavy industry (a part it still plays) to a leadership position in technology, research and development, and advanced manufacturing. Baltimore continues to be a "great seat of commerce," as the *Maryland Gazette* characterized it more than 200 years ago—but its commerce is evolving and adapting to the challenges it faces on the edge of the twenty-first century.

Baltimore is raising its sights and widening its horizons, seeking to forge a place for itself in the forefront of biotechnology, biomedicine, aerospace, electronic and computer systems, telecommunications, and financial services, not just nationally but internationally.

The tools that the Baltimore area has in its possession to help accomplish these goals are impressive—as are the results achieved so far. The Greater Baltimore region has one of the highest concentrations of scientists and engineers in the United States; it receives the largest amount of federal research and development funds in the country; and it has obtained high marks for the vibrancy of its economy and the performance of its government, businesses, and industries. In April 1990 *Financial World* magazine hailed Maryland's state financial management as the best in the country, and the nonprofit, Washington-based Corporation for Enterprise Development earlier gave Maryland straight A's in the four key categories for economic development: performance, vitality, capacity, and policy. Performance is the category covering such areas as employment growth, per capita income, job quality, and quality of life; vitality refers to the competitiveness of existing businesses and the birth of new enterprises; capacity covers the financial and human resources in the area, as well as its infrastructure and ability to attract and retain talent; and policy is the category that relates to such things as tax policies, government regulation, educational improvements, and aid to distressed communities.

The Baltimore-Washington corridor now is among the most important high-tech areas in the U.S., according to an analysis by the Johns Hopkins Institute for Policy Studies. The institute's report, released in 1989, defined a company as "high-tech" if a significant number of its employees and funds were devoted to research and development. Sometimes a firm also is defined as high-tech if its manufacturing techniques are innovative or if it is highly specialized. High-tech services include communications and data processing and noncommercial research groups. Within the Baltimore-Washington corridor some 57 percent of the nearly 150,000 employees in its high-tech companies are engaged in service industries—compared to 17 percent for the country as a whole.

Another study by the Washington/Baltimore Regional Association found that the region is experiencing a boom in information technology, with growth in printing and electronics manufacturing. It also is becoming a "major player" in commercial biotechnology. Approximately 10 percent of the country's biotech firms—some 130 companies—already can be found in the Baltimore-Washington region. And by June 1990 the Baltimore-Washington corridor passed California's Silicon Valley and Boston's Route 128 as the biggest employer of computer service workers in the country, according to the regional group.

In order to do more than merely maintain that record but enhance it, Maryland created a state office of technology development in 1989. Its task is to provide grants to establish and strengthen research and development ties between private high-tech companies, universities, and the state's 42 federal research and development laboratories—the highest concentration of such facilities in the country.

Maryland knows the competition is tough, with some 30 other states already investing mammoth sums in development of high-tech businesses. But J. Randall Evans, secretary of the Maryland Department of Economic and Employment Development, has written that Maryland has "distinct advantages" over its competitors.

"With a diverse industrial base already in place, Maryland is home to 291 high-tech manufacturing companies, 713 computer-service companies and 80 of the top 100 electronic firms in the United States," Evans wrote in 1989.

"And with new federal programs that allow the transfer of unclassified technology to the private sector, Maryland's more than 40 federal research laboratories . . . are practically overflowing with potential products, techniques and services, just waiting to become commercially productive," according to Evans. He says his department will provide technical outreach to existing and prospective companies by establishing regional development centers throughout the state, as well as plan and oversee technology conferences.

Even as it gears up to enhance its status as a high-tech heartland, Maryland—in particular, the Baltimore-Washington corridor—already is home to dozens of high-tech corporations along the Interstate 270 route through Montgomery and Frederick counties, a highway known to the more than 80,000 scientists, technicians, engineers, and computer savants who traverse it daily as "Satellite Alley." Many of the firms for which this extraordinary concentration of biomedical, genetic, electronic, environmental, and telecommunications experts work are among the leaders in their fields.

The typical high-tech business in the state is young—less than 10 years old—but growing. Many are Maryland-born but have a diverse federal and commercial clientele that comes from across the country and overseas. And while some forms of heavy manufacturing are no longer done in the state, "reports of the death of manufacturing in Maryland are greatly exaggerated," *The Sun* reported in 1989. Nearly half—48 percent—of the state's high-tech firms are engaged in some sort of manufacturing, according to a *Sun* poll.

More than 80 percent of the high-tech firms told the pollsters that the quality of life in Maryland—its natural beauty and broad recreational and cultural opportunities—have a positive effect on their businesses, particularly on their ability to recruit employees from elsewhere in the country. Many of the businesses said the large base of engineers and scientists already in Maryland's labor market was another significant advantage possessed by the state. "There's a higher concentration of brainpower here than anywhere in the world," said one local economic development official. Maryland's business climate, sound infrastructure, and good school systems received positive marks as well in the poll.

The technical support and financing programs run by the state also were viewed favorably—by the 10 percent or so of the high-tech companies that have used them. At the University of Maryland, these include the Maryland Industrial Partnership Program (MIP), which provides funds for companies that are trying to place new products on the market; the Technology Advancement Program (TAP), an incubator operation that supplies office space and technical assistance to new businesses; the Technical Extension Service (TES), which provides on-site technical advice to businesses around the state; and the Technical Initiative Program (TIP), which helps to shape research agreements between the university and industries.

At The Johns Hopkins University a new sort of university-industry collaboration has been formed to speed up, if possible, the commercialization of research done at the university and the laboratories of its medical school. Triad Investors Corporation, a "venture services" firm launched in 1989 with approximately $10 million in equity commit-

This microwave tower exemplifies Baltimore's involvement in such high-tech industries as electronics and telecommunications. Photo by Greg Pease

ments from corporate board members and Hopkins, will seek to assist often-reluctant researchers in developing ideas that have the sort of commercial applications corporations may be willing to turn into marketable products. (Additional private investments are expected to boost Triad's equity commitments to $30 million.) Triad's staff and support personnel are not comprised of pie-in-the-sky whiz kids. They are technological experts who use an extensive, time-consuming review process to test potential products and services.

"Triad will let researchers stay in the laboratory while [it] develops their technology in facilities such as the Bayview Research Campus" of Hopkins' Francis Scott Key Medical Center, according to James McComas, Triad's chairman.

Central to the Bayview Research campus is the $16-million, 110,000-square-foot Triad Technology Center, a unique facility that already has in place for its tenants a collection of state-of-the-art "wet labs" for chemical and biological research. The research park's connection to the Hopkins health system and university are seen as a critical factor in persuading new or established biotechnology firms to locate at Bayview. In particular, concentration of research into respiratory ailments, gerontological problems, and drug and alcohol abuse at Bayview provides unprecedented opportunities for compa-

Left: Catalyst Research is but one example of the high-tech and biotech research and development being done in the Baltimore-Washington corridor. Photo by Greg Pease

Below: Maryland is home to over 700 computer-service companies, many of which are located in the Baltimore area. Photo by Greg Pease

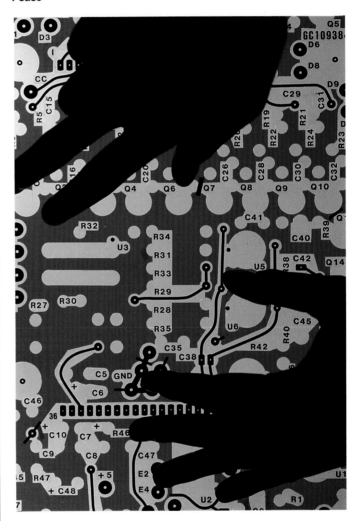

nies seeking access to clinical trial developments, institutional resources, and key personnel.

The newest technology available is also being employed now in Baltimore's oldest industry: the port.

The Seagirt Marine Terminal, a $250-million, high-tech facility opened in September 1990, is among the world's most advanced and efficient port facilities. With its computerized, 230-foot-tall, high-speed cranes, a computerized entry gate to 14 trucking lanes, and a specialized rail yard, the 265-acre terminal in Canton has been designed to accelerate the movement of cargo from ships to trucks to trains. At Seagirt the new cranes should be able to double the amount of cargo previously processed by the older cranes at the port. And the modernization of the port has not been confined to Seagirt; the port's largest terminal at Dundalk has also been reorganized to facilitate efficiency and expedite the flow of cargo. Brendan W. "Bud" O'Malley, the executive director of the Maryland Port Administration, told *The Evening Sun*'s Jon Morgan that Baltimore's port now has facilities that are "unrivaled in the United States" —and essential to the continued vitality of an industry that generates annual revenues of $1.5 billion and creates 50,000 jobs. Quite simply, *The Sun* once observed, the port is "the state's economic engine."

In recent years rivals such as Charleston, South Carolina, and the triumvirate of Virginia ports in Norfolk, Newport News, and Portsmouth that is collectively known as Hampton Roads have siphoned off significant volumes of important cargo categories. In 1988 Hampton Roads handled more international general cargo than Baltimore—although when cargoes of bulk commodities and ship service to Puerto Rico are added to the figures, Baltimore retained a lead in overall tonnage handled. General cargo includes goods and merchandise—automobiles and steel, as well as products packed in standardized cargo containers. General cargo statistics exclude bulk commodities such as grain and coal, for which Baltimore remains a major distribution center. In 1989 Baltimore's strong export trade boosted its general cargo to 6.1 million tons, up 6.5 percent from 1988 (but below Hampton Roads' 6.91 million tons of general cargo).

So far the state and federal governments have spent approximately

$160 million to dredge the shipping channels linking Baltimore to the Chesapeake Bay. The deepening of the channels to 50 feet benefits the large carriers of bulk goods. The Army Corps of Engineers also has undertaken a major study, scheduled to be completed about 1994, to examine the economic and environmental feasibility of deepening and otherwise improving the venerable Chesapeake and Delaware (C&D) Canal. About a third of the ships that call at Baltimore travel through the 35-foot-deep C&D, originally built in 1829. It is a critical shortcut to the Atlantic that can save shippers six hours or more on their way to and from the ocean—a vital marketing point in Baltimore's competition against Hampton Roads, which lies on the lip of the bay, less than 20 miles from the sea.

While down as a port, Baltimore is far from being out—and some analysts see it as poised to bounce back.

Baltimore still has a significant lead in storage space along the wa-

terfront for stowing and handling the most lucrative types of cargo. Some 1,120 acres can be loaded with automobiles and other general cargo goods. (Hampton Roads has just 794 acres of storage area and is not expected to expand beyond 1,000 acres for several years.) Baltimore remains a superlative gateway for international commerce, with an extensive transportation network in place to speed goods to inland markets. For.cargo that is shipped by truck, Baltimore still has an advantage because rates are largely based on mileage, and the city not only remains the East Coast port closest to Midwest manufacturers but sits at the center of an expansive cluster of highways that reach key cities, a transportation network far superior to the roads emanating from its Virginia rivals. In 1913 James H. Preston, Baltimore's mayor at the time, wrote: "The rumble of the freight car is prosperity's favorite music." It remains a tune to which the city hums today. A state-of-the-art dockside rail yard was opened in 1988, bigger and possibly better than the railhead at Norfolk's International Terminal. Long-range plans for Baltimore's Dundalk Terminal also call for a rail yard there.

Baltimore's song of national and international commerce is punctuated by more than just the blast of steamship whistles and the rumble of railroad freight cars today; now it vibrates with the roar of jet engines, too. During the late 1970s a five-year, $70-million redevelopment project transformed what had been a sleepy, if cozy, Friendship Airport into Baltimore-Washington International Airport (BWI), a high-tech terminal with a first-in-the-nation air-rail link and limousine service to downtown Washington.

Baltimore-Washington International now handles more than 119,000 tons of freight a year. Only 20 minutes from downtown Balti-

Above: The Dundalk Marine Terminal is an important gateway for international commerce arriving in the United States. Photo by Walter Larrimore

Facing, top: The rail yards at Locust Point provide gleaming proof of how quickly freight can be shipped from Baltimore to much of the country. Photo by Edwin H. Remsberg

Facing, bottom: Walbrook Lumber is among the city businesses that in many ways keep Baltimore as a hands-on kind of town, where enough of the older crafts and industries have adapted to present-day, high-tech conditions. Photo by Greg Pease

more, BWI also serves more than 10 million passengers annually with direct connections to the West Coast and overseas.

All of these factors have combined to boost Maryland's growth in foreign trade far beyond the pace set nationally. Some 914 affiliates of foreign companies now are located in the Baltimore-Washington region, employing more than 87,000 people and accounting for an estimated investment of $6.9 billion in property, plants, and equipment; and export growth statewide jumped by 134 percent between 1983 and 1989, compared to a national export growth of 58 percent. International trade is a top priority of Governor William Donald Schaefer, who has traveled to Europe, the Orient, and the Middle East on economic development missions to promote the port, tout BWI, develop overseas markets for Maryland foods, and encourage investments in the state. In August 1990 *World Trade* magazine ranked Baltimore among the top 10 cities in North America for firms

involved in international trade. "We
are not a local economy," Schaefer
has said, "we are a global economy."

One of the more intriguing
examples of Maryland's "global"
economy was the decision in 1989 of
Phoenix Sea Farms to build the
largest indoor fish farms in the
United States on Maryland's Eastern
Shore. Its first computerized plant,
scheduled to open in 1991, will produce a half-million pounds of hybrid
striped bass (called "rockfish" by
Marylanders), plus another half-million pounds of other fish species a
year. "Aquaculture is big business,"
Schaefer told *The Evening Sun*'s
Leslie Walker, "and I mean *big* business." Clearly Maryland will become
a player in it in a big way, perhaps

changing the nation's seafood industry in the process.

The world of Baltimore's industry and business is changing, too. For
years Baltimore was viewed as a town of branch offices and beer-and-a-
shot, blue-collar jobs. Of branch offices there certainly are many—
more than ever in recent years, with many major Baltimore-based
companies being absorbed by larger out-of-state firms. Of blue-collar
jobs there are considerably less, with retrenchment in the smokestack
industries that once were the core of Baltimore's economy.

Nevertheless, a number of Fortune 500 corporations still call Baltimore home; the number of publicly held companies headquatered in
the Baltimore-Washington "common market" grew from 159 in 1988
to 163 in 1989; the "branches" the city hosts are enormous, and its
blue-collar industries are endeavoring to adapt to the restructuring
that manufacturers around the country are being forced to undergo.
The business climate in Baltimore not only remains excellent, it has
been judged superior by the likes of *Fortune* magazine itself, which in
1989 ranked Baltimore as the best city in the Northeast in which to do
business and fifth overall in the U.S., ahead of New York, Boston,
Philadelphia, and the San Francisco Bay Area.

Business giants that still have their headquarters in the Baltimore
area include McCormick & Co., which controls about 40 percent of
the nation's $2-billion spice business; Black & Decker Corp., the
world's most famous power tool company, which sells some 40 percent
of the power tools marketed in the U.S.; Crown Petroleum, with more
than $1.1 billion in annual sales; Londontown Corp., the world's
largest manufacturer of rainwear and outer garments; Parks Sausage
Co., the largest black-owned meat-processing company in the United
States; T. Rowe Price, one of the country's largest mutual fund firms;
Legg-Mason, the national brokerage company; RTKL Associates, an

architectural firm with many overseas clients; and the Rouse Company, the urban redevelopment pioneer that manages—and in most instances owns—downtown marketplaces in 14 American cities. These marketplaces include Boston's Faneuil Hall; New York's South Street Seaport; Philadelphia's Gallery at Market East; Washington's Shops at National Place and the National Press Building; Atlanta's Underground; Miami's Bayside; New Orleans's Riverwalk; Saint Louis's Union Station; Santa Monica Place—and, of course, Baltimore's Harborplace and Gallery at Harborplace.

Baltimore's banking business is similarly strong. *Bank Financial Quarterly*, in a survey of the industry prepared by the IDC Financial Publishing Co. of Wisconsin, gave Maryland a high "excellent" rating, within a few points of the "superior" category reserved for the finest financial institutions in the country. Such an accolade reflects the strong, balanced economy in the state.

The diverse financial resources in the Baltimore area include venture capital firms such as New Enterprise Associates, Emerging Growth Partners, and ABX Ventures, which manage some $1.5 billion; leading insurance firms such as USF&G Corporation, Sun Life of America, Maryland Casualty Co., and the Fidelity and Deposit Company of Maryland; and such investment bankers as Ferris Baker Watts Inc. and Alex. Brown & Sons, which was founded in 1800 and is the oldest investment banking firm in the country.

Being a "branch town" is by no means a disadvantage in the view of some Baltimore-area business development officials. They cite with approval the arrival of the branch offices of several major Washington, D.C., law firms as being among the city's successes in recent years, as well as the opening in town of the branches of such megabanks as Chase Manhattan, Mellon Bank, and Citibank. And such major nonprofit, charitable organizations as the Catholic Relief Services and the National Association for the Advancement of Colored People have moved their headquarters from New York to Baltimore during the past decade, taking advantage of the city's proximity to Washington but far lower operating costs.

In Baltimore's once-predominant heavy industries, painful changes have preceded what many now hope is a new era in scaled-down—but

Above: Companies like Locke Insulator earn Baltimore high marks as a place to do business. Photo by Greg Pease

Left: Once a sleepy little facility appropriately named Friendship Airport, Baltimore-Washington International Airport now has a sleek terminal that represents its expansion into a major regional airport that gets its share of European freight and passenger flights. Photo by Greg Pease

Below: Bethlehem Steel's Baltimore facility was once the largest steel plant in the world and remains a significant part of the local economy. Capital improvements are helping ensure that Beth Steel can remain competitive with other plants in this country and abroad. Photo by Roger Miller

still significant—manufacturing. Job training and retraining are key features of the cooperative development effort recently undertaken by the five political subdivisions that make up the Greater Baltimore region.

Bethlehem Steel's Baltimore facility was once the largest steel plant in the world; during the Second World War its Sparrows Point shipyard built more tankers and Liberty and victory ships than any other shipyard in the country. By 1957 it had nearly 30,000 workers at Sparrows Point alone. Now the payroll there is down to some 7,900 men and women, and for the first time in the city's history, the port of Baltimore is without a yard that builds ships.

The cutbacks are hardly exclusive to Baltimore. Throughout the nation the commercial shipbuilding industry is moribund. Not only is Baltimore without ships on the ways; when Bethlehem Steel announced in 1989 that it would stop building ships at Sparrows Point, not a single commercial ocean-going vessel was being built anywhere in the country.

The "Beth Steel" shipyard in Baltimore has hardly shut down. It remains in the ship repair and renovation business, with Sparrows Point "awash in work" as *The Sun's* John H. Gormley, Jr., reported in June 1990. "For the first time in years, the yard is making money." And it awaits the day when the fortunes of the U.S. shipbuilding industry revive. Baltimore's future as a steel-making center also is secure, with Bethlehem Steel continuing to pour millions of dollars into capital improvements at its Sparrows Point plant, including $300 million for a state-of-the-art continuous slab-caster.

Major economic shifts and technological advancements have forced similar changes on other members of Baltimore's manufacturing community. General Motors, for example, transformed its 54-year-old Baltimore plant on Broening Highway into a production facility for minivans. Roger B. Smith, former chairman of General Motors, hailed the plant's rapid adaptation—and subsequent productivity—at a May 1989 ceremony marking completion of the factory's 10-millionth vehicle—a blue, two-tone minivan with plush velour seats and air-conditioning. The speed with which the plant shifted its production lines, with no downtime, "set a record for GM," Smith said. And while Baltimore's large smokestack industries are contracting, the number of industrial parks, providing homes for more compact businesses, is growing. The buildings that once housed Western Electric's Baltimore plant now serve as the Point Breeze Industrial Park; Fort Holabird, once a major U.S. Army station, now is the Holabird Industrial Park; and the Sparrows Point Industrial Park is planned for acreage that once brought forth steel.

At the 135-acre Port Covington site in South Baltimore owned by CSX Transportation, the city is investing $36 million towards creation of a "corporate showpiece comparable to the Inner Harbor," in the words of Mayor Kurt L. Schmoke. Two million square feet of office space—plus a hotel, a marina, restaurants, and retail outlets—will rise on the site, which already has a $112-million, state-of-the-art production plant and office built by *The Baltimore Sun* (due to open in late 1991 or early 1992). The city hopes Sun Park will be just the beginning of a business development that will create 8,000 to 10,000 jobs and produce annual tax revenues of more than $5 million.

Baltimore also has experienced the flowering of an industry that old-timers never anticipated: tourism. Once a city that was just a blur to passengers riding through on trains or in cars, Baltimore and the attractions around it now draw a growing swarm of conventioneers and casual visitors. In 1988 tourists had an economic impact of $8.3 billion in Maryland; in Baltimore alone more than 20,000 jobs are linked directly to convention business. A $130-million plan for doubling the size of the Baltimore Convention Center by 1993 has been recommended in order

The promenade around the Inner Harbor is often packed with, both, tourists and nearby office workers. They are walking testimony that the waterfront, which had slipped into seedy decline, has been reborn as a tourist mecca. The food stalls, restaurants, and shops of Harborplace also attest to how much people like to gather by the water's edge. Photo by Greg Pease

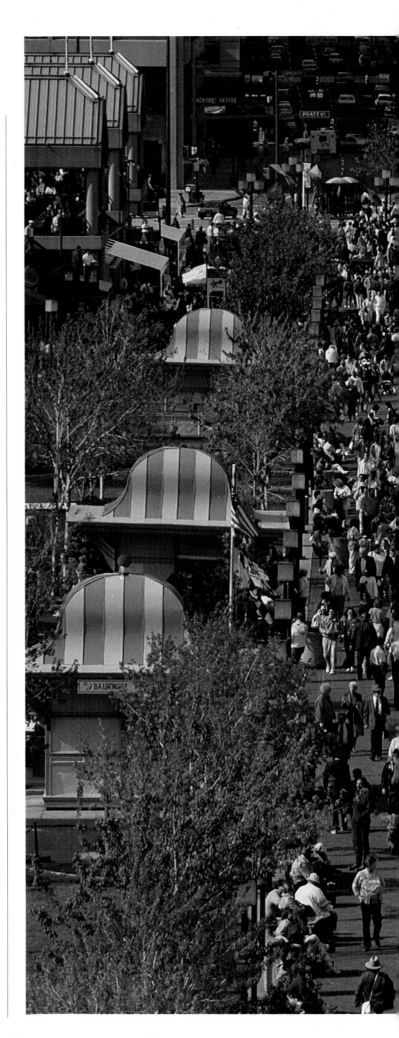

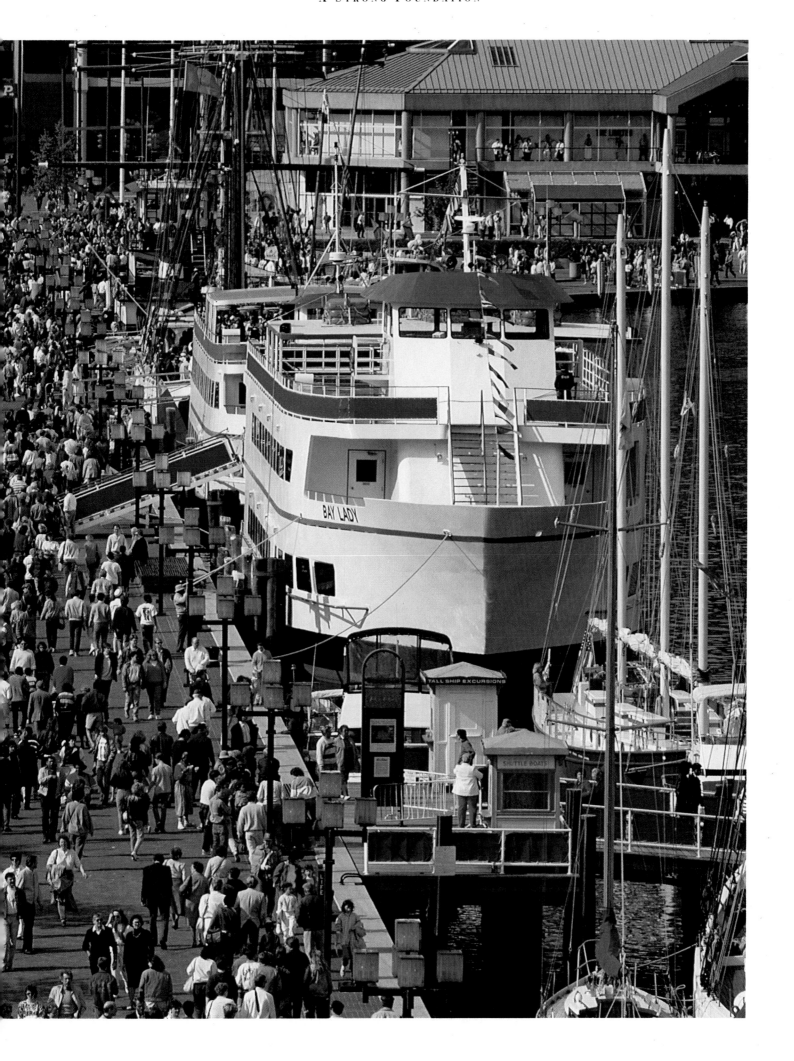

to meet the demand for space and time in it and to counter the competition from other cities and states for convention business.

"Consolidation" may combine with "continued growth" as the watchwords of the future for Baltimore's business and industry.

In July 1989 the city's two top downtown development agencies, the quasi-public Charles Center-Inner Harbor Management Corporation and the Market Center Development Corporation, were merged to form the Center City Development Corporation. Like its predecessors, the new agency oversees downtown redevelopment efforts under a contract with the city. At the time the merger of the two agencies was announced, Mayor Schmoke observed: "In order to carry forward Baltimore's downtown renaissance in an era characterized both by tremendous opportunity and diminished federal resources, we must redouble our efforts, stretch our creativity and use all available resources with maximum efficiency."

As the economy of the Baltimore metropolitan area expands, it finds itself merging with that of the city right down the parkway: Washington, D.C. In fact, figures from the 1990 census may prompt the U.S. Census Bureau to combine Baltimore and Washington into a Consolidated Metropolitan Statistical Area (CMSA) in 1992. That will make Baltimore, Washington, and the 15 counties and small cities surrounding them the nation's fourth-largest metropolitan region, behind only New York, Los Angeles, and Chicago. It will be an economic behemoth packing the power of 6 million residents.

The Baltimore-Washington region already ranks second only to Los Angeles as the fastest-growing urban area in the country, according to figures compiled by the Washington/Baltimore Regional Association (W/BRA). Between 1987 and 1988 the Baltimore-Washington "common market" gained 140,800 residents, a jump of 2.3 percent. "Only the nation's healthiest metropolitan areas exhibit consistently strong population growth such as we see here," said William C. Harris, chairman of W/BRA.

With the opportunities that the statistical merger of Baltimore and Washington may afford come the challenges that both metropolitan areas already face: unchecked, undisciplined growth, traffic gridlock, and intractable pockets of poverty in the midst of some of the wealthiest communities in the country.

The solutions for these problems will be neither simple nor short-term. One solution requires a revitalization of the inner-city school systems, which now seem largely unable to prepare students for entering the work force. As a start, at least, the city governments of both Washington and Baltimore have formed coalitions with local churches, civic groups, and businesses to create programs that are aimed at upgrading the working skills of students.

These are problems that afflict all major metropolitan areas. What the Baltimore-Washington region also has are unique attributes that give it an enviable appeal—an appeal so special that the two cities comprising the area are at odds over which can claim credit for its most enticing allurements. (Debate also is intense over what the new metropolitan entity should be called: Baltington? Washingmore? Baltiwash?)

Once looked down upon by its neighbor to the south as gritty, quaint, and unfashionable, Baltimore has seen its urban ethos become *chic*. In turn, Washington, dismissed even by John F. Kennedy (and others) as a sleepy town of "Northern charm and Southern efficiency," now has a lively mix of cultural diversions that make it a capital city of truly international class.

The Washington Post's Jonathan Yardley, one of the estimated 100,000 workers who commute between the two cities, has written that since he moved to Baltimore in the late 1970s, he has taken "a certain smug pleasure, after all those years of contemptuous dismissal, in the enthusiasm with which Washington suddenly discovered Baltimore. Visitors accustomed to the capital's company-town emphasis on government, lobbying, and influence-peddling looked at Baltimore's mixture of industry and commerce, poverty and prosperity, ethnic and racial groups and exclaimed, 'Why, this is a *real* city!' . . ."

Differences between the two cities will endure ("Baltimore will still have the best crab cakes and Washington the best fireworks display," Yardley contends), but between them they also comprise what *The Sun* has aptly called "an uncommon market."

Facing: The office towers ringing this downtown intersection show how lofty the banks and other financial institutions are. Photo by Greg Pease

Below: Economic changes and technological advancements in the automotive industry required General Motors to transform its 54-year-old plant into a production facility for minivans in 1989. During the quick and efficient shift in the assembly lines, productivity remained high. Photo by Roger Miller

7

LIFE ON THE CHESAPEAKE

■ ■ ■

Participants in the annual Governor's Cup race relax and catch up
on their sleep after an overnight sailing race between Annapolis
and Saint Marys City. Photo by Greg Pease

The advocates of economic development in Maryland have come up with a variety of slogans over the years to promote the advantages of Baltimore and its environs: "Baltimore's Best"; "Charm City"; "Maryland: More Than You Can Imagine"; "Memories Are Made in Maryland."

The success and staying power of each of these boosterisms have been equally varied. Some stuck, and others sank beneath the ripples of the Chesapeake Bay. Perhaps ironically, the most enduring catchwords coined to reflect the attractions of the Baltimore region were not devised by the economic development wizards of either the city or the state but by the marketing mavens for a local beer. In 1958 the National Brewing Company, a major sponsor of the Orioles, launched an award-winning advertising campaign built upon a slogan that continues to embody the amenities of Maryland: It is "The Land of Pleasant Living."

That understated expression, devoid of drumbeat, endures because it captures the essence of the Baltimore area's ambience: prosperous, cultivated, unhurried. The city can dance to the latest music at popular nightspots but also pause to listen to the measured tolling of the 200-year-old bells in the Otterbein Church. Baltimore is a small-town city in the best sense of those words. It is a place where the "rush hour" lasts only 45 minutes; where cultural and recreational opportunities are easily accessible; where excellent housing remains affordable; and where the cost of living in general is less than in comparable cities on the East Coast or elsewhere.

It is an area with traditions that are entrancing—and contagious. All of the bounty of the bay and rich farmlands—the hot, steamed crabs in summer; the cool, salty oysters in winter; tangy Maryland tomatoes; fresh local sweet corn and strawberries; wild game and homegrown hams—is found here. Baltimore has all the excitement of a cosmopolitan city—with live theater, art galleries, and museums—and all the tranquility of small towns and rural retreats. With more than 100,000 acres of parkland in the Greater Baltimore region alone, recreational opportunities abound; within easy driving distance are either the ski slopes or the seaside. It is an area with the pride of a heritage and accomplishments born of three centuries of local history. And with all the glories of a storied past, here also can be found the prospects of a sparkling future.

Partners for Livable Places recently named the Greater Baltimore area as the most livable place on the Eastern Seaboard, extolling its fine educational institutions and medical care facilities along with all of the attributes cited above. The U.S. Conference of Mayors bestowed its Annual City Livability Award on Baltimore in 1989, while to a writer for *Life* magazine, Baltimore's superiority was not limited to the East Coast. It was deemed "the most downright livable major city in the U.S."

Although the housing market is notoriously volatile, as of late 1989, prices in the Greater Baltimore area appeared to be stabilizing, with homes still available in the realm of reasonableness, given residential prices in many other major metropolitan areas. The average cost of a home in Baltimore City was just $71,000—figuring into that average the price of modest row houses (which can go for as little as $30,000), as well as large, detached residences in the city's suburb-like communities and new luxury townhouses and condominiums with average prices of more than $200,000.

In Baltimore County the average home price was $127,382; in Anne Arundel County, $156,594; in Carroll County, $128,650; in Harford County, $120,962; and in Howard County, $175,485.

Overall, according to surveys conducted by the American Chamber of Commerce Researchers Association, the costs of housing, groceries, transportation, and health care in the Greater Baltimore area are among the most affordable along the East Coast, better than Boston, Philadelphia, Washington, D.C., and Atlanta. Office space and labor also are readily affordable.

Yet, as one leader of the Greater Baltimore Committee stated: "It's not enough to simply say that you're cheaper, because eventually you'll lose that argument to some place overseas. We've tried to emphasize quality—quality universities, quality technology." Indeed, quality everything.

Perhaps as characteristic a symbol as any of the quality of life in Baltimore proper are the city's seven historic markets. Of course Baltimore has modern, gleaming supermarkets and trendy specialty shops, but the venerable city markets offer not only a cornucopia of provender but the sort of personal service and unique neighborhood flavor that reflect the city's special warmth and character.

The grande dame of these victual extravaganzas is the Lexington Market, first opened in 1782 and now the oldest continuously operating market in the United States. With some 160 stalls offering everything from fresh-shucked Chincoteague oysters to made-on-the-premises Polish sausage, canvasback ducks, prime meats, handmade chocolates, and highly polished apples, Lexington Market caters to all of Baltimore from its downtown location.

Lexington Market's six sisters, set in smaller quarters, each serve up a sense of their neighborhoods along with all their wares. To a writer for *The Washington Post*, the merchants and patrons at the Broadway Market, opened in the heart of Fells Point in 1784, form "a microcosm of ethnic Baltimore: Greek, Polish, Korean; black; young professionals and older people moving back to the city; and the families of men who work the tugboats berthed in the harbor a block from the market." Similarly, the Cross Street Market, opened at Cross and Light streets in 1842, serves the white-collar professionals of Federal Hill and Union Square, as well as the blue-collar workers and urban homesteaders of the Otterbein neighborhood. Competing for the Union Square trade is the Hollins Market, opened in 1835 at 26 South Arlington Avenue. The Belair Market, opened in 1818 in the 400 block of North Gay Street, caters to urban homesteaders from Stirling Street as well as longtime residents of East Baltimore. The Lafayette Market, opened in 1869 at 1700 Pennsylvania Avenue, now is a centerpiece of Pennsyl-

vania Avenue renewal, and the baby of the bunch (at only 106 years of age!), the Northeast Market, opened in 1885 at Monument and Chester streets, is the largest of the neighborhood markets in the area.

Just as the neighborhood markets supply the ingredients for tables in many a private home, so do they service some of the city's superb restaurants. Nearly 20 years ago the exacting food critic of *Esquire* magazine, Roy Andres De Groot, drew a parallel between Baltimore's eateries and exuberance: "I have been developing a theory that any city which has claims to being well run, which is energetically tackling its problems, which has a strong and concerned leadership, is almost

bound to be a city of fine restaurants," De Groot wrote. "Nowhere have I found this to be truer than in Baltimore."

The abundance and diversity exemplified by Greater Baltimore's markets and restaurants are reflected in all aspects of its life in every season. In the city alone, for example, beginning in December, the Baltimore Office of Promotion and Tourism and local businesses sponsor a 2-1/2-month Winter Festival, with a temporary ice rink in the Inner Harbor, a parade of lighted boats, and sculptures of ice and snow, among other attractions. May brings Baltimore's original celebratory rite of spring, the Flower Mart. Begun in 1911, it offers arts, crafts, food (with such exotic local treats as lemons impaled on peppermint sticks), as well as flowers and plants, of course, and entertainment, all in historic Mount Vernon Square. May also means the Preakness and the Chesapeake Bay Bridge Walk. With summer comes such disparate diversions as the Piscataway Indian Festival and Powwow in Pinefield, near Waldorf; the Annapolis Wine Festival; a Blue Bayou rhythm 'n' blues festival in Upper Marlboro; derby and fair in Crisfield; farmers' markets throughout the state; jousting competitions; a chicken-clucking contest in Fells Point; and construction of the world's largest sandcastle in Ocean City. Fall brings the Baltimore City Fair; Oktoberfest out at Garrett County's Deep Creek Lake; the Autumn Glory Festival in Oakland; the Kunta Kinte High Heritage Day in Annapolis; and the New Market Days Festival in New Market, the "antiques capital of Maryland."

Above: Notable for its northern Italian cuisine, the Brass Elephant is located along what's known as Restaurant Row on North Charles Street in Mount Vernon. The restaurants here cater to just about every ethnic taste. Photo by Greg Pease

Facing: Faidley's Raw Bar is among the gustatory delights in Lexington Market, which opened in 1782 and is the oldest continuously operating city market in the United States. For locals, the personable ambience always seems to enhance the flavor of the seafood. Photo by Greg Pease

Something that is entertaining and interesting appears to be happening every day—and all of it is within easy access of Greater Baltimore. "Day-tripping"—making a roundtrip visit to an intriguing place close to home—is a Baltimore tradition.

Following the course of the sun from east to west, Baltimore daytrippers can find that the ancient occupations of the sea and land still are pursued by watermen who ply the bay and farmers who plow the fields. In Southeast and Southern Maryland much of the land appears as it did when the first European settlers arrived in 1634. The southeastern counties of Worcester, Somerset, Wicomico, and Dorchester were the main setting for James Michener's historic novel, *Chesapeake*. Here crabbing, oystering, clamming, and fishing remain the foundation of the picturesque, tranquil life in communities such as Cambridge, Smith Island, Deal Island, and Crisfield, which bills itself as the "Seafood Capital of the World."

In the summer tens of thousands of Baltimoreans enjoy excursions to Ocean City, which does all it can to offer something for every visitor. With its broad, 10-mile stretch of beaches and three-mile boardwalk, its fishing tournaments, its boating opportunities and nightlife, Ocean City has been a favorite family (and singles) destination for decades.

On the Upper Eastern Shore the crownstone of the Mason-Dixon Line, commonly considered the official demarcation between the North and the South, can be found in Caroline County. (Many less elaborate stones placed by surveyors Charles Mason and Jeremiah Dixon between 1763 and 1767 can still be seen by travelers to other Maryland sites.) In Talbot County's Wye Mills, Maryland's official state tree, the majestic, 400-year-old Wye Oak, the largest of its kind in the U.S., can be found. Queen Anne's County has Centreville's eighteenth-century courthouse, in continuous use since 1792, and a bronze statue of England's Queen Anne, dedicated by her present-day namesake, Princess Anne.

While many Baltimoreans head to Ocean City in the summer, others prefer the quieter Victorian bed-and-breakfast accommodations of Chestertown. Just a two-hour drive from Baltimore, but a virtual trip back in time, Chestertown has stately Georgian homes lining its cobblestone streets, antique shops, a port on the Chester River that is popular with sailors and boaters, and, in the fall, seemingly inexhaustible flocks of Canada geese and other waterfowl for sportsmen. The Eastern Shore is considered perhaps the finest duck- and goose-hunting area on the Atlantic Flyway, and Chestertown is right in the heart of it. Chestertown also exudes the sophistication of a metropolis along with the comforts of a small town, being home to Washington College. The 10th-oldest chartered college in the country, it is the only one to which George Washington personally gave permission to use his name—as well as 50 guineas in gold to help the college get started in 1782. He later served on its board of governors.

With only 850 students, Washington College is a striking example of the educational opportunities still available at small liberal arts institutions. It has an acclaimed English department that benefits from a substantial bequest from Sophie Kerr, a novelist, whose legacy is an annual $30,000 literary prize awarded to a graduating senior, as well as a series of lectures by prestigious visitors. These lectures, along with art exhibits, concerts, and plays at the college give Chestertown a

Left: The Polish Festival is one of the largest of the summer ethnic festivals that have thrived during Baltimore's renaissance. Baltimoreans enjoy returning downtown, to their old neighborhoods and ethnic roots. Photo by Greg Pease

Below: Ray Charles, seen here, performs at a music festival at the Pier 6 Concert Pavilion. This concert tent's Inner Harbor location makes it an ideal place to hear music on a balmy summer night. Photo by Walter Larrimore

Above: The annual Greek festival, held at Festival Hall near the Inner Harbor, attracts many lively and fun-loving residents of Greek ancestry who come in colorful ethnic attire to enjoy the tradition, food, and music of their homeland. Seen here are members of the Hellenic Golden Coin dancers. Photo by Greg Pease

Above: The Preakness Balloon Race is but one of the colorful activities that swirl around the running of the horse race itself. Photo by Greg Pease

Facing, top: The Piscataway Indian Festival and Powwow in Pinefield, near Waldorf, is a feather-bedecked reminder of the continuing presence of Maryland's original residents. Photo by Greg Pease

Facing, bottom: Charles Street is Baltimore's grandest of streets, with many chic shops and cultural institutions among its attractions. So what better place for the costumed wit provided by a parade. Photo by Greg Pease

cosmopolitan air that blends easily with its Eastern Shore coziness.

The Southern Maryland counties of Calvert, Charles, and Saint Marys, located on the western side of the Chesapeake, still have the strong Southern charm born of the area's origin as a tobacco-growing region in the mid-seventeenth century. Saint Marys, "the Mother County of Maryland," is the site of the state's first capital, Saint Marys City, surrounded by 800 acres of unspoiled tidewater. A replica of the *Dove*, the square-rigged ship that brought the first of Maryland's settlers to its shores, is docked on the Saint Marys River, and a reproduction of the original statehouse of 1676 welcomes visitors. The Calvert County Maritime Museum offers cruises on a converted 1899 bugeye sailboat and allows visitors into the Drum Point Lighthouse, built in 1883. It also has samples of the primordial fossils found at Calvert Cliffs, now the site of the state's nuclear power plant, which also is open to visitors.

Just south and west of Baltimore proper are the Central Maryland and Greater Washington counties which gave birth to the nation's capital, harken to the country's past, and herald its future. Prince George's County donated part of itself to create Washington, D.C.—the District of Columbia—in 1791 but retained much that remains splendid for itself, including the 341-acre Fort Washington National Park on the Potomac River. The entire history of aviation, from the Wright brothers to the space age, also can be found in Prince George's County. Beginning in 1909 Orville and Wilbur Wright taught the basics of flying at the College Park Airport, now the world's oldest operating airport; and nearby at the Goddard Space Flight Center in Greenbelt, NASA has its hub of tracking operations.

In Montgomery County the C&O Canal National Historical Park offers transportation of a more tranquil nature: mule-drawn boat rides along the bucolic, man-made waterway that begins in Georgetown and wanders more than 184 miles west to Cumberland.

Shrines to patriotism and religion are among the attractions of Frederick County. The Emmitsburg home of Elizabeth Ann Seton preserves the memory of the first American-born saint. In the county seat, Frederick, the Barbara Fritchie House and Museum honors the exploits (possibly apocryphal) of the aged lady whose defense of the Stars and Stripes during the Civil War was immortalized by John Greenleaf Whittier's stirring poem. Given the homes of Mother Seton and Barbara Fritchie, it is not surprising that Frederick County likes to call itself "the land of

Saints . . . Poets and Patriots," but it also admits to a few moonshiners by preserving the Blue Blazes Whiskey Still in the Catoctin Mountain Park near Thurmont; and it discreetly avoids trumpeting the presence of U.S. presidents since Franklin D. Roosevelt who have relaxed in their Catoctin Mountain retreat, Camp David.

In the center of Central Maryland, of course, is Baltimore City itself, but immediately surrounding it are the focal points of Maryland's fabled horse country, its wine industry, some of the region's oldest towns, and the most successfully planned modern community—Columbia—the country's youngest major city.

Northeast of Baltimore are Cecil and Harford counties. Cecil lays claim to being the site of the country's most successful man-made waterway, the still-vital Chesapeake and Delaware Canal, as well as the National Steeplechase and Hunt Association and the Thoroughbred

Racing Association of North America. Harford County boasts the oldest continuously used lighthouse at Concord Point (built in 1829), the U.S. Army Ordnance Museum at the Aberdeen Proving Ground, and the spectacular (and occasionally whimsical) Ladew Topiary Gardens.

Baltimore and Carroll counties, directly north and northwest of Baltimore City, feature some of the nation's loveliest horse country; vineyards and wineries such as the Boordy Vineyards, Montbray Wine Cellars, Whitemarsh Cellars, and Wood Hall Vineyards; and museums devoted to farming, fire fighting, and Maryland's great railroading heritage.

Immediately west of Baltimore City is Howard County, where the B&O Railroad's first passenger terminal in Ellicott City now houses a museum, and the old mill town's historic flavor is retained by its rough stone structures, antique stores, and the Howard County Courthouse, which was built of large granite slabs and white oak beams in 1843. Not far from Ellicott City's winding streets are the carefully planned roads of Columbia, strategically situated between Baltimore and Washington on what had been Howard County farmland.

To the southwest of Baltimore lies Anne Arundel County, where Annapolis maintains its colonial atmosphere while being an active, vibrant city, an important center of the pleasure craft industry, a popular port of call on the Inland Waterway, and, of course, Maryland's capital.

Facing: Maryland horse country may be the breeding ground for some top race horses, but the pace of life is itself agreeably slow and tranquil here. Photo by Walter Larrimore

Below: Boordy Vineyards in Baltimore County may surprise those who don't realize that there are a dozen or so small wineries in the state. Photo by Keith Weller

All of central Annapolis is a National Historic Landmark. As Stewart Udall, former secretary of the U.S. Department of the Interior, noted, it contains "the greatest concentration of eighteenth-century buildings in the United States." George Washington slept here—often. So did Thomas Jefferson and most of the Founding Fathers. It was one of the social and political centers of the young United States and served briefly as the nation's capital when the city named for Washington—now only a 45-minute drive down the highway—was little more than a mosquito-infested bog.

The centerpiece of Annapolis is the Maryland State House, still the political hub of the state. It is the oldest capitol building in continuous legislative use in the country and the only statehouse to have served as the nation's capitol. Built between 1772 and 1779, the State House was the meeting place of the Continental Congress from November 26, 1783, to August 13, 1784. It was the site of the last great events of the American Revolution: George Washington's resignation of his commission as commander in chief of the Continental Army and the ratification of the Treaty of Paris, which ended the Revolution.

Looming over the State House's legislative chambers—and Annapolis itself—is its 200-foot-high, octagonal dome, the largest wooden structure of its kind in the country. Constructed entirely of cypress, completed in 1793, and painted white, the dome does not contain a single nail. It is held together by wooden pegs.

The city's eighteenth-century proportions make Annapolis a casual perambulator's dream. Its key points of interest—the Georgian mansions built by wealthy merchants, tobacco planters, lawyers, and patriots (three of Maryland's four signers of the Declaration of Independence lived in Annapolis, and their homes still stand), as well as its bustling harbor, the Naval Academy, and historic Saint John's College—all are within a short stroll of each other.

Founded in 1696 as King William's School, Saint John's is, according to the education editor of *The New York Times,* the "one remaining outpost of classical liberal arts education in the nation." The college's 380 students spend four years pursuing a course of study that consists entirely of reading and discussing 100 great works of literature, philosophy, science, mathematics, music, and language. The texts include books by renowned Western thinkers ranging from Plato to Einstein to Freud.

The waterways surrounding Annapolis prompted the move of the colony's capital there from Saint Marys City in 1695. Commerce gave Annapolis life, but a somber reminder of a grim aspect of early colonial trade can be found at the head of the City Dock, where a plaque has been placed to commemorate the involuntary arrival there from Africa of Kunte Kinte, the enslaved ancestor of *Roots* author Alex Haley. The plaque notes that the unhappy passengers on Kinte's slave ship and those who followed contributed mightily to the growth of the new land.

Abutting the City Dock is Market Space, a collection of shops, food stalls, and restaurants. Crab, oyster, and fishing boats bob at the quayside throughout the year, providing local restaurateurs with seafood that—they like to boast—"slept last night in the Chesapeake Bay." There may be as many eateries per square foot in Annapolis as in any comparably sized area of Manhattan, with specialties ranging from haute cuisine to homemade fudge and overstuffed delicatessen sandwiches.

Crowned with an octagonal dome that is the largest wooden structure of its kind in the country, the Maryland State House in Annapolis was the site of the last significant events of the American Revolution. Photo by Roger Miller

The two decades immediately preceding the American Revolution are considered Annapolis' "Golden Age," when the wealthy gentry built the elegant homes that gave the city its eighteenth-century sobriquet, "The Athens of America." After its role as the center of the concluding dramas of the Revolution, Annapolis lost its position as economic capital of Maryland to the bustling port of Baltimore.

During its long, twilight somnolence, Annapolis' burghers, secure in their old money, were content to live life as it had been led and resisted changes in their town. Consequently, when Annapolis began to awake to a new era of growth and prosperity, enhanced by its untouched colonial atmosphere, preservation more than restoration was required to burnish the qualities that have attracted tourists and businesses in increasing numbers. In the past 15 years more than $25 million has been spent to spruce up the city.

Annapolis now is the site of the nation's largest sailboat show, which is to Annapolitan merchants what Christmas is to non-nautical retailers. A Florida-based sailor once stated: "Moslems want to go to Mecca. Sailors want to go to the Annapolis boat show."

Now entering its third decade, the Annapolis Boat Show draws 500 boat-makers and dealers from all over the world. They bring their yachts and catamarans, motor-sailers and ketches to the city's waterfront—and are followed only a week later by the U.S. Powerboat Show.

Stretching west from Baltimore, the more than 75,000 acres of forests, parks, rivers, and lakes within the Blue Ridge and Allegheny mountain ranges of Western Maryland make Washington, Allegany and Garrett counties a favorite retreat for Baltimoreans. Here they can ski on land in the winter and on water in the summer; raft down some of the most challenging whitewater in the East; fish, hunt, hike, and camp; and enjoy the riotous blooms of spring or the brilliant colors of autumn's glory.

Glories—and tragedies—of the nation's military history also can be found here. Out in Garrett County, Braddock's Trail, a remnant of the French and Indian War, was built in 1755 by the army of British general Edward Braddock, under the direction of Braddock's young aide-de-camp, George Washington. Closer to Baltimore, only an hour's drive away in Washington County, is the rolling, now-quiet landscape

Above: Spice-encrusted hard crabs and a cool beer from Baltimore's own National Brewery make the perfect summertime meal in the land of pleasant living. Photo by Walter Larrimore

Previous page: The annual Annapolis Boat Show, the largest sailboat show in the nation, draws boat-makers and dealers from all over the world and boating enthusiasts from all over the Baltimore area. Photo by Greg Pease

Right: The Washington Monument serves as an architectural symbol of the city's proud past. Photo by Roger Miller

on which the bloodiest single-day battle in American history, Antietam, was fought.

There, on September 17, 1862, Confederate forces under General Robert E. Lee and Union troops commanded by Major General George B. McClellan met and turned the earth red with their blood. By day's end nearly 23,000 men were dead, wounded, or missing. In no other battle—not Gettysburg, Belleau Wood, Pearl Harbor, Normandy, or Tarawa—were there as many American casualties. The Antietam Battlefield Park, unsullied by commercialism, has dozens of regimental monuments, a reception center with a splendid film describing the battle (which Southerners still call Sharpsburg, naming their battles after the closest town, not the nearest river), and the solemn dignity that enables visitors to reflect upon the profound tragedy that was the Civil War, and the courage of the men who fought it.

Washington County (which is named for the Father of Our Country) also celebrates what it contends is the first true monument to George Washington. The structure was built of rough stones near Boonsboro in a single day—July 4, 1827. That the Boonsboro monument was finished first is undisputed; that Baltimore's monument was the first begun—in 1815—and was nearly complete when the Boonsboroans went on their one-day frenzy of monument-building is also uncontested. Those of a diplomatic inclination who wish to give each monument its due acknowledge the initial completion of the rough-hewn Boonsboro edifice and call the Baltimore structure the first *architectural* monument to Washington.

Back when many Baltimoreans suffered a colossal inferiority complex about their city, a debate over the supremacy of the Mount Vernon Square Washington Monument could raise a ruckus. Now, while revered, it is just one of the attractions that draw millions of visitors to Baltimore each year—an estimated 18 to 20 million to Harborplace alone.

What might be even more astonishing to Baltimoreans of an earlier generation is the fact that many of those visitors come up from

Washington, long the haughty younger sister down the highway. "I think Washingtonians like Baltimore better than Baltimoreans like Washington," late night talk-show host Larry King has said. "Washingtonians love the Inner Harbor, the Orioles, the restaurants. Baltimore has become a unique attraction," said King, who lives in Arlington, Virginia. "I love Baltimore. It's one of my favorite cities in America."

Baltimore endures, wrote Hank Burchard of *The Washington Post*, "because it has soul as well as brains, and a heart as well as muscle."

"The city is mannered and muscular, cultured and crude, sedate and swinging, crumbly old and sparkling new, beautiful and damned ugly. It's a great place to go with your sweetheart, your drinking buddy, your spouse, your children, your shipmates, your garden club . . . It's Bawlamer, Bawlmer, Baldimer, *Baltimore*, the city that won't quit," Burchard wrote. It is "fun, endlessly interesting, inexpensive and uncrowded."

Today, if Baltimoreans long to search for their heart's desire, they can, like Dorothy in *The Wizard of Oz*, find it in their own backyards.

8

AROUND THE CORNER

▪ ▪ ▪

The Inner Harbor has changed remarkably since 1970. Once the rotting wharves were cleared away, and open public space and Harborplace took their place, the harbor became an immense tourist attraction. Banana boats may not call here any longer, but expensive yachts do. Photo by Greg Pease

n 1929, on the 200th anniversary of Baltimore's founding, the *Baltimore Municipal Journal* published a 300-page celebratory "book of memories." It featured a cover drawing depicting the tiny Baltimore Town of 1729; the wharves, steamboats, and waterfront skyline two centuries later; and a fanciful projection of the Baltimore of the future, with elaborate, arched walkways connecting huge office buildings and even a large dirigible anchored to the tower of one skyscraper.

The path of prognostication is furrowed with pitfalls. A little more than a month after the *Municipal Journal*'s book was published in September 1929, the stock market crashed. The Baltimore Trust Company's landmark headquarters, the centerpiece of the cover drawing on the *Municipal Journal*'s book, opened in December 1929—not long before stock market losses caused the Trust Company to collapse. (The skyscraper, still a jewel of the skyline, is now called the Maryland National Bank building.) And the age of dirigibles went down in flames with the *Hindenburg* in 1937.

Although the *Municipal Journal*'s cover artist did not foresee these setbacks, he also did not—and surely could not—predict the triumphs of Harborplace, the National Aquarium in Baltimore, the Maryland Science Center, the Constellation, or any of the other glories that now adorn Baltimore's waterfront. So it is with any look to the future. Anticipating triumphs may prove just as elusive as foreseeing tribulations.

In terms of the Baltimore skyline alone, plans currently on architectural drawing boards suggest the 1990s may witness the most spectacular development in nearly a century. Perhaps not since the Great Fire of 1904 leveled the city's business district have so many blueprints for new office buildings been prepared. No less than 30 sites have been targeted for the erection of new "headquarters-caliber" developments. As Edward Gunts, *The Sun*'s architecture critic, observed late in 1989, "Even if only a fraction of the proposed projects get built, Baltimore could see a new wave of development representing more than one billion dollars worth of private investment in the early 1990s."

Construction has already begun, or ground-breaking appears imminent, for buildings that will herald what one city development official calls "the second phase of the renaissance" downtown.

The flurry of announcements featuring elaborate architectural renderings may have been prompted by the developers' desire to get their projects on track before a new development plan for downtown is finalized in early 1991 by a special 35-member advisory committee to the mayor. But some leading developers have said that optimism about their projects' prospects was due to Baltimore's emergence as an attractive alternative to other East Coast cities as a place for out-of-town businesses to relocate, with better housing, better labor, and office space rental rates that are very competitive.

Striking new office towers may not be the only edifices altering Baltimore's face within the next few years. A $37-million, 11-story federal office building is due to be built at Baltimore and Howard streets downtown. Announced in September 1990 and scheduled for completion in 1992, the new building will house some 1,300 workers for five federal agencies. As of September 1990 Congress also has authorized $1.5 million in federal funds to begin design work for the proposed $200-million Christopher Columbus Center of Marine Research and Exploration in the Inner Harbor. Richard Rogers, a British architect who worked on such controversial landmark buildings as Paris' Pompidou Center and the new Lloyd's of London headquarters in England, has been selected to design the first phase and master plan for the center, which would be his first major project in the United States.

The Columbus Center, planned for some 11 acres on the north side of Piers 5 and 6, would have a center of marine biotechnology with laboratories and offices; a center for marine archaeologists; and a maritime museum—with relics going back to Columbus' time. Researchers have told Congress that the Columbus Center—a "Smithsonian of the Seas"—would make Maryland a world leader in such research fields as marine pharmacology and aquaculture, disciplines used to cleanse the environment and increase fish production.

While the Christopher Columbus Center may make Baltimore a focal point of marine exploration and research, the Space Telescope Science Institute on the campus of The Johns Hopkins University promises to put the city in the vanguard of space research and exploration, making Baltimore a herald of the heavens as well as the seas.

At the Space Telescope Science Institute, astronomers design the mission and direct the eye of the $1.5-billion Hubble Space Telescope, orbiting 380 miles above the earth. If the data reaching the Space Telescope Science Institute "does not exactly make Baltimore the center of the universe," wrote John Noble Wilford in *The New York Times*, "it [the data] insures that it [Baltimore] will be a center of cosmic exploration well into the next century."

That will be so despite the Hubble Space Telescope's mirror-induced myopia. Even with its flaws, the Hubble "still has 100 times greater sensitivity to ultraviolet light than any other telescope, on earth or in space, [and] 100 times greater spectral resolution . . . ," according to NASA. It remains capable of "unprecedented scientific work on spectroscopy, photometry, astrometry, and in ultraviolet wavelength imaging . . ."

In December 1990 Hopkins astrophysicist Samuel Durrance went aloft on the Space Shuttle Columbia with the Hopkins Ultraviolet Telescope (HUT) to probe the invisible universe of ultraviolet light. In addition to the HUT, the so-called Astro 1 observatory on the shuttle carried three other telescopes, two of which, like the HUT, were built in Maryland, the Ultraviolet Imaging Telescope developed at the Goddard Space Flight Center in Beltsville, and the Broad Band X-Ray Telescope, also a product of Goddard. (The fourth telescope was the Wisconsin Ultraviolet Photo-Polarimeter built at the University of Wisconsin.) Among the civilian astronomers to accompany Durrance was another Marylander, Ronald A. Parise, of the

Computer Science Corporation in Silver Spring. The HUT and its companions returned to Earth with the shuttle having gathered data that will engage astronomers for years.

Baltimore and Maryland have great prospects for advancing in the arts as well as the sciences during the 1990s. Governor William Donald Schaefer has pledged to increase support for artistic organizations. The Maryland Arts Council, proudly acknowledging the extraordinary accomplishments of the city's artistic community during the 1980s, now aims to ensure the continued vitality of these already thriving enterprises and enhance their ability to reach even more people.

The arts community hopes to do more, however, than merely maintain the *status quo*. The Baltimore Museum of Art (BMA) plans to begin construction early in 1991 on a $7-million, 39,500-square-foot west wing to house twentieth-century art; the Walters aims to complete transformation of the Hackerman House on Mount Vernon Square into its new Museum of Asian Art; a new Museum

Above: A number of significant buildings are expected to be added to the downtown skyline in the 1990s. So the familiar features of renaissance Baltimore will be spruced up even more in time to greet the twenty-first century. Photo by Greg Pease

Facing: A jewel in Baltimore's Harborplace is the USS *Constellation*. The oldest U.S. warship continuously afloat, the historic vessel was launched from Baltimore in 1797 and active as late as World War II as an auxiliary flagship. Photo by Ira Wexler/Folio

Maryland's first light rail system, the $469-million, 27-mile Central Corridor Line that is planned to run from Hunt Valley in the north to Glen Burnie in the south, with an offshoot to Baltimore-Washington International Airport. The first stations, originally scheduled to open in late 1991, may now not accept their first passengers until 1992. Whenever the line opens, it may prove to be the first installment in a network of light rail lines crisscrossing the state. Light rail, a modern incarnation of old-time trolleys, is expected to influence the design of suburban commercial development, as well as facilitate the commuting of city dwellers to jobs in the counties and county dwellers to cultural and retailing centers in the city. It is estimated that 34,000 riders will use the initial line every day.

Perils as well as prosperity can accompany growth. Although more residents of the Greater Baltimore area of Anne Arundel, Baltimore, Carroll, Howard, and Harford counties believe their communities are better places to live now than a decade ago, even more fear that further growth will

for Contemporary Arts, providing exhibition space for visual artists as well as performance space for concerts, theater, dance, video, and multimedia works, is due in 1992; Center Stage is scheduled to add a new theater, with a small but expandable seating plan, for more intimate productions; and the Baltimore Symphony plans to tour Europe again during the 1991-92 season and visit the Orient in 1993-94.

Such artistic advances require money as much as inspiration. The BMA is in the midst of a $21-million fund-raising campaign, Center Stage is hoping to raise $13 million before this decade ends, and the Walters met its $7-million fund-raising target in 1990. The major Baltimore-based artistic institutions also are hoping to convince other metropolitan-area jurisdictions to increase their financial contributions to the city's cultural centerpieces, even as major projects are being launched and completed in the surrounding counties.

The regions surrounding Baltimore experienced phenomenal growth in the 1980s. Certain to spur additional development will be

detract from their quality of life if it goes unchecked. A poll by *The Sun* in late 1989 suggested that the effort to curb suburban sprawl and preserve the region's livability will become a significant political movement in the 1990s.

Sprawl, in fact, is not a concern limited to the suburbs. Development within Baltimore City, particularly along the waterfront, has the potential to greatly increase the tax base and perpetuate the renaissance—but fears have been voiced that the 27-mile waterfront gold mine could become a strip mine if care isn't taken to create an updated, unifying development plan. The Schmoke administration's citizens advisory committee is reevaluating the existing plan (or lack of one) for downtown development and devising a strategic framework to guide its future for the next 20 years. The head of the latest planning effort is Walter Sondheim, Jr., whose vision and leadership helped shape the initial Baltimore renaissance. The committee, with representatives from the business, educational, cultural, and civic com-

munities, is expected to produce its strategy for progressive downtown development by April 1991. Advance reports indicate the committee foresees a doubling of downtown office space over the next 20 years; construction of 2,700 new hotel rooms by 2010 (adding to the 4,000 built in the 1980s); 4,000 new residences downtown—and some 11 million tourists, compared to 7 million in 1990.

That there are problems facing the city, no one would deny. A local foundation study reported in late 1989 that the community groups which once played a crucial role in Baltimore's rejuvenation have weakened, for a variety of reasons. (Ironically, one of the reasons cited by the report was the creation of city agencies to deal with problems the community groups once addressed.)

City officials recognize the important contribution community groups make to Baltimore. They have met with representatives of the existing organizations in an effort to devise ways to rebuild them and encourage creation of new ones to deal with whatever difficulties continue troubling neighborhoods throughout the city.

Baltimore's leadership still have faith in the attractions of city living. A new public-private partnership, Baltimore Community Development Financing Corporation, plans to make $40 million available for converting vacant, derelict houses into inhabited, desirable homes. A dozen private lending institutions, including Maryland National Bank, the Mercantile-Safe Deposit and Trust Company, Rosedale Federal Savings and Loan, and the Harbor Bank of Maryland, are providing $30 million of that money. It is, said *The Sun*, "an unprecedented financial commitment to the city's older, struggling neighborhoods," an effort to make the "urban homesteading" of the 1970s a movement of the 1990s as well.

At the upper reaches of Baltimore's housing market, local real estate developers expect to build approximately 4,000 new waterfront units during the 1990s. These include the $350-million Inner Harbor East, a six-block, eight-acre neighborhood of low- and mid-rise buildings at the edge of the Jones Falls and the Inner Harbor. Bounded on the north by Fleet Street and on the east by Central Avenue, the development's planners aim to build "an authentic Baltimore neighborhood" from scratch. It will feature some 800 apartments, condominiums, and townhouses; office buildings; 300 boat slips; waterfront shops, restaurants, and a hotel; plus a waterfront promenade. The planners of Inner Harbor East have

Above: Baltimore has attracted many new companies and new hotel guests because the Inner Harbor offers an appealing combination of retail stores, tourist attractions, civic services, and relatively low office rents. Photo by Greg Pease

Facing: Portions of Baltimore County seem even farther away from Baltimore City than what the actual mile count indicates. However, construction of a 27-mile light rail line from Hunt Valley above the city to Glen Burnie below the city will make commuting between Baltimore, its suburbs, and the countryside a fast and easy ride for the many folks who will likely choose to leave their cars at home. Photo by Roger Miller

placed an emphasis on public spaces and streets, making it an accessible attraction to visitors as well as residents. Portions of the development may be ready for occupancy by late 1991.

Far greater in scale than Inner Harbor East will be the 1,590-unit HarborView condominium project, a $600-million, 42-acre "city within a city" development for which ground was broken in September 1989 on the site of the old Bethlehem Steel Corporation Key Highway shipyard in South Baltimore. Also projected to have shops, restaurants, offices, and a 400-slip marina, HarborView may take up to a decade to complete. More than $16 million in real estate taxes for the city are expected to be generated by it.

With plans for six buildings that will rise between 20 and 30 stories, including a 27-story residential tower due to be completed by mid-1992, the HarborView project has worried the residents of exist-

ing waterfront neighborhoods, who fear that the atmosphere of their area—not to mention traffic patterns, public access, and property taxes—may be irrevocably disrupted and altered. A citizen group sought to put stricter height limits on future development, assure continued views of the harbor, create more open space, and guarantee greater community involvement in the review of new developments.

The city planning commission elected to let the HarborView project proceed as planned but gave assurances to community residents that they not only would be given a greater role in development processes but that future housing on the former piers would be subject to stiffer controls.

Canton, an East Baltimore working-class neighborhood, has become a prospective "Gold Coast" for development, with luxury housing and the East Coast's largest marina on the drawing boards and one award-winning project, Canton Cove, a $14-million, 89-unit luxury condominium in a recycled loft building, already in place.

Despite the exciting prospects of these new central-city housing, retail, and recreational developments, the fact remains that the population of Baltimore City proper has been declining while that of the metropolitan area surrounding it has been on the rise. The city, home to 720,100, according to preliminary 1990 Census figures, is projected to lose more than five percent of its population within the next 20 years, while Baltimore County is expected to grow by four percent;

Anne Arundel County by 14 percent; Harford County by 15 percent; Carroll County by 40 percent; and Howard County by 42 percent. Overall, the population of Maryland is expected to grow by only 583,000 between 1990 and 2010, but it is the type of growth, not its size, that has local planners—and politicians—concerned.

What is at stake, of course, are the very qualities that make Greater Baltimore and Maryland itself "the land of pleasant living." And as it was when the city and state were founded, much concern and hope are focused on the Chesapeake Bay. The water, always the water, mirrors

Facing: Baltimore demonstrated its commitment to urban renewal in 1975 with the complete renovation of the city hall. Constructed in the French Baroque Revival architectural style in 1875, this ornamental building supports a dome that was considered to be the largest iron-structured roof of its time. Photo by Roger Miller

Below: Canton is a waterfront neighborhood in which longtime residents and newcomers are trying to strike the right balance between upscale new housing and the original neighborhood texture. Photo by Greg Pease

Maryland's past and may prove a harbinger of its future.

"We can't continue to allow the sprawl we have allowed in the past," Governor Schaefer said in October 1989 when he appointed an 18-member state commission to explore ways to protect the bay. "We have to think differently and act differently."

The Commission on Growth in the Chesapeake Bay Region, chaired by Michael D. Barnes, a former U.S. representative, has been given the task of studying and recommending regulatory, legislative, and other means for protecting the environmentally fragile bay from a projected 800,000 or more new residents who are expected to flock to its shores by 2020.

What is to come for Baltimore and for Maryland as the twentieth century draws to a close engages the interest and challenges the imagination of leaders at every level of state and local government, as well as the private sector.

The population of the Greater Baltimore area is expected to continue growing—but at a slower pace than in the 1980s. High-tech jobs will become more plentiful, but it will be necessary to overcome a shortage of skilled labor to keep the economy booming.

The labor shortages offer young city dwellers a "window of opportunity," said community leader Arnie Graf. "The population curve has changed, and employers have to find a work force that is more than basically educated, people who can think, compute and communicate."

Windows of opportunity abound for Maryland businesses overseas. A survey of the largest firms in the Baltimore-Washington region in late 1989 found that 75 percent of the companies that responded now earn income from international trade, up from 52 percent five years earlier. And high-tech firms, particularly in the Baltimore area, are especially interested in beginning or expanding their markets in a trade barrier-free Western Europe by 1992 and, within a few years, Eastern Europe, Latin America, the Middle East, and Asia.

In the surrounding counties that comprise Greater Baltimore, many opportunities for growth exist, but care must be taken to manage development wisely. The Baltimore County Council has adopted a 10-year master plan for regulated growth; in Anne Arundel County, high-tech office park construction means greater employment opportunities, and new housing brings a more urbanized environment; in Carroll, Harford, and Howard counties, more public services, new roads and schools, and adoption of specific growth plans are key public issues.

As for the city itself, the extraordinary changes of the past two decades will be a tough act to follow.

The potential for further advancements is great, but it may hinge on what city planners call "the big-bang scenario," a combination of "special happenings" and high-profile projects that spark demand for new offices, residences, hotels, stores, or tourist attractions.

A study prepared jointly by the city's department of planning and the Legg Mason Realty Group, Inc., cites a variety of possible spurs to future development, including a high-speed rail service between Balti-

Performing at Harborplace, the group "Up With People" projects optimism that characterizes the spirit of the Baltimore renaissance. While keenly aware of pressing problems in education, housing for the poor, and other areas of social concern, civic officials are nonetheless confident that Baltimore can meet these challenges and provide a better life for all its citizens. Photo by Edwin H. Remsberg

more and Washington, which would increase the appeal of Baltimore's more affordable office space; a downtown football stadium to complement the Orioles' sparkling new nest; a 3,500-seat waterfront performing arts center, double the size of the 1,600-seat Mechanic and capable of housing grand opera and similar major productions; and a 20,000-seat arena for major-league winter sports or a trade mart.

Such spectacular developments are by no means certain for the 1990s, but the city's planning process for downtown is capable of responding promptly to them if the opportunity arises.

City planners also have devised other "scenarios" for Baltimore besides the "big-bang." A "baseline scenario" assumes that city and state support will assure continuation of the development trends of the 1980s. An "opportunity scenario" foresees an increase in downtown development that prompts even greater market activity than anticipated in the modest "baseline scenario." Among the factors that might shift development from a "baseline" to an "opportunity scenario" would be expansion of the Convention Center, bigger tourist crowds, more downtown business activity, and tighter controls on suburban growth.

During the 1980s Baltimore experienced a mind-boggling emergence as a symbol of urban revitalization and as a tourist mecca. Sustaining that momentum will require considerable effort; matching or exceeding it will call for all the creativity and enterprise the city and state can muster.

Above: An endless variety of attractions, such as the National Aquarium and the Maryland Science Center, draws thousands of visitors and residents to the water's edge at Baltimore's breathtaking Inner Harbor. Photo by Walter Larrimore

Below: Harford is just one of the many rural counties surrounding Baltimore that is slowly attracting more residents. But as the population climbs, the Commission on Growth in the Chesapeake Bay Region continues to establish regulations that will ensure the environmental protection of the bay. Photo by Edwin H. Remsberg

PART TWO

...

BALTIMORE'S
ENTERPRISES

NETWORKS

Baltimore's energy and communication providers keep power and
information circulating inside and outside the area.

■ ■ ■

Photo by Roger Miller

CITY PAPER

A successful newspaper that speaks with a strong voice, *City Paper* is Baltimore's largest weekly and second largest newspaper, after the *Baltimore Sun*. It is also a product that many people thought would not make it in a small city. But the alternative newspaper has developed a loyal following, with circulation growing over a six-year period from 16,000 to 91,000.

Founded as *City Squeeze* in 1977, it became *City Paper* with its fifth issue. It is one of 52 alternative newspapers in the United States, but it is the only corporate-owned one. Its parent, Times-Shamrock, a family-owned company headquartered in Scranton, Pennsylvania, also operates radio stations around the country, including WGRX-FM and WTTR-AM in Maryland. Times-Shamrock has established a clear mission for *City Paper*: "To be indispensable to the people it serves."

Fulfilling its mission, the newspaper focuses upon what goes on, good and bad, especially news that local dailies do not cover. Unswayed by pressure, *City Paper* publishes such articles as "Baltimore's Sacred Cows," which took a hard look at a number of local "untouchables," among them the 1989 Orioles, hard crabs, and the Walters Art Gallery.

Liberal minded and controversial, *City Paper* is also life-style oriented and humorous. It offers the most comprehensive arts and entertainment coverage in town, listing more than 1,000 recreational items in its calendar every week. Its papers encompass a broad diversity of subjects, from local to national politics, Inner Harbor plans and happenings, marketing news, interviews, poetry, comics, and quality advertising. Each September, a "Best of Baltimore" issue running well over 200 pages singles out a multitude of top-flight places, people, and services of interest to its upscale young readers.

Those readers are divided almost equally between men and women and are mainly aged 18 to 49, with average household incomes of $40,500. More than half own their own homes. They pick up their copies of the free paper where they work, eat, and play—at any of 1,600 distribution points, including 400 gray-and-maroon street boxes. Circulation is audited quarterly by Verified Audit Corp.

City Paper's role in the community extends to a variety of charitable and civic causes. It supports the Multiple Sclerosis, Cancer, and Heart associations, and the Kidney Foundation. Growing increasingly Baltimore oriented, the paper also supports city neighborhoods, from street fairs to businesses.

An urban, modern alternative newspaper, with a new, colorful appearance, *City Paper* has won both journalistic and community awards. It anticipates continued progress as it completes the move from an underground paper to the voice of Baltimore.

BALTIMORE GAS AND ELECTRIC COMPANY

Providing power to the dynamic and highly diverse Baltimore regional market, the Baltimore Gas and Electric Company counts on an aggressive management team, dedicated work force, and efficient generating facilities to keep up with expanding demand for energy.

Founded in 1816 by the artist/entrepreneur Rembrandt Peale, BG&E is the nation's oldest utility. It is also one of the most cost efficient, charging lower rates than most utilities serving major East Coast metropolitan areas. BG&E customers pay less than half the rates charged in New York City and less than two-thirds of those in Boston and Philadelphia.

To meet the electricity needs of its Central Maryland territory, BG&E relies on nuclear, coal, hydro, and natural gas. This makes the utility virtually free of dependence on the uncertain supply and pricing of foreign oil. BG&E operates 10 local electric generating plants, including the Calvert Cliffs nuclear power plant, which can generate up to 50 percent of BG&E's electricity. Run in a safe and environmentally sound manner, Calvert Cliffs has saved customers an average of $360 million in fuel costs every year since it began operations in 1975. The company also shares ownership of three generating facilities in Pennsylvania and belongs to the Pennsylvania/New Jersey/Maryland interconnection, allowing access to pooled capacity.

In addition, BG&E purchases from pipeline suppliers and natural-gas producers, and maintains facilities in three of its plants for the production and storage of liquefied natural gas and propane.

Conservation of precious resources is critical to all of today's consumers—residential, industrial, and commercial. BG&E's numerous load management programs help customers save money by using energy more efficiently. The Conserve 2000 campaign promotes a wide variety of conservation measures for residential and

Above: This painting by Rembrandt Peale recreates Peale's first demonstration of gas lighting. Peale founded The Gas Light Company of Baltimore in 1816. Today that same company is known as the Baltimore Gas and Electric Company.

Left: BG&E's Education Coordinator talks to local schoolchildren about community volunteer programs.

commercial customers.

Using the slogan "Let BG&E Power Your Expansion," the Baltimore Gas and Electric Economic Development staff assists companies wishing to expand or relocate into their service territory. Using a broad base of technical knowledge, coupled with a business view of the marketplace, BG&E encourages stable technical, scientific, and manufacturing development in a region offering a sound business climate and quality of life conducive to attracting and retaining employees. BG&E is a major participant with local, regional, and statewide business development organizations.

At the same time the company is an integral part of the social structure of the community, and it has the credentials to prove its good corporate citizenship. BG&E is a winner of the Edison Medal, awarded each year by the Edison Electric Institute to the most outstanding electric utility in the United States in terms of

Above: Baltimore is 200 miles closer to the Midwest than any other East Coast port. More than 60 steamship lines serving about 350 overseas ports call at the Port of Baltimore. Photo by David Lavine. Courtesy, Maryland Port Administration

Left: This satellite was assembled at the Applied Physics Lab at Johns Hopkins University in a joint project with Germany and England. The project explores solar winds in relation to the earth's magnetic field. Courtesy, Johns Hopkins University

Right: Bethlehem Steel Corporation utilizes the state-of-the-art continuous slab casting process. This totally computerized system, with an annual capacity of 2.9 million tons of slab, has improved the quality of steel products and recognized energy savings. Courtesy, Bethlehem Steel Corporation

contributions to the community and industry. The highest honor the institute confers went to BG&E for a wide range of outreach programs as well as excellence in management.

The utility's outreach programs are broad based and highly visible. The company is built on the premise that since it operates within a franchised territory, its corporate health can be only as strong as the territory's. That makes it to BG&E's advantage to support education, economic development, senior citizens' services, child care, energy conservation, and a multitude of other causes. Ready to use all the resources at its command, the company responds to emerging needs with its own initiatives and cooperative programs with local agencies.

Education has been a priority issue at BG&E since the 1970s. The company is convinced that helping children stay in school improves the quality of life for all Marylanders. School sponsorships, teacher workshops and incentives, and scholarship programs are some of the ways BG&E addresses this important issue.

For senior citizens the company runs the Gatekeeper Program, a referral service in cooperation with the Maryland State Office on Aging. For children it offers an informational Latchkey Program and is also a major supporter of Downtown Child Care Inc., a private nonprofit organization. To help low-income consumers, the company conducts a job-skills program in conjunction with the Human Resource Development Agency of Baltimore County. BG&E modifies control knobs on appliances with braille-like markings at no charge for the blind. And for the hearing impaired the utility maintains a special telecommunication device and keeps trained representatives on 24-hour duty to answer these calls. More than 2,000 of BG&E's 9,000 employees have walked for the handi-

capped, raised money for the homeless, fed the poor, cared for abused children, and much more.

For all its customers, the company offers many kinds of assistance. Its service reliability program keeps customers informed of efforts to improve the service they get; its special assistance line helps customers who do not know where to get the help they need. A 24-hour meter-reading telephone service allows customers to call in their readings at their convenience. A speakers bureau, cultural arts group, series of helpful publications, billing assistance, and energy conservation programs are also offered.

Baltimore Gas and Electric also owns a nonutility subsidiary, Constellation Holdings. Constellation is made up of nine companies focusing on four major business lines: energy and environment; real estate; senior living and health care; and investments and financial services. Started in the mid-1980s, the Constellation companies make significant investments in the community, and BG&E plans to expand further in these areas.

As an energy supplier for nearly 200 years, Baltimore Gas and Electric Company has a long tradition of superior service and reliability. The utility intends to maintain that tradition and its status as one of the lowest-cost gas and electric producers and suppliers in the region.

WLIF-FM

Chosen by a large group of people as "their" station, WLIF-FM Lite 102 takes the responsibility seriously. For more than 20 years it has been serving Baltimore listeners as a prime source of entertainment and information and as a friend as well. The station's mix of light contemporary music, news, and service programming fits right into its adult audience's lives. Lite 102 makes sure to stay on target by keeping in touch with listeners through extensive, ongoing local research.

On the air since Christmas Eve 1970, WLIF was aquired by Infinity Broadcasting Corporation in May 1989. The new ownership, well known and respected in the industry, has added strength and expertise to the operation.

The essence of the station's music format is a blend of soft, familiar "adult contemporary" hits of the past 25 years, reproduced from the highest-quality compact discs. Every piece is carefully tested for local appeal before becoming part of the Lite 102 music library, resulting in the relaxing flavor the audience delights in.

Along with entertainment, Lite 102 provides the news and information that its listeners need to pursue their busy, active lives. Twice an hour during morning drive time and regularly throughout the afternoon, the station's award-winning news department presents both local and world news. At 6 p.m. a business report features stock-closing information and stories of special importance to the local business community.

Left: The Lite 102 Summer Sunday Concert Series consistently draws record crowds to Baltimore's Inner Harbor between April and September. Photo by Ronald Hube

Above: Lite 102's Life Around Maryland Calendar exemplifies the station's history of community service by raising more than $20,000 each year for charity. Photo by Richard Smith

Lite 102's information segments also include hourly weather and stock market updates. And, in light of continuing repair work on the beltway and other major arteries and downtown streets, the station broadcasts 20 traffic reports daily.

More than a source of entertainment and information for its listeners, Lite 102 is also their friend. Its on-air personalities are warm, lively, and well informed, making it easy for the audience to get involved with them. Some announcers have been with the station for a decade or more; all know Baltimore and Maryland well.

Augmenting its listener services, Lite 102 offers various kinds of information on a call-in basis. Its SnoPhones, with a single statewide number, provide weather-related, school-closing information. The Lite 102 Life Around Maryland Events Line offers news of festivals, concerts, and happenings all over the state in three-minute reports compiled from such sources as the Maryland Department of Tourism.

Life Around Maryland is also the theme of an annual Lite 102 community project, a calendar promotion for the benefit of a local charity. Launched in December 1984, the promotion promptly won a major industry group's award for the Best Radio Promotion in the United States. The calendars, illustrated with prize-winning photographs from the Lite 102 annual Life Around Maryland photograph contest, are sold, with all proceeds going to charity. A joint effort of the station and its advertisers, the promotion raises more than $20,000 every year.

WLIF Lite 102 also supports a long list of other community organizations and events, including Santa Claus Anonymous, the Maryland Food Committee/Maryland Food Bank's "Food For All," the Kennedy Institute's "Festival of Trees," and United Cerebral Palsy's "Casual Day." A strong advocate for the arts, the station does promotions with the Mechanic Theater, Baltimore Symphony, Baltimore Opera, National Aquarium, and Maryland Academy of Sciences. On Sunday evenings from April through August, the station invites Baltimore families to the Harborplace Amphitheatre for the Lite 102 Summer Sunday Concert Series. Entertainment includes big band and brass, ragtime, jazz, and classics, all set against the backdrop of Baltimore's beautiful Inner Harbor.

With its large base of listeners and 5,000-square-mile coverage, from southern Pennsylvania to northern Virginia, Lite 102 is a full-service station committed to quality of sound as well as the best in entertainment and information. In 1989 it completely rebuilt its production studios, installing state-of-the-art equipment to make its facilities among the finest in the state.

A consistent market leader and broadcast institution, WLIF Lite 102 plans to work hard to maintain that position and continue to grow for Baltimore.

BALTIMORE BUSINESS JOURNAL

Tailored to the needs of a select management audience, the *Baltimore Business Journal* covers business news, trends, and features in the city and its five surrounding counties. The newspaper's objective is to provide this audience with the most complete and accurate local business information available.

It has been doing just that since it was founded by the Vittert Group of St. Louis in 1983. Mark Vittert, the entrepreneur who headed the organization, envisioned a market for in-depth business news in growing communities and chose five cities to put the idea to the test. In addition to Baltimore, he started newspapers in St. Louis, Indianapolis, Philadelphia, and Cincinnati. Vittert's idea worked. All five newspapers are still going strong.

In 1986 the Vittert Group sold out to American City Business Journals, a coast-to-coast network of business tabloids in the nation's major markets. The company, based in Charlotte, North Carolina, now owns 26 newspapers, each one published in the community it serves. In 1989 Shaw Publishing Inc. became a major shareholder. Its president is Ray Shaw of Charlotte, North Carolina. Shaw, a former president of Dow Jones, also serves as American City Business Journals' chief executive officer.

Reflecting its readers' interests, the Baltimore newspaper concentrates on banking and finance, high technology, real estate, government contracting, health care, retail, public relations and advertising, and personal finance. It treats these subjects from several angles. In addition to thorough news coverage, the paper, which comes out every Monday, publishes special editorial sections on various topics, regular columns, and a weekly list of the top 25 companies in a designated industry. The industries covered range from private corporations and homebuilders to executive search and venture capital firms.

Regular special sections include industry reports focusing on a single industry and growth reports targeting Baltimore's dynamic geographic growth areas. The reports provide comprehensive coverage of each industry's or area's people, trends, and companies, identifying both established firms and brand-new players. These sections within the newspaper are complemented by glossy magazines covering the key industries of real estate and health care.

Weekly columns in the paper deal with real estate, marketing and media, and high technology. The small business adviser section offers "how-to" advice to the entrepreneur.

Additional weekly features include "People," which highlights area appointments and promotions; "For the Record," which reports on individual and company achievements, the state bank commissioner's actions, and land sales, among other items; and "Portfolio," which analyzes local public companies.

The newspaper's top 25 lists appear in every issue. Each list serves as a snapshot of the industry as it exists in Baltimore, showing its size, major players, and economic impact. The lists are compiled by a research staff according to yardsticks that vary with the industry. In some fields, such as office supplies, the top is measured by volume of sales; in others, such as ad agencies, by billings; in still others, such as travel agencies, the top is determined by the

Above and Facing page: *The Baltimore Business Journal* **covers business news, trends, and features in the city and its five surrounding counties, providing its readers with the most complete and accurate local business information available.**

size of the staff. At the end of each year, the newspaper publishes the *Book of Business Lists*, a collection of all the lists that have appeared during the preceding 12 months.

This format serves the *Baltimore Business Journal*'s purpose well, judging by its readership quality, circulation growth, and national awards. The newspaper draws a top-management audience. Company owners,

chairmen, presidents, vice presidents, general managers, and treasurers make up 64 percent of its readers. Middle management comprises another 23 percent. Most of these executives are with small companies, although 27 percent work for companies with 1,000 or more employees. Readers' median age is 41 years; the average annual household income is $134,800.

Circulation growth has been dramatic, exceeding 20 percent a year to make the *Baltimore Business Journal* the second fastest-growing newspaper in the American City chain.

Virtually from the outset, the paper has been winning awards; its editorial integrity has been recognized by its parent company as well as professional news associations. In 1989 it was voted the company's second most-

improved business journal. In 1988 and 1989 it won five separate awards for editorial excellence from the Maryland/Delaware/D.C. Press Association, plus several other local and national awards.

The newspaper plays an active role in the business community it writes about. In 1990 it joined Ernst & Young and Merrill Lynch to bring Baltimore into the nationwide Entrepreneur of the Year program. Previously run in other cities but new in Baltimore, the program identifies outstanding entrepreneurs in their communities and, from their number, selects a national winner. In further business-related activities, the paper works with several local chambers of commerce, in Baltimore and the surrounding counties, and the local office of

the Small Business Administration with which it cosponsors annual awards. The newspaper is also a participant in the state Department of Economic Development's Maryland with Pride program.

In addition to business and civic causes, the paper supports a variety of charitable groups. Among them are the Baltimore AIDS Walk, the Maryland Special Olympics, and the March of Dimes.

For the future, the *Baltimore Business Journal* projects continued growth. To ensure that growth, it will continue to rely on the mission that has guided it from the beginning: "To build upon our leadership as Baltimore's authoritative source of balanced, accurate, timely, and essential business news and information."

THE DAILY RECORD

In its first issue on October 2, 1888, *The Daily Record* promised "to provide a comprehensive digest of events transpiring in legal and commercial affairs for the information and reference of lawyers, real estate agents, merchants, bankers, stockbrokers, and the general public."

For more than a century the newspaper has been delivering on its promise. The four-page tabloid launched by Edwin Warfield has grown into a comprehensive business newspaper under the leadership of his family. Today the fourth

generation is in charge, and major progress has been made in the past few years. Publisher Edwin Warfield IV presides over an expanding organization, which includes *Warfield's*, the highly successful Baltimore business magazine he introduced in 1986, and a printing operation with a specialty in legal work.

The original Warfield, a lawyer, banker, and politician who served as Maryland's governor from 1903 to 1908, turned over control of the *Record* to his brother, John, also a lawyer.

Within six months of its start, the paper, which sold for two cents, had attracted many advertisers and grown to six pages. Its bread and butter was legal notices—public notice advertising—for everything from property sales to divorce decrees, name changes, and foreclosures. The early *Record* also printed Baltimore and New York stock exchange reports, bank

Edwin Warfield IV (left) and Edwin Warfield III. Photo by Peter C. Howard

financial statements, news of real estate transactions, and reports on court cases docketed and decided—still a major feature.

By 1909, when John Warfield succeeded his brother as president, the paper had expanded to eight pages and added theater notes and a column on amusements. Seven years later, the *Record* sold its St. Paul Street building to the city and moved to its present location, 15 East Saratoga Street.

Edwin Warfield died in 1920. In 1923 his son Edwin, Jr., a World War I veteran, succeeded his uncle John as president of the company. Edwin, Jr., took over a changing business. The newspaper had become a broadsheet; the company had diversified into a commercial printing business. It prospered throughout the 1920s, buying the adjacent building at 11 East Saratoga Street for additional office and printing space.

In 1929, just before the stock market crash, daily circulation was up to 2,300, with lawyers making up 60 percent of the list. No jobs were lost at the *Record* during the Depression. Under the steady guidance of Edwin, Jr., it reached its 50th anniversary as a 10-page paper that ran news briefs on the front page.

The Daily Record raised its price to five cents in the mid-1940s. Edwin, Jr.'s, son, Edwin III, a decorated World War II flyer, took up command of the family company on his father's death in 1952. With a coterie of dedicated people to help him, Edwin III was also able to follow in his grandfather's footsteps and enter politics. He represented Howard County in the Maryland House of Delegates from 1962 to 1970, when the governor appointed him adjutant general of Maryland, in charge of the National Guard. Since retiring in 1979 with the rank of U.S. Air Force major general, he has served as chairman of the company's board.

In 1983, as the company was undergoing both technological and managerial reassessment, the founder's great-grandson, Edwin IV, joined the staff. Under his direction *The Daily Record* has confirmed its status as Baltimore's

business executives as well as lawyers.

Toward that end, the *Record*, which became a tabloid again in 1987, has revised its editorial content to include a contemporary mix of news articles, features, local columns, and cultural reviews. Capsules on personnel moves around town, building profiles, graphics, and photographs also spruce up its pages.

Monthly supplements run the gamut from health care and construction to advertising and the port. Today the *Record* reaches an estimated 20,000 readers, about half of them lawyers.

Its sister publication, the biweekly *Warfield's*, is a glossy, four-color magazine with striking photography. With a local emphasis on Maryland and the Baltimore/Washington common market, *Warfield's* has won wide readership among a cross-section of area business leaders, chief executive officers, lawyers, and sales and marketing professionals. In its short life it has also won the notice of professional organizations that have honored it with numerous awards. Running more than 100 pages per issue and heavy with advertising, *Warfield's* adds a new dimension to the company as it reflects the vitality of the region.

A local organization with deep Baltimore roots, The Daily Record Co. is a prominent supporter of many community causes. Its major efforts are devoted to the Lawyers' Campaign Against Hunger, run in conjunction with the Maryland Food Committee; House of Ruth, a halfway house for abused women; *Lady Maryland*, the schooner built to give schoolchildren sailing experience and knowledge of

Together, *The Daily Record* and the monthly magazine *Warfield's* provide comprehensive coverage of legal and commercial news and commentary.

second daily by becoming an authoritative, alternative source of news for professionals. It is committed to meeting the specialized information needs of Maryland's developers, bankers, real estate brokers, architects, and

the history, economics, and ecology of Chesapeake Bay; and the Fund for Educational Excellence.

"In this era of media consolidation, *The Daily Record* takes pride in its independent and local ownership," says Edwin Warfield IV. "We have survived through four generations, demonstrating a respect for tradition yet taking innovative steps where our readers have looked to us for expanded coverage."

10

INDUSTRY

A rich industrial tradition combines with technological skill to spell success
for many Baltimore firms.

■ ■ ■

Photo by David S. Lavine

BLACK & DECKER

One of the strongest brand names in the world, Black & Decker is a global manufacturer and marketer of power tools and other quality products used in and around the home and in commercial applications. The company, which sells in more than 100 countries, is the world's leading producer of most of those products, and enjoys a strong reputation for quality, value, and innovation.

It all started with an investment of just $1,200, made by S. Duncan Black and Alonzo G. Decker in 1910 to form The Black & Decker Manufacturing Company. Located in downtown Baltimore, it made special machinery, including milk bottle cap and candy dipping machines. The new venture prospered and by 1913 was paying cash dividends. The company entered the consumer market in 1930 with the Cinderella washing machine. Over the following decades the firm continued to expand, acquiring other manufacturers and building plants. Overseas sales and operations, begun in 1918, also gained momentum.

Black & Decker has always been known as an innovator. In 1914 it produced the world's

Above: Founding partners S. Duncan Black and Alonzo G. Decker.

Left: Black & Decker is one of the strongest brand names in the world, a reputation built by the quality of the power tools and other products it manufactures.

first portable power drill. Among other major innovations are the world's first electric hammer, in 1936; the first cordless drill, 1961; the now-famous Dustbuster® cordless vacuum, 1979; and the Univolt™ universal battery charging system, 1988. From 1986 through 1989 the number of introductions totaled more than 250 new products, and accessories accounted for thousands more. In worldwide sales of power tools alone, Black & Decker is twice as large as its biggest competitor.

The company's long history of success has been interrupted just once, by the same problem confronting many other American manufacturers: foreign competition. Since 1985 it has been attacking the problem from several angles and solving it. Achieving notable success in 1988, it reported record sales and earnings, double-digit revenue growth in all major product lines, and a growth rate twice that of

the markets it serves. One year later Black & Decker acquired Emhart Corporation, fulfilling the company's objective of broadening its earnings base and more than doubling its size while infusing new strength, scope, and opportunity throughout operations. Emhart's products, nearly all ranking at the top in their markets, are a good fit; they add locks and hardware, faucets and fixtures, and bolts and rivets to the power tools and household products lineup.

A market-driven company led by a talented management team, Black & Decker has built partnerships with its distributors and retailers. It has proved itself willing to listen and able to respond with products and programs tailored to the demands of each channel of distribution.

With its long tradition of operating in Baltimore, the company supports a variety of cultural, educational, health, and civic organizations. Black & Decker's heritage is in Baltimore and it plans to maintain its local presence while continuing to develop its position in international markets.

THE POOLE AND KENT COMPANY

One of the largest and best-known mechanical contractors in the United States, The Poole and Kent Company has been a city institution since 1947. Robert R. Poole and E. Robert Kent, friends at Baltimore Polytechnic Institute and roommates at the University of Maryland, formed a partnership that year to supply heating, ventilation, and air conditioning services (HVAC).

Starting out with just one employee in two third-floor rooms of a converted Charles Street residence, the partners quickly made their mark. Within two years they had added a plumbing capability and were supplying complete mechanical contracting services. In 1952, when revenues rose to more than $2 million, they incorporated.

Today Poole and Kent's annual revenues, which have been growing by nearly 20 percent a year, exceed $200 million. In its first 40 years the company's aggregate sales topped the $2-billion level. The work force includes 100 office employees plus 500 regular field workers and double that in peak periods. In addition to its headquarters and one division in Baltimore, the company, whose parent company since 1980 has been Monumental Investment Corp., has offices throughout the Southeast.

Its reach goes well beyond that. Besides jobs as far south as Key West in Florida, Poole and Kent has performed work in nearly every mid-Atlantic state and as far north as New England and as far west as Texas. Its overseas projects can be found in Bermuda, the Caribbean, Central and South America, and in the Middle East.

Along the way Poole and Kent has picked up numerous awards for craftsmanship. The Baltimore Building Congress and Exchange has recognized the company's Baltimore office for the excellence of its work for such clients as Westinghouse, Johns Hopkins University, Patapsco Waste Water Treatment Plant, the National Aquarium, and the Peabody Institute.

The company attributes its steady growth to its key personnel. From the start its founders recognized they were in a people business; they drew up their personnel policy to attract and keep highly qualified specialists. Only employees may be stockholders, and they are

Above: In addition to plumbing, heating, ventilation, and air conditioning, Poole and Kent provided all the life-support systems for the various exhibits in the National Aquarium. Photo by Sydney S. Sussman

Below: The four 200-foot-diameter clarifiers, clustered in the center, are the heart of the system installed by Poole and Kent at the Patapsco wastewater treatment plant owned and operated by the City of Baltimore. Photo by Sydney S. Sussman

One of Poole and Kent's Inner Harbor projects was Harbor Court, a mixed-use facility consisting of a hotel, restaurants, office space, condominiums, and a parking garage. Photo by Sydney S. Sussman

given, not sold, their shares as a reward for good work and an incentive to stay on. In consequence, Poole and Kent's top management specialists average 20 years or more in the construction industry while project managers average 15 years in actual design and

America, they include the Mechanical Contractors Association of Maryland, Associated General Contractors, Engineering Society of Baltimore, Baltimore Building Congress and Exchange, American Society of Heating, Refrigeration and Air Conditioning Engineers, American Society of Plumbing Engineers, American Subcontractors Association, and Subcontractors Association of Baltimore. Company executives spend weeks of their time every year in serving on these organizations' boards and committees.

As a prominent corporate citizen, The Poole and Kent Company engages in many charitable activities, such as a scholarship fund at the University of Maryland's College of Engineering, usually awarded to a graduate

Poole and Kent was happy to work at Harborplace, part of the Inner Harbor and said to have more visitors each year than Disney World. Photos by Sydney S. Sussman

installation of mechanical systems.

Every year since 1965 *Domestic Engineering*, a national mechanical trade magazine, has ranked the top 200 mechanical contractors. Poole and Kent is one of only two contractors to be ranked in the top 20 every year, and it was ranked number three in 1990.

Over the years Poole and Kent has developed a variety of techniques that have been widely adopted throughout the industry. These include job cost controls, labor planning and scheduling techniques, managerial cost accounting and forecasting, and work-hour standards for estimating. Key company individuals have served on national committees for the Mechanical Contractors Association of America and contributed to *Managerial Accounting and Cost Control System* and *Labor Estimating Manual*, two manuals found in the offices of every major mechanical contractor in the United States.

Poole and Kent's clients include some of the biggest and most demanding names in the construction industry, private business, government, education, and health care. In the past three decades, no other mechanical contractor in the nation has done more hospital work; in the Baltimore area it has worked at most major hospitals. The company has also done a great deal of airport work and played a role in Harborplace, Meyerhoff Symphony Hall, and the remodeled Lyric Opera House, all components of the new Baltimore.

A sampling of the myriad kinds of jobs Poole and Kent performs includes air circula-

tion and temperature control for electronic equipment rooms, storage and piping for large propane gas installations, low-humidity rooms for laboratory testing, hydrant fueling stations for jet aircraft, cryogenic and related exotic gas storage and handling facilities, constant humidity and temperature control for manufacturing processes, and chemical cleaning of pipelines.

As a leading member of the industry, Poole and Kent belongs to a long list of its professional and trade organizations. In addition to the Mechanical Contractors Association of

of Baltimore Polytechnic Institute. The University honored Bob Kent in 1984, presenting him with its Distinguished Alumni Award.

Now retired from the company he founded, he keeps his hand in, maintaining an office, serving as a director, and setting his sights on the future. Singling out pollution control as the firm's likely focus in the years ahead, Bob Kent says, "Every smokestack that I see I visualize as a mechanical contractor's job someday to clean up what's coming out of there and put it into usable form."

A A I Corporation

A unique approach to anticipating and meeting customer needs characterizes AAI Corporation, one of the nation's top-ranking defense contractors. The company, which also serves corporate customers, is well known for delivering reliable, innovative products not only on time but also within budget. These products range from state-of-the-art training systems for the military to light-rail vehicles for Maryland's light-rail system.

Founded in 1950, AAI is a subsidiary of United Industrial Corp. of New York, which also produces energy systems and plastic products. The broad-based engineering firm, which was organized primarily to serve the U.S. Department of Defense, started life as Aircraft Armaments, Inc., indicating its major line, aircraft weaponry, and fire control. By 1966 the company had diversified and the new name was adopted to reflect its broader mix of products and activities.

Today with 2,300 employees around the world, AAI designs and manufactures a wide range of highly sophisticated products in four operational divisions: training and simulation, electronics, unmanned systems, and mechanical systems.

Right: AAI, headquartered in Hunt Valley, Maryland, supports worldwide operations in the defense and commercial markets.

Below: AAI's on-site child-care center is considered one of the finest examples of a child-care facility in the country.

Training and simulation products are geared to ensuring military readiness through systems that save both lives and money. One such product, the Pierside combat system team trainer, which was developed for the U.S. Navy's use, provides a realistic, economical alternative to at-sea exercises. Another, the advanced first-term avionics maintenance trainer, uses interactive video to train U.S. Navy test equipment maintenance technicians. AAI is building on its experience with this product to develop a cost-effective trainer for the defense satellite communications sys-

tem. It has also developed a unique fire-fighting training system for the U.S. Navy and several municipalities.

AAI's electronics division is the country's leading producer of modular automatic test equipment systems, a U.S. Air Force program designed to standardize test equipment for greater efficiency. The company's second-generation system, which has multiple applications on various military aircraft avionics, ground-based radar systems, and tactical missiles, runs 10 times faster than its predecessor. The division also produces three highly differ-

entiated threat generation systems that provide distinctive capabilities and a broad spectrum of applications in laboratories, anechoic chambers, training facilities, and on the flight line.

Unmanned systems makes the Pioneer the world's only combat-proven remotely piloted vehicle; it has logged thousands of flight hours in support of U.S. military forces, including in Operation Desert Storm. Used extensively by the U.S. Navy, Marine Corps, and Army, the Pioneer has demonstrated its battlefield potential, providing real-time reconnaissance, battlefield surveillance, target acquisition, artillery/naval gunfire adjustment, and battle damage assessment.

Mechanical systems products include the munitions handling trailer, which provides precise control for loading cruise missiles onto aircraft. The trailer utilizes an easily controlled hydraulic system that is both accurate and efficient, reducing load time. AAI is also the sole

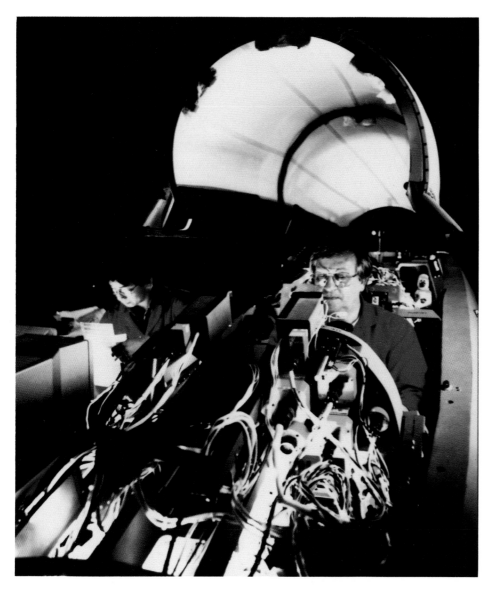

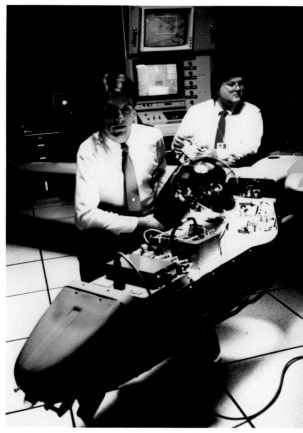

subsidiaries, Systems Management Inc. and Manufacturing Assembly Inc., immediately began to capitalize on the unique advantages of small businesses. The former has won a contract for a sophisticated helicopter flight simulator for the Coast Guard, while the latter is moving into such business areas as waste management, emissions control, and urban mass transit.

As a well-established Baltimore company, AAI supports many local nonprofit organizations. Major beneficiaries of its contributions include Baltimore Goodwill Industries, Baltimore Museum of Art, Baltimore Symphony Orchestra, Cockeysville Volunteer Fire Co., Johns Hopkins University, Junior Achievement of Metropolitan Baltimore, Maryland

supplier of shipboard cargo-handling systems for the U.S. Navy; its orders for the product continue into the next century.

AAI's nonmilitary customers include the National Weather Service, Center for Disease Control, Maryland Department of Transportation, and Baltimore Gas and Electric Co. The company has been awarded a contract from the Weather Service for the design, development, and implementation of an automated weather observation system aimed at making the nation's airports safer places. The product, the automated surface observing system, automatically collects and transmits weather data every minute, replacing antiquated manual collection each hour.

AAI Medical Corporation, a new subsidiary, takes advantage of AAI's experience as a leader in maintenance and support of sophisticated electronic equipment to provide complete clinical equipment management.

Above: This simulated cockpit for the U.S. Navy's A-6E and F-14D aircraft includes electronic combat systems, threat analysis and modeling, cockpit hardware, instruments, displays and panels, aerodynamic modeling, and software.

Right: The Pioneer unmanned aerial vehicle is the only operational UAV system in the U.S. military.

In Maryland AAI builds truck assemblies for the cars that run on the state's light-rail system. The company is also working with the Baltimore Gas and Electric Company on the production of a transportable unit to increase the availability of electric power within the Baltimore metropolitan area. The new unit will enable the utility to increase capacity and keep up with its customers' growing needs.

To expand its business base, AAI set up two new units in 1989. These wholly owned

Academy of Sciences, Maryland Public Television, Maryland Special Olympics, National Aquarium of Baltimore, and United Way of Central Maryland.

Looking to the future, AAI Corporation plans to continue doing what it does best: providing quality products and services in the military defense environment while expanding its nondefense work by translating its technical expertise into such areas as medical equipment support, firefighter training, light rail, and weather systems.

ENVIRONMENTAL ELEMENTS CORPORATION

Environmental Elements Corporation is a leading worldwide supplier of engineered air pollution control systems and services to the utility, municipal, and industrial markets. The company has enjoyed years of steady growth, advancement in technologies, and a widening national and international customer base.

The company was incorporated in 1974 under the direction of its current chairman of the board, Richard E. Hug, as a subsidiary of the Koppers Company. At the time, Koppers was a large multinational firm with diverse operations in the areas of engineering/construction, road materials, forest products, chemicals, and metal products.

The need for environmental protection was emerging as a major national concern when Environmental Elements Corporation was formed, but its underlying business antedated that concern. Its products were based on technology and experience that Koppers had developed and demonstrated as far back as 1945.

Today as a publicly held company under the leadership of its chairman, Richard E. Hug, and its president and chief executive officer, F. Bradford Smith, Environmental Elements Corporation enjoys a reputation as a well-focused and technically competent organization among its *Fortune* 500 customer base. It is also respected throughout the Maryland community as a company that cares. Environmental Elements and its staff support a wide variety of local, civic, cultural, and charitable causes. Senior management has been particularly active in civic affairs. Richard E. Hug has served as chairman of the board of several nonprofit organizations, including the Maryland Chamber of Commerce, United Way of Central Maryland, and The Kennedy Institute. Currently, he serves as chairman of the board of the National Aquarium in Baltimore. With management leading the way, the company encourages volunteerism on the part of all its employees. It communicates a strong sense of the importance of "doing for others" as a way of enriching the quality of life throughout the region.

The engineered systems supplied by the company for the enhancement of air quality are offered on a turnkey, performance-guaranteed basis. These systems include particulate collection equipment (electrostatic precipitators and fabric filters), gaseous removal systems (wet and dry scrubbers), and continuous emission monitoring devices.

Precipitators, in use for several decades, are known for their reliability. Environmental Elements custom designs this equipment to exacting standards and particular applications. The data bank of more than 1,200 installations, coupled with the expertise housed at its Technical Center, assures equipment that is not only cost effective but also "works the first time."

As the cost of new installations continues to rise, the company's concept of rebuilding and replacement of precipitators and their components has won increasing attention. Environmental Elements utilizes experienced teams of trained engineers to assist its customer base in evaluating its air pollution control equipment needs to meet today's stringent air emission requirements.

The company takes great pride in the state-of-the-art technology that it has developed and applied to its product offerings over the years.

This has enabled Environmental Elements to gain a significant share of the distinct markets it serves. Technology combined with product quality, customer service, and committed people is the essence of the company's success.

Environmental Elements Corporation looks forward to a bright future as the nation's concern for clean air intensifies. The company expects to be in the forefront in providing "environmental solutions" for the country's clean air goals—balancing business objectives with good corporate citizenship and community participation as it helps society achieve an improved environment.

Top: Environmental Elements Corporation's headquarters in Baltimore.

Bottom: Electrostatic precipitators at Atlantic City Electric's Beesley Point Station.

Above: Recovery boiler precipitators at Champion International's Pensacola, Florida, facility.

Left: A Virginia Electric Power Company facility utilizing ENELCO® precipitators.

Below: ENELCO® dry scrubbers and fabric filters on the Indianapolis resource recovery plant.

LOCKE INSULATORS, INC.

The second century of helping to deliver electricity into American homes and businesses is about to begin for Locke Insulators and its 500 employees. Porcelain insulators, Locke's products, make it possible to transmit and distribute unseen, powerful electricity.

Locke began in 1893 in Victor, New York. Its founder, Fred Locke, developed the world's first "wet process" porcelain insulators because glass insulators, which were then in common use, lacked reliability for the transmission of electricity.

Locke moved the operation to Baltimore in the early 1920s to take advantage of the city's active port. The move laid the foundation for progress for many years to come. Named Locke Insulators Corporation by its founder, the company is still in the same location he chose, at the north end of the Hanover Street bridge, where Charles Street begins. The factory occupies 27 acres of land on the east side of the bridge, and it has more than 700,000 square feet under roof.

As the nation's demand for electrical power grew over the years, so did Locke's role, and the company established itself as a major supplier to electrical utility companies. As such it became an important link in the chain that has contributed so much to the standard of living this nation achieved through the use of electricity. Locke also sells overseas. Doing its best to help the U.S. balance of trade, the company exports hundreds of thousands of insulators each year to other nations.

After moving to Baltimore Locke became

Locke Insulators is located in the heart of Port Covington, minutes from downtown Baltimore. Photo by Blue Moon, Pasadena, Maryland

affiliated with General Electric Co., and several years later it became a wholly owned General Electric operation. Through the years the Locke plant continued to serve the insulator needs of utility companies and at the same time provided an intra-company source for high-quality porcelains for power equipment. General Electric used these insulators in transformers, circuit breakers, switching equipment, lightning arrestors, and other power products that it supplied to utility companies all over the world. Gradually sales of porcelains were extended to other original equipment manufacturers.

In 1974 NGK Insulators Ltd. of Nagoya, Japan, purchased 60 percent of Locke from General Electric. A program of innovations, technology transfers, and new product introductions followed, strengthening Locke and preparing it for the demands of the twenty-first century. In 1989 Locke became a wholly owned operation of NGK.

To be on the cutting edge of technology in the insulator industry means supplying a product that either provides a new way of doing a job or delivers better performance. Locke

started in 1983 with that first "wet process" porcelain that continues to this day to be the basis for high-quality electrical porcelain, not only for Locke, but for other manufacturers around the world.

During the past 100 years, many changes have occurred in the electric utility industry and in the products it purchases. The industry started with direct voltage but rapidly changed to an alternating voltage. It also began with voltage levels substantially less than much of today's distribution voltage levels and then shifted to transmission voltages for moving power at the 500-kV and 765-kV levels and even to the 1,100-kV levels in some of the offshore installations. The electric utility industry has come full circle, back to direct voltage for moving bulk power in certain circumstances.

The procelain insulator industry also has matured. Product scope and capability continues to be mainly evolutionary, with an occa-

These custom-assembled suspension insulators will be hung from high-voltage transmission towers to support electrical power lines. These are the first of three major Locke products.

The many hoods of an apparatus bushing are cut on a green finishing machine like a bowl on a potter's wheel. Afterwards they are glazed, placed on large flat cars, and fired in periodic kilns. These bushings are the second of three major Locke products.

sional touch of innovation. Locke persists in honing its design skills and expertise to provide products that respond to the mechanical and electrical necessities, be they ordinary or unique in essence. These skills have a proven record of being able to address all types of natural and human-related environmental problems. As the electrical industry and the equipment it uses have evolved and become more sophisticated, Locke has kept pace with insulators and porcelain components that are responsive to both.

Locke's forte has been, and continues to be, in the higher voltages, such as the transmission class. As such, Locke's products generally reflect the larger end of the porcelain industry. The degrees of sophistication, quality, and reliability are required to be on the higher levels. Locke's products are severely tested, whether by customers or by Mother Nature, and it has been imperative that continuing stress be on growth in a quality image. Thus, Locke's product scope primarily includes suspension insulators for transmission lines, post insulators for station facilities, and a variety of porcelain hous-

ings for the original equipment manufacturers.

Locke's product quality owes just as much to improved processing technology as it does to design. In fact, the stability of quality of proven designs is solely due to having manufacturing consistency in producing these designs. Locke and its parent company have made a long-term commitment to the future to continue to upgrade the insulator technology, complete with equipment and processes to back up this technology. Recent factory investment has included both brick and mortar expansion as well as a continuation of mechanization, consolidation of processes, and realignment of facilities for better and more efficient production.

The Locke factory is situated at the gateway to the new and exciting Port Covington development area, a multiple industrial/commercial/

Post insulators support conductors and switching equipment in substations. The electrical integrity is proven in the laboratory in tests such as this one in which the service performance requirements are greatly exceeded, resulting in a flashover.

recreational area designed to complement the Inner Harbor and related waterfront communities. The project area's only heavy industry, Locke Insulators, Inc., expanded its factory and other facilities as part of a continuing effort to manufacture products that are on the leading edge of technological development and fine quality.

The products, porcelains and assembled insulators, depend mostly on the dedication, experience, and skill of each member of the Locke team. Locke's employees, who hold the key to the company's success, look forward to the challenges of the future. The company is proud to enter its second century of progress in 1993.

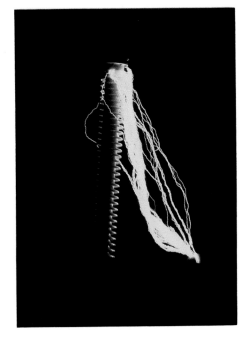

FMC CORPORATION

FMC is a multinational corporation headquartered in Chicago, Illinois, with annual sales of $3.7 billion. The corporation is composed of five operating groups that produce a wide variety of products including agricultural and industrial chemicals, defense systems for the armed forces of the United States and other allied governments, and specialized machinery. FMC's 24,000 employees work in 90 manufacturing and mining facilities located in 25 states and 16 other countries.

The Baltimore plant of FMC Corporation's Agricultural Chemical Group is one of the largest chemical manufacturing facilities in Maryland. Located in the Fairfield/Curtis Bay area, its nearly 300 employees produce a variety of intermediates used to produce crop protection chemicals. These products protect the crops from harmful and destructive pests, increase crop yield, and improve the quality of the food we eat.

The plant has a long history in the community. The 90-acre plant has been the site of chemical business since 1915. Its roots go back to a joint venture between the Hercules Powder Company and U.S. Industrial Alcohol Company to make chemicals used in the production of smokeless gunpowder. Subsequently, U.S. Industrial (USI) took over sole ownership of the plant and concentrated on two principal product lines, sterno and automobile antifreeze.

In 1954 the facility was acquired by FMC Corporation. FMC is one of *Fortune* magazine's 200 largest corporations and a worldwide producer of machinery and chemicals. Since its purchase of the Baltimore facility, FMC has made a significant investment in people, product technology, and capital to modernize the facility, enhance working conditions, and service customers.

Throughout the 1950s and 1960s, the plant made a wide variety of specialty chemicals. In the late 1970s the plant became part of FMC's Agricultural Chemical Group, which marketed a number of crop protection chemicals. By the early 1980s FMC had become a leader in the field of synthetic pyrethroids. FMC is continually improving this new generation of pesticides similar to nature's own insecticide found in African chrysanthemums. Other products produced at the plant are used to safely remove unwanted grasses and plants from soybean fields and to treat many pests associated with the destruction of corn crops.

At the Baltimore plant each employee strives to meet customers' current and future needs as part of FMC's goal to become the

Above: The Baltimore plant of FMC Corporation's Agricultural Chemical Group covers 90 acres and employs nearly 300 people.

Facing page: Committed to excellence, FMC anticipates new challenges by developing new and better products and ways to use them.

"customers' most valued supplier." Significant progress is evident over the years in product quality and delivery as well as plant safety and environmental protection.

That progress has been achieved by a motivated work force. The employees at the plant have worked to increase their own growth potential by accepting increased responsibility for plant operations. Each develops his own "can-do" attitude and couples it with a good understanding of the competition. This understanding has led to increased productivity, innovation, and a strong concentration on safe work behavior. Using the capabilities of all of its employees is the competitive edge that makes the Baltimore plant a leader in its field.

The high morale and productivity of the Baltimore plant is evidence that the philosophy works. "Since we implemented our plant programs around the corporate goals, our employees have steadily gained a deeper insight into our business strategies and our position in the global marketplace," said Frank Solecki, plant manager. "It created a greater sense of teamwork here in Baltimore."

One of the clearest indications that this process is working is the plant safety record. The employees of the Baltimore plant have virtually eliminated lost-time accidents. Excellence in safety performance is the result of a motivated work force that continually undergoes educational and hands-on training programs. The skills developed can then be applied in the workplace and at home. In addition, employees at all levels are involved in process hazards reviews, systems safety analysis, periodic facilities design reviews, and field safety audits. Employ-

ees accept responsibility for their safety and the safety of their coworkers.

Protecting the environment is a part of each employee's responsibility. FMC and its employees go to great lengths to safeguard the public health and community environment. Sophisticated and effective environmental controls and waste minimization methods are used throughout the operation. In both waste minimization technology and emergency response practices the Environmental Protection Agency selected FMC Baltimore as a site for training videos and tour opportunities.

These and other accomplishments have earned wide recognition for FMC's Baltimore plant. The Chemical Manufacturers Association presented the company one of its first Community Awareness and Emergency Response awards. It recognized FMC's role in organizing the South Baltimore Industrial Mutual Aid Plan (SBIMAP), an association of more than 55 companies, government agencies, and community groups working with local fire departments and the Baltimore mayor's office to provide a community response group.

As a member of the Baltimore community, FMC is committed to being both a responsive and responsible member of the Baltimore business community.

11

BUSINESS AND FINANCE

Building on the past while planning for the future, Baltimore's business and financial community demonstrates its innovative leadership.

■ ■ ■

Photo by Walter Calahan/Folio, Inc.

ALEXANDER & ALEXANDER SERVICES INC.

Charles B. Alexander

William F. Alexander

Charles B. and William F. Alexander were pioneers in the American insurance industry in the late nineteenth and early twentieth centuries. The two brothers complemented each other perfectly. C.B. was the astute, conservative administrator, while W.F. was the bold, extroverted salesman. Together they made innovation and client service the cornerstone of their work ethic. Growth came from pioneering new insurance, identifying exposures for which there was no standard policy, and developing special coverages to solve them.

The company originally won recognition by designing coverages in the natural-gas industry. Willingness to obtain coverages to meet clients' specific requests is still a company hallmark. It has helped make Alexander & Alexander Services Inc., one of the largest global insurance brokerage, risk management, and human resource management consulting firms.

The Alexander brothers launched their company in Clarksburg, West Virginia, in the 1890s. In 1914, when William Alexander sought the Baltimore & Ohio Railroad account, railroad officials turned him down because his company had no Baltimore office. He immediately went out and established an office on St. Paul Street, across from the B&O, then returned to announce his action. The railroad's executives were sufficiently impressed to award him the account.

With B&O's business, Alexander & Alexander was well on its way to national prominence in the insurance industry. It became a Maryland corporation in 1922, and its Baltimore office is today one of the largest offices worldwide. A&A was also one of the first major firms to relocate to the Inner Harbor when that area's renovation began. Today the company maintains corporate headquarters in New York City, with administrative and finance offices in Owings Mills, in addition to the Baltimore office.

A&A is a strong supporter of charitable endeavors in the community. The company has had long-term commitments to organizations such as the United Way.

Since it went public in 1969, A&A has experienced a period of growth unparalleled in the insurance brokerage industry, merging with more than 200 other insurance brokers, agencies, and consulting concerns worldwide. It serves a wide range of businesses, governmental entities, and individuals.

Two acquisitions in the 1980s greatly enhanced A&A's ability to serve clients globally. It acquired Alexander Howden Group plc in 1982 and Reed Stenhouse Companies Ltd. in 1985.

Before the decade ended A&A went on to strengthen its presence in Japan, China, and other Asian countries. It also anticipated opportunities arising from a unified European market in 1992 and made further organizational adjustments to meet client needs in a changing global marketplace.

Approaching its centennial, A&A remains driven by the values its founders instilled: innovative thinking, prudent foresight, and service to clients.

IBM

In Baltimore since 1915, just one year after the company was founded, International Business Machines Corp. viewed its relationship with Baltimore as a partnership. If the community is not solid, its corporate thinking goes, then the business cannot be solid. This fundamental unity between company and community underlies IBM's extensive participation in civic and charitable activities.

IBM takes a similar view of its customer relationships. A market- and customer-driven company, it believes that customers must do well before the company can hope to profit. It sells by developing a thorough understanding of the goals, needs, and problems of its customers; in effect, forming "partnerships" with them. The idea is that the greater its understanding, the more help it will be able to give, and that as its customers succeed, IBM will succeed. The company is committed to leadership in the markets it addresses and to demonstrating excellence in the services and products it can bring to bear on customers' business problems.

These ideas are not new at IBM. When the fledgling company opened its first local office with a handful of people in the Baltimore Gas and Electric Company building on Liberty Street, it produced computing, calculating, and recording machines. Over the years it evolved from manufacturing accounting machines through stored-program computers into today's state-of-the-art networking computers. Its customer orientation throughout the entire period has engendered loyalty and strong business ties. IBM still preserves relationships that originated in the 1920s with many public- and private-sector companies.

Growing along with Baltimore, IBM has benefited from the city's diversified, balanced economy. Since its customers reflect this balance, the company has enjoyed steady rather

Two views of IBM's two-acre Pratt Street location: close up (Above) and in the larger context of Baltimore's Inner Harbor (Facing page).

than cyclical growth.

IBM has demonstrated its concern for Baltimore many times over. Only part of this concern is self-serving and designed to further its business objectives. A large part has a high moral basis. Many of the company's executives are natives of Baltimore and eager to help solve community problems. The company takes a two-pronged approach, encouraging both volunteerism and donations. Its own giving is substantial. Major beneficiaries include the arts, education, science, and job formation programs.

A long list of nonprofit organizations is supported by IBM people with funds, services, and gifts of furniture and equipment. The list includes the arts, organizations to help the homeless, children's programs, hospitals, and colleges.

Through the Fund for Community Service program, IBM provides financial support for local projects and activities and encourages IBMers to be partners in the betterment of their communities.

Under the matching grants program, IBM matches on a two-for-one cash basis the contributions of active and retired employees and their spouses to eligible post-secondary educational institutions, hospitals, and cultural institutions.

In addition, IBM employees are deeply involved in the activities of the Baltimore Urban League, Baltimore County Community Center, League for the Handicapped, and Our Daily Bread, a local soup kitchen. They also serve as volunteer fire fighters and paramedics. Each Christmas all the company's local branch offices join in the Adopt-a-Family program sponsored by the Baltimore Services Agency, donating food, clothing, toys, and checks. United Way gets special company attention as an umbrella organization for "have-nots." IBM

holds a position of community leadership in both employee and corporate giving to United Way, and it has served as a pilot for an innovative program to get more businesspeople involved in the organization's activities.

IBM has also played a major role in the revitalization of downtown Baltimore and continues to invest in the area. From its original quarters it moved several times, to Cathedral, North Charles, and St. Paul's streets and, in 1970, to Hopkins Plaza. A few years later IBM decided to break with tradition and put up its own building instead of following its ordinary practice of leasing space from a developer. The decision reflected the depth of its commitment to Baltimore.

The Inner Harbor project had just kicked off, but progress was slow until IBM came in to help. After the company purchased the two-acre Pratt Street site and got ready to build, interest in the project heightened and other companies announced plans to buy in the area. IBM broke ground for its 10-story, 320,000-square-foot building in 1973 and moved in two years later. The building, which also has

a 940-car garage, was designed to blend new technology with respect for Baltimore's historic vitality. IBM occupies 40 percent of the space; its major tenant, T. Rowe Price, occupies 45 percent.

In 1989, when both companies found business growing and more room was needed, IBM and T. Rowe Price Associates, Inc., formed a partnership to expand the building. They worked out plans to enlarge the existing 10 stories and top the new space off with a 28-story tower designed to call to mind Baltimore's maritime heritage. The addition nearly doubles the building's square footage, making it one of the largest in the downtown business district. IBM and T. Rowe Price continue to occupy the same proportion of space while the tower provides quarters for new tenants.

To IBM, the future looks extremely bright because the city is on the move and the company is in step with it. Local management states, "We have 575 people here focusing on one thing—solving customer problems with the best products and services we can offer to enable both of us to profit."

CHICAGO TITLE INSURANCE CO. OF MARYLAND

One of the oldest title insurance companies in America, Chicago Title Insurance Co. of Maryland is also one of the strongest. It has the state's largest and most experienced legal department, most extensive title plant, and largest agency servicing staff, as well as a completely computerized judgment reporting system. Chicago of Maryland is also a member of the nation's most powerful family of title insurers, which gives it impressive financial resources. It leads all of its competition, capturing approximately 27 percent of all title insurance policies written in Maryland.

The company's precursor, Maryland Title Insurance and Trust Co., was founded by a special act of the General Assembly in 1884. Two decades later, in the aftermath of the Great Fire, the company played a significant role in Baltimore history. Its records helped officials redraw property lines and determine ownership, facilitating the city's restoration. Soon after, the company outgrew its original quarters on South Street and in, 1913, moved into its own spacious new building on St. Paul Street. It still occupies, although no longer owns, the building.

The company's acquisition in 1978 by SAFECO Corp., a large real estate and insurance firm, resulted in a name change to SAFECO Title Insurance Co. of Maryland. Nine years later Chicago Title and Trust Co.

Above: After the 1904 fire, the company's records helped officials redraw property lines to determine ownership and facilitate the city's restoration. Courtesy, The Peale Museum, Baltimore City Life Museums

Below: The Title Building in 1945.

acquired SAFECO Title, which took on the Chicago Title Insurance Co. of Maryland name in May 1988. John M. Obzud, executive vice president and chief operating officer, explains, "With this name change we are now recognized as part of the strongest family of title in-

surance underwriters in the country with not only the technological and financial backing but the flexibility of decentralized control to respond to local market conditions."

The parent company, Chicago Title and Trust, traces its roots back to 1847. Other members of its family, in addition to Chicago of Maryland, include Chicago Title Insurance Co., Security Union Title Insurance Co., Chicago Title Insurance Co. of Oregon, and Chicago Title Insurance Co. of Idaho. The organization, which also operates in Puerto Rico, the Virgin Islands, and Canada, has a nationwide network of offices and agents. It offers the most comprehensive and geographically well-balanced distribution in the industry, backed by unrivaled corporate resources.

The security of its policyholders is CTIC's

Above: Chicago Title Insurance Co. believes that now is the time for sound financial management. Photo © 1991 Tom Guidera III

Chicago Title Insurance Co. has played a significant role in Baltimore's history of growth and prosperity. Photo © 1991 Tom Guidera III

main concern. Commitment to quality and sound financial management are its watchwords—quality in the services and products provided by its offices and agents, and prudent management of the assets that support its title insurance policies. This commitment has assumed added importance in this time of concern over the stability of financial institutions. CTIC believes that it is now essential for customers to evaluate the financial strength of title insurers and the assets behind the policies that protect interest in title.

For the further protection of its customers, CTIC maintains an additional reinsurance policy with Lloyd's of London to cover it for losses of up to $30 million. Not the title insurance industry's typical single transaction reinsurance agreement, the Lloyd's coverage is

instead a blanket policy covering all title insurance policies issued by CTIC.

Chicago of Maryland, similar to its sister companies, has separate reserves and separate assets for title losses. An independent operating entity, its assets cannot be reached to satisfy claims against another of the related companies.

In the later 1980s, as growth heightened the demands on its accounting and computer systems, CTIC took action to maintain customer service standards. It launched a new branch automation system, known as TEAM, and accelerated the development and installa-

tion of a new agency accounting system and a new title plant system integrated with TEAM, full implementation of its new claims system, and refinement of its National Business Group system. Chicago of Maryland began to benefit from these new programs early in 1991.

Well into its second century in Baltimore, the company supports a variety of local civic, charitable, and educational causes. They include the Greater Baltimore Committee, Baltimore Better Business Bureau, Maryland Chamber of Commerce, Maryland Home Builders, Greater Baltimore Board of Realtors, United Way, Maryland Special Olympics, Maryland Mortgage Bankers Association, Maryland Land Title Association and American Land Title Association, Maryland Institute College of Art, and Baltimore Educational Scholarship Trust (BEST).

The company's symbol, a castle surrounded by a ring, reflects the age-old notion of the home as a castle, protected by a moat. Chicago Title Insurance Co. of Maryland stands behind America's property owners, ready to defend them swiftly and firmly, summoning its strength from resources hard won by consistent and prudent business practices over its long history.

MERCANTILE-SAFE DEPOSIT AND TRUST COMPANY

A local bank serving the Baltimore community for more than 125 years, Mercantile-Safe Deposit and Trust Company concentrates on building long-term customer relationships. The bank believes customers are best served when the decision makers are part of the community it serves. The bank has grown with Baltimore and, although it now has $2 billion in assets, senior management remains accessible to customers.

The bank took on its present form in 1953, when the Safe Deposit and Trust Company, the state's largest trust institution, merged with the Mercantile Trust Company, a prestigious banking and trust company. The institution operates under Safe Deposit's charter, which was granted on March 10, 1864, during the Civil War. The objective of the founders, who included such prominent Baltimore citizens and benefactors as Enoch Pratt and William T. Walters, was to provide a safe repository for valuables during those uncer-

Headquarters for Mercantile-Safe Deposit and Trust Company and its parent company, Mercantile Bankshares Corporation, are in downtown Baltimore's Hopkins Plaza.

tain times. In 1876 the bank moved from rented quarters to a new fireproof and burglar-proof building, which would later demonstrate its durability.

Mercantile Trust, the other forerunner, was founded in 1884 as a kind of financial department store—then a new concept in banking. Pratt was also a founder of this bank, which offered savings and checking accounts, loans, fiduciary services, foreign banking, and safe-keeping facilities. The institution went on to play an important role in the postwar reconstruction and development of the South. In 1886 it erected a Romanesque, fortress-like building, now a historic landmark, with impregnable vaults that proved of inestimable value to Baltimore.

During the 1904 fire that destroyed much of the city's business district, Safe Deposit and Mercantile Trust invited local merchants to preserve their records and valuables in their great vaults. Although the buildings around them burned to the ground, both the Safe Deposit and Mercantile buildings remained intact, justifying their claims and their customers' faith.

The Safe Deposit was granted trust powers in 1876, the first corporate fiduciary in Mary-

The contents of our vaults were **unharmed** *by the* **Baltimore Fire in 1904**

On the morning of February 8, 1904, the Mercantile Trust building stood intact amidst the ruins of the Baltimore fire.

land and one of the first in the nation. Today Mercantile's Trust Division provides fiduciary services to corporations, charitable institutions, and individuals. Its large personal trust department manages a large portion of the personal trust funds in Maryland.

As a venerable Baltimore establishment, the bank has a tradition of involvement in civic, educational, human service, and cultural organizations. Its executives hold or have held top posts in many organizations, such as chairman of the board of trustees of the Johns Hopkins Hospital, chairman of the Maryland Historical Society, member of the Maryland State Racing Commission, president of the board of the Community Foundation of the Greater Baltimore Area, member of the board of directors of the Baltimore Symphony, and chairman of the board of trustees of Goucher College. The bank itself makes significant contributions to Baltimore civic, cultural, and human service organizations, and is a charter member of the Five Percent Club of Greater

Baltimore, a group of companies with a goal of giving 5 percent of earnings to charity. Emphasizing commitment to the community, the bank also encourages employees to volunteer their services to nonprofit groups.

In 1955 Mercantile's management joined forces with several other business leaders in an all-out effort to halt and reverse the deterioration of downtown Baltimore. They helped form the Greater Baltimore Committee, an early and pivotal body in the public/private partnership that has rejuvenated the city over the past few decades. Mercantile's president served as the group's first vice chairman. Its planning council designed Charles Center, where the large, modern Mercantile Building is located. Early on, the bank committed to be its prime tenant and made the move in 1970.

Mercantile is an affiliate of Mercantile Bankshares Corporation, Maryland's first multibank holding company. Founded in 1970, the corporation has combined assets of almost $5 billion. Affiliate banks are community banks, locally managed. Their combined results have been impressive.

Return on average assets and capital-to-asset ratios run well above industry norms.

Management credits five main principles.

First, it extends credit prudently. It does not want to enlarge its loan portfolio by reducing underwriting standards. Second, it knows its customers. The bank believes that the traditional customer/banker relationship is a personal one developed over time, and that managements who make customer-related decisions locally are in the best position to foster those relationships.

Third, the bank maintains capital strength. It recognizes that banks must be prepared to meet reversals, which requires maintaining a conservative capital-to-asset ratio. Mercantile Bankshares' ratio, more than 10 percent, is one of the nation's strongest for institutions its size. Fourth, it focuses on delivering those services it knows how to perform well and at a reasonable profit. The bank does not try to be all things to all people but prefers to concentrate on doing what it knows how to do well. Fifth, it guards its reputation for integrity.

From that perspective and its position in an economically viable area that it understands, Mercantile-Safe Deposit and Trust Company expects to remain a conservative, well-managed, and profitable institution as it extends its long and deep involvement in the economy and growth of Baltimore.

T. ROWE PRICE ASSOCIATES, INC.

T. Rowe Price Associates is a Baltimore native and proud of it. Founded by Thomas Rowe Price, Jr., himself a native son, the firm has grown from one man with a a pioneering investment philosophy into one of the nation's premier investment management companies.

Starting out in 1937, Price's goal was to grow to 25 employees and $60 million in assets under management. Today, from its headquarters at 100 East Pratt Street overlooking the Inner Harbor, the firm has more than 1,000 employees and manages more than $30 billion in assets.

T. Rowe Price provides a broad range of investment management and related serveces for more than one million individuals and institutional investors, such as corporate pension, profit-sharing, and other employee benefit plans, as well as endowments and foundations. Its clients include some of the country's largest corporations.

In addition to its diverse family of no-load (no sales cahrge) stock, bond, and money-market mutual funds, the firm manages limited partnership investments in real estate, venture capital, and small public companies and offers discount brokerage services.

This broad spectrum of products has grown from a single investment concept that was generally unknown and untested in the 1930s, a time when stocks were considered cyclical investments. Price championed the growth stock theory of investing, which held that investors should concentrate on well-managed companies whose earnings and dividends were expected to grow at above-average rates and stick with them through "thick and thin ".

This investment philosophy was well-suited to capitalize on the prosperity America

Above: T. Rowe Price headquarters in Baltimore's revitilized Inner Harbor. Photo by Bill Harr, Hedrich-Blessing

Below: Investment managers place orders at the firm's equity trading desk.

enjoyed following World War II. As the economy expanded, many of the growth companies previously identified by T. Rowe Price performed so well that the firm attracted national attention.

A strong commitment to research played a significant part in the firm's success. Price believed it was critical to visit companies and explore other sources of information before investing in them. This approach enabled the firm to identify some big winners at relatively early stages in their development—such well-known companies as Dow Chemical, 3M, Monsanto, Merck, and IBM.

By the time Price retired in 1971, he had earned a reputation as one of the great investors of the twentieth century. *Forbes* magazine dubbed him the "sage of Baltimore," and wrote in 1975: "They come and they go—with brief torrents of publicity and a moment or two of glory. But very few money managers stand the test of time. One of the handful that has is T. Rowe Price."

Although the leadership has changed, the company continued to thrive. A fixed-income division was started in 1971 by George J. Collins, who joined T. Rowe Price that year and now serves as its president and chief executive officer.

The firm was innovative in taking a more active approach to bond management based on anticipating interest rate trends. It also applied the same research commitment to the fixed-income area that it had to equities and earned a reputation for its in-depth credit analysis.

In the 1970s T. Rowe Price created both taxable and tax-free money-market and bond funds. This strategy positioned the company for the trends that emerged in the decade as investors became increasingly risk averse and more aware of alternatives to fixed-rate deposits.

When inflation and short-term interest

Left: Thomas Rowe Price, Jr., founded the firm in 1937.

Below: T. Rowe Price Financial Center in Owings Mills, Maryland.

rates soared to double-digit levels at the end of the 1970s, for instance, the firm capitalized on the flood of new investors and assets that poured into money-market funds.

In 1979 T. Rowe Price further broadened its scope, forming a joint venture with Robert Fleming Holdings Ltd., a London-based merchant bank, to offer international investment services. Today Rowe Price-Fleming serves as investment adviser to the T. Rowe Price family of international stock and bond mutual funds and to large institutional clients in the United States.

Rowe Price-Fleming has grown into one of the largest managers of overseas assets for U.S.-based investors, with more than $4 billion under management.

In recent years much of the firm's growth has been driven by the broadening appeal of mutual funds. In addition to direct purchase by individual investors, mutual funds have become an increasingly popular investment option for participants in corporate-sponsored defined contribution plans, such as 401(k) and other profit-sharing programs.

Through its subsidiary, T. Rowe Price Retirement Plan Services, the firm has become one of the most successful full-service managers in the mushrooming 401(k) market, providing a full array of administrative and investment management services.

Reflecting this growth, the firm opened the T. Rowe Price Financial Center in Owings Mills, Maryland, in 1991 to enhance service for mutual fund investors and to accommodate continued expansion in its defined contribution plan business.

T. Rowe Price Associates has expanded far beyond Price's dreams, but it continues to be guided by the principles that formed the cornerstone of its original operations, especially the commitment to provide high-quality investment services that meet the needs and goals of its investors.

"Profitable operations are essential," Price advised his colleagues many years ago, "but profits must follow a job well done and result from the goodwill of the investing public. That is our most important asset, one that is so difficult to build up and so easy to lose. My experience shows me that the best way to maintain it is to make your client's interest your top priority."

BLUE CROSS AND BLUE SHIELD OF MARYLAND, INC.

Blue Cross and Blue Shield is one of the most successful private business initiatives in the United States. Blue Cross and Blue Shied of Maryland is part of the nationwide network of insurers that, with its collective power, has made the Blue Cross and Blue Shield membership card the universally recognized symbol of quality health coverage.

For more than 50 years, Blue Cross and Blue Shield of Maryland has helped employers and individuals effectively finance the cost of health care. The company offers a wide range of products and services—from traditional indemnity to managed care alternatives such as

flexible benefits plans and the largest health maintenance organization in the state.

The Blue Cross and Blue Shield concept—prepaid, guaranteed medical coverage—was born of necessity in the 1930s. At that time the cost of health care was a financial burden for families struggling through the Great Depression. Times were also hard for hospitals, which were obligated to treat the poor but had no way to collect fees. In Dallas, Texas, an innovative plan fulfilled the needs of both. A group of schoolteachers agreed to pay 50 cents each monthly to the Baylor University Hospital in return for 21 days of health care at no

additional cost when they needed it. The prepaid hospital care, considered the first "Blue Cross" plan, was so popular that similar plans sprang up around the country at an astonishing rate.

In 1937 a nonprofit community health-care service plan was begun in Baltimore. Within two years it expanded to include subscribers and hospitals throughout the state. To cover the charges of doctors not employed bt hospitals, a "Blue Shield" plan was also created in 1950. In 1969 the two companies officially changed their names to Blue Cross of Maryland, Inc., and Blue Shield of Maryland, Inc.

Above: Individuals visit the customer's service lobby in Owings Mills for assistance in filing claims or to get information about the many products offered by Blue Cross and Blue Shield.

Left: Blue Cross and Blue Shield of Maryland's corporate headquarters is located in Owings Mills, Maryland.

In 1984 they consolidated as a single corporation, Blue Cross and Blue Shield of Maryland, Inc.

Over the years, Blue Cross and Blue Shield of Maryland has worked hard to ensure that its products and services keep pace with customers' needs, rising health care costs, and dramatic advances in medicine. Programs now include dental and vision care, prescription drug coverage, alcohol and drug rehabilitation, mini-group and individual coverage, home and hospice care, student coverage, catastrophic coverage, long-term care insurance, programs for the uninsured, flexible benefits plans, and

support for health maintenance and preferred provider organizations. Blue Cross and Blue Shield of Maryland also provides claims administration services to more than 650,000 Maryland residents for the federal Medicare program.

Blue Cross and Blue Shield of Maryland is dedicated to quality service for its customers. Group discussions and one-on-one interviews with clients provide valuable feedback on how to make coverage information clear and easy to use. Customers aid in the develpment of new products and evaluate the effectiveness of existing ones. To help Medicare recipients understand and use their coverage better, the company conducts special workshops, seminars, and presentations.

In keeping with its long history of social responsibility, Blue Cross and Blue Shield of Maryland further serves its customers by giving back to the community. During open enrollment each year, it makes individual coverage available to all Maryland residents—even those whom other insurers are unwilling to

cover. For children whose family income is below poverty level but above medical assistance levels, the company offers primary care and prescription drug coverage through The Caring Program. Other community health-related events sponsored by the company include the Constellation Classic, a 10-kilometer run around Baltimore's Inner Harbor; the Maryland Senior Olympics, a yearly athletic competition for citizens over 55 years old; and Maryland's AIDS walk, a fund-raising trek across the city to benefit AIDS research. Blue Cross and Blue Shield employees volunteer nearly 50,000 hours of their own time to the community each year.

Throughout its history, Blue Cross and Blue Shield has been helping people of Maryland protect their most important asset—their health. Today, the company continues to focus on meeting customer's needs by addressing contemporary health-care issues: quality, cost, and access. Its managed care apporach to these issues matches the most appropriate care with the most appropriate setting and encourages patients to be better health-care consumers. To help its customers take better care of themseoves, Blue Cross and Blue Shield as added coverage for preventive care, such as mammography screenings consistent with American Cancer Society guidelines.

Blue Cross and Blue Shield of Maryland, Inc., served more than 1.5 million people—nearly one in every two Marylanders—and its reputation for innovation, quality, and dependability remains unsurpassed.

TRAVEL GUIDE

A travel management service for business, Travel Guide is committed to delivering the highest level of service available. The company is unique in its industry. It is privy to special knowledge and opportunities by virtue of membership in the Travel Guide Group of companies, which include Dial Travel, a supplier of travel services to agencies, and Trade Tourism Marketing, Inc. (TTM), U.S. and U.K. marketing and consulting representatives for airlines, hotel chains, and government tourist boards.

The name Travel Guide traces its roots to 1951, when Eugene Fisher, who still works with the group, founded it. A pioneer in recognizing the special-interest market, Fisher chartered whole aircraft and cruise ships, enabling him to undersell his competition.

David J.B. Wallis, now president, came over from England in 1967 under the sponsorship of Fisher, who had worked with his father. Wallis stayed for about four years and then left to start his own hotel marketing business. In the mid-1970s he founded TTM in Washington, D.C. By 1981 the company had proved its ability to generate business for its clients, and its consequent growth demanded more management depth. Wallis brought in Charles L. Anderson, Jr., as a consultant. Within six months, Anderson became an equal owner of TTM, and the company continued to expand, taking on government tourist agencies, car rental companies, and other clients. Among present clients are the Scottish Tourist Board, the State of Virginia, Florida's Pinellas County, Sarova Hotels worldwide, the Hotel Dorset in New York, Tradotel in Paris, Palmas del Mar in Puerto Rico, and Busch Gardens, Florida.

In the mid-1980s Wallis and Anderson

Views of Travel Guide's corporate headquarters from the courtyard (Left) and street (Above). The building is a historic old tin foundry located in Baltimore's Inner Harbor.

went to Fisher to review some new aircraft chartering opportunities. Finding him ready to retire from Travel Guide, they bought him out. The company was still in the business of arranging group travel to Europe—a tough sell in 1986 when terrorism was at its height. The new owners began to concentrate instead on developing corporate business, and soon acquired Wareheim Travel Services, Inc., a travel agency already well positioned in the Baltimore business travel market. Shortly thereafter,

For many corporate managers, one of the most attractive features of Travel Guide is its professional approach to pricing and planning. Not a product vendor, the company utilizes fee-based pricing for its services rather than a commission on travel and lodging costs. This approach provides unique funding and management resources for clients.

Travel Guide focuses on organizations headquartered in the Baltimore/Washington corridor, although it services the nationwide operations of such clients as McCormick and Co. Other major clients include Johns Hopkins University, Monumental Corp., National Academy of Sciences, Noxell Corp., and T. Rowe Price & Associates.

An aggressive supporter of many worthy local causes, Travel Guide finds that its best vehicle is to work with clients who are heavily committed to a variety of nonprofit organiza-

Travel Guide's corporate reservationists at work.

the company adopted Travel Guide as its trade name.

Since early 1986 the company has provided travel services almost exclusively to businesses. At the start it tried to serve all businesses, but by the end of that year it changed direction to serve only companies with annual travel expenditures of more than $200,000. "We said goodbye to 300 accounts that did not fit," Wallis says. "We won't serve everyone, but those we do handle get the finest level of service available."

Travel Guide performs an advocacy role for clients, working closely with them to control costs, analyze patterns and needs, and bring in travel suppliers such as airlines and hotels. "We're facilitators," Wallis explains.

For many major clients, Travel Guide provides on-site services, establishing a proactive partnership to help manage the entire travel function. It works with these clients to set, administer, and evaluate travel policy; modify policy as corporate needs change; and negotiate with travel providers. Travel Guide also offers back-up support, sending in substitutes when client personnel are out of the office and taking on management reporting and accounting functions. It was first in its industry to install stand-alone, PC-based accounting and management reporting systems in clients' offices, as well as to respond to clients' specific, unique needs with proprietary software. With ticketing and reservations systems on-site,

Travel Guide also handles regulatory filing with the Airline Reporting Corp. in Washington, D.C., and International Airlines Travel Agency Network in Canada.

An innovator in the use of technology, the company employs the most sophisticated reservations management system available today, and the automated document printer (ADP) as a satellite ticket printer. This technology enables Travel Guide to process travel arrangements 70 percent faster than any other system in current use while dramatically mitigating human error. ADPs, more reliable and cost effective than messengers, can deliver boarding passes and tickets within 30 seconds of a reservation.

tions, including United Way, the Heart Association, and the Boy Scouts of America. Travel Guide contributes significant travel components to its clients' charitable fund-raising efforts. These contributions generate substantial interest in the fund-raising programs, helping to ensure their success.

In a service and knowledge business, Travel Guide takes as its motto, "Sterling Service Through Excellence." On that basis, Wallis and Anderson anticipate major growth in the company's special market niche in the Baltimore/ Washington area. They also predict increasing synergy in the years ahead between Travel Guide and Trade Tourism Marketing as TTM adds more hotel chains to its client roster.

BASELINE SOFTWARE GROUP

Baseline Software Group, led by Bill Gaertner and Rick Straub, has offered unique consulting, recruiting, and software development services to the Baltimore/Washington data processing community since 1983. With 90 percent of its business devoted to on-site consulting, Baseline creates a variety of customized systems including relationship banking, insurance policy writing and rating applications, hospital patient care and accounting, and computer integrated manufacturing. Baseline's comprehensive abilities enable the company to perform as a single point of contact for their clients, who range from insurance companies and banks to hospitals and manufacturers.

As a quality–oriented organization, Baseline emphasizes its role as consultant in client relationships. That emphasis also drives its people

Partners Bill Gaertner (far left) and Eric Straub (third from right), along with the management staff of Baseline Software Group.

policy. The company only hires thoroughly experienced professionals with a minimum of eight years in the field; its staff of 30 people averages 15 years' work experience. This depth of experience gives Baseline a sense of technical history, along with the advantages of combining proven data processing skills with progressive technology.

Pacing that technology, Baseline actively encourages its staff to upgrade their skills and knowledge. In-house training seminars are supplemented by outside programs, and employees are entitled to one week's leave annually for education with the company paying the tuition. Reinforcing the experience and training, Baseline's consultants are armed with an extensive array of technical tools, equipping them to serve their clients accurately, effectively, and professionally.

Baseline's proficient staff enables the company to bid on highly technical contracts. While mainframes are the bulk of the business,

capabilities also extend to PCs, artificial intelligence, and expert systems. One measure of Baseline's success is its status as an IBM business partner: a software application specialist teamed with the computer giant to deliver the best possible service to its customers. Business partners must meet stringent professional and customer service standards while supplying their own products and services as well as those of IBM.

As a Baltimore-based company staffed by Baltimore people, Baseline has a long-standing commitment to the city. The firm is a participant in a number of local and national professional and business associations, including the Engineering Society of Baltimore, the Greater Baltimore Committee, the Association for System Management, and the Data Processing Management Association, as well as several technical user groups in the Mid-Atlantic area. Baseline also supports a number of charitable groups with its employees playing a major role in fund-raising.

Baseline Software Group will continue concentrating on dynamic software technology. Spurred by its highly trained staff and the latest development tools, Baseline goes beyond traditional value-added services. It forms partnerships with clients and vendors to be their local expert. Baseline's accomplishments are best expressed by one of its long-term Baltimore clients:

"My organization has been a client of Baseline since its inception. During that time I have found the management to possess both a high degree of integrity and business acumen. The quality of the professional technicians they provide has been unsurpassed by any of their competitors. An additional plus I have experienced in dealing with Baseline is their empathy and synchronization with our business objectives."

W.B. DONER & COMPANY

Over the past 35 years, what W.B. Doner & Company calls "the power of a simple idea" has vaulted many of its clients to national prominence.

One such idea, for Colt 45 malt liquor, featured a man sitting serenely in the middle of a bull ring, calmly sipping the product. For World Wildlife Fund's anti-poaching appeal, it was a single, stark question: "How many elephants can you fit in a box?" For the Baltimore Symphony Orchestra, it was transforming the players into "Baltimore's Other Major League Team."

These and other powerful, compelling ideas have won the agency virtually every major advertising award in the United States and overseas. But the true measure of Doner's success is results. Either Doner's ideas make the cash register ring or they don't.

Obviously, Doner's clients like what they get. Founded as a three-man outpost of the company's Detroit office in 1955, Doner's

This ad, created by W.B. Doner & Company for the World Wildlife Fund's Elephant Action Campaign, brought attention to the problem of the poaching of African elephants.

Baltimore billings mushroomed to more than $100 million by 1990, and the office now shares headquarters status with Detroit. And growing up in Baltimore—instead of New York or Los Angeles—has sharpened the agency's skills.

Traditionally, Doner clients haven't been the ones with the biggest budgets. The agency can't simply outspend its clients' competitors, so they've had to outthink them. A case in point: Klondike Ice Cream Bars, a Doner client that shot past competitors from Kraft, General Foods, Nestle, and RJR to seize the number-one spot in the industry—on a fraction of their budgets—all based on the question, "What would you do for a Klondike bar?"

Success stories such as these have spurred many regional and national clients to bypass larger cities—and larger agencies—for W.B. Doner. Still, some of Doner's most memorable successes have been on behalf of local causes. For the Baltimore Burn Center the agency filmed a burning Polaroid of a small child—then played the film backward. As the fire dwindles and the picture restores itself to normal, an announcer quietly delivers the spot's only spoken line: "The Baltimore Burn Center works wonders."

"Baltimore's Other Major League Team," a television ad for the Baltimore Symphony Orchestra, featured musicians, Baltimore sports personalities, and symphony-goers describing the symphony as if it were an athletic team. The spot won a Gold Lion award for W.B. Doner & Company at the 37th Annual International Advertising Film Festival at Cannes.

This simple, eloquent statement exemplifies Doner's approach, no matter what the project or the size of the client. It sounds like a very basic approach. But then, as Doner has demonstrated in Baltimore, a simple idea can take you a long, long way.

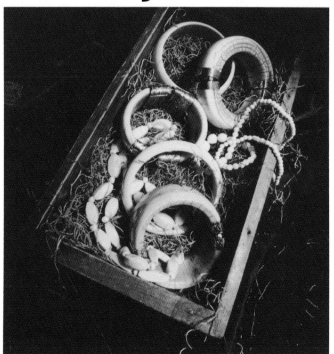

How do you fit five elephants in a box?

First find someone who'll do the killing. Arm him with a machine gun and an axe. Send him off to slaughter elephants. Pay him for the tusks. And ship them away to be carved into bracelets and necklaces.

The African elephant is being driven from the face of the earth for the sake of consumer demand for ivory trinkets. In just 10 years, the population of African elephants has been more than halved. If this rate of killing continues, the African elephant could be extinct in just 25 years. The killers and the people who pay them don't care about elephant deaths. They don't hear the world's outrage. They just want money. They're the people we must stop.

Please join World Wildlife Fund's Elephant Action Campaign. Help us put these killers and the people who finance them out of business. Your donation of $15 or more will help us support increased anti-poaching patrols. And supply equipment to those rangers who are already in the field – desperately trying to stop the senseless slaughter of one of the world's great species.

Time is running out. 143 African elephants are dying every day. So their tusks can be turned into jewelry. You can stop this. Before it's too late.

Call 1-800-453-6100 to make a donation.

YES! I'll gladly join World Wildlife Fund's Elephant Action Campaign. I've enclosed my tax-deductible gift of:

☐ $100   ☐ $50   ☐ $25   ☐ $15   Other $_____

Mr. Ms.
Mrs. Miss _____

Address _____

City/State/Zip _____

Phone _____

Please enclose your tax-deductible check made payable to World Wildlife Fund along with this coupon to **World Wildlife Fund,** Dept. ZB2, 1250 24th Street, N.W., Washington, D.C. 20037. Or, call **1-800-453-6100** and use your VISA® or MasterCard®.

World Wildlife Fund

NCNB National Bank of Maryland

With a presence in Baltimore since 1854, NCNB National Bank of Maryland is well known in the community for its superior service. Among its customers, the bank counts individuals and businesses of all sizes. Its private banking operation has won national recognition.

Chartered as the Dime Savings Bank of Baltimore, it changed its name in 1866 to Central Savings Bank, a name it kept for well over a century. In 1982, reflecting a change in mission and direction to become more like a commercial bank, it became CentraBank. That name lasted six years. In 1988 the bank took on its present name after merging with NCNB Corp. of Charlotte, North Carolina.

NCNB also traces its roots back to the nineteenth century. Organized in 1874 as Commercial National Bank, it merged in 1957 with American Trust Co., the largest bank in the Carolinas. Two years later, another merger brought in First National Bank of Raleigh; in 1960 Security National Bank of Greensboro was merged into the institution. The new bank

Headquarters of NCNB National Bank of Maryland, part of NCNB Corp., the largest banking company in the region and the seventh-largest bank holding company in the nation.

(From left) K. Michael Kines, senior vice president of private banking; Molly Olbrich, vice president of community affairs; H. Lee Boatwright, president; and Miles Coffman, vice president of retail banking.

that resulted, North Carolina National Bank (NCNB), grew rapidly and, after several additional mergers, became a one-bank holding company in 1968. Over the next two decades it expanded across the Southeast.

Today NCNB Corp. is the largest banking company in the region and the seventh-largest bank holding company in the nation. With more than $60 billion in assets, it operates in seven states—Maryland, North and South Carolina, Virginia, Georgia, Florida, and Texas—and maintains offices around the United States and overseas.

NCNB of Maryland, stronger than ever since the merger, is deeply involved in the community it has been serving for so long. "To be a good corporate citizen, you have to put back into the community, not just take

out," says H. Lee Boatwright, president. The bank has a partnership with Graceland Park/O'Donnell Heights elementary school, and more than 25 percent of its 150-member staff does volunteer work at the school. Among other causes supported by NCNB and its people are United Way, Baltimore Symphony, Baltimore Museum of Art, and local soup kitchens. Boatwright is also involved with Union Memorial Hospital.

Deeply committed to the area, NCNB has opened four new offices since 1987, offering mortgage banking, auto financing, leasing, and asset-based lending. Looking ahead, Hugh L. McColl, Jr., chairman of NCNB Corp., says, "We are committed to doing business with consumers and individual customers, small and medium-size commercial businesses, and large multinational corporations. We intend to be a leading factor in all three markets wherever we have a geographical presence. Our standing goal of being a significant national banking company is being realized because of this commitment."

THE WORLD TRADE CENTER BALTIMORE

A variety of unique features distinguish the WTC Baltimore. On the seventh floor, the Maryland International Division has gathered representatives and resources from eight state agencies standing ready to serve international business.

On the 21st floor the WTC Multimedia Conference Center, available for rent, offers expansive views of the harbor and city, as well as a world-class boardroom.

Top of the World, the 27th-floor observation deck and museum, offers Baltimore's only 360-degree panoramic view, extending 13 miles in every direction. Permanent exhibits dramatize the history of the port and the city and introduce visitors to displays from Baltimore's nine international sister cities. Revolving exhibits feature paintings and photographs, often sponsored by the embassies of foreign nations.

Constantly seeking new ways to serve Maryland's business community, the WTC is also planning a World Trade Club, to encourage networking at home and abroad, with information services and restaurant facilities. Well loved by residents and visitors alike, The World Trade Center is a Baltimore landmark with a solid tradition and a bright future.

The symbol of Maryland's commitment to international trade, The World Trade Center Baltimore is constantly alive—its lines of communication humming through the day and night, in touch with commerce across the globe. As the state charts new courses, opening and expanding trade delegations, the WTC serves as a one-stop shop for business and exchange.

Two decades ago all this was just a dream for then-mayor, now governor, William Donald Schaefer. He envisioned a great building rising out of the waterfront, dedicated as a gathering place for international business. An extraordinary partnership that he helped fashion between the city, state, and private industry

Above: The World Trade Center Baltimore at twilight. Photo by Greg Pease

Right: The Top of the World observation level and museum is located on the 27th floor of the WTCB. Photo by Karl M. Ferron

eventually made that vision a reality, and the 30-story World Trade Center opened in 1977 as the seventh such center in the world. The award-winning building, designed by I.M. Pei, soars 423 feet above the original port of Baltimore, matching its appropriate location with its unique design as the world's tallest pentagonal structure. Today there are more than 200 world trade centers in 54 countries.

PROFESSIONS

Greater Baltimore's professional community brings a wealth of service,
ability, and insight to the area.

▪ ▪ ▪

Photo by Greg Pease

DAFT-MCCUNE-WALKER, INC.

Experts in land planning and development in the mid-Atlantic region, Daft-McCune-Walker, Inc. (DMW), takes a multidisciplinary approach to every project. The firm's professional staff includes landscape architects, environmental scientists, land planners, computer specialists, civil engineers, and land surveyors. Together they give DMW a singular ability to solve problems creatively and economically, realizing each site's greatest potential.

In 1970, when the firm was established with a staff of three people, its services were confined to landscape architecture. Over the years it has added other functions in response to growing client needs. Civil engineering services were introduced in 1977 to support the land planning effort and provide better overall design implementation to clients. In 1984 DMW set up a surveying division and, three

years later, an environmental division, enabling it to supply fully integrated services.

Today, with 95 specialists including 30 landscape architects, DMW is Maryland's largest landscape architectural/site civil engineering firm, known for providing the highest quality of service. Its clients include *Fortune* 500 corporations, financial institutions, and quality developers along with such nonprofit organizations as universities, hospitals, and state and county governments and agencies. As a mark of its standing, the firm is regularly invited to participate in statewide seminars on land planning, environmental design, and civil engineering by the major organizations in the field, including the Urban Land Institute and the National Association of Industrial and Office Parks.

DMW's success is traceable to its mission, which stresses a commitment to service as well as the team approach to problem solving. The mission statement also recognizes that "land planning and implementation services carry vital implications for our natural and community resources, and thus help determine future quality of life. We bear responsibility for the

wider, long-term impact of our work, which we approach as dedicated stewards of the natural environment."

DMW worked with United States Fidelity and Guaranty Company to create an in-town country setting for its training and development and computer-center conference facility at Mount Washington in Baltimore. Formerly the campus of a women's college, the 70-acre site held an octagonal building that was built

Above: "The Pond" provides a visual focal point for United States Fidelity and Guaranty Company's Mount Washington corporate campus.

Far left: The master plan of the 70-acre USF&G campus.

Left: Computer technology is the centerpiece of DMW.

in 1855. DMW evaluated master-plan uses to create a land plan sensitive to the old and new buildings, including the new 500,000-square-foot life division headquarters on the north campus.

Computer technology is the spine of what drives DMW. The firm initiated a CADD (computer-aided drafting and design) strategy in 1985 to enhance its core services of land planning, environmental assessment, engineering, and surveying. By integrating various hardware platforms from Intergraph, Hewlett Packard, Compaq, and Macintosh, DMW utilizes the best software packages available, including ARC/INFO and HASP, to create

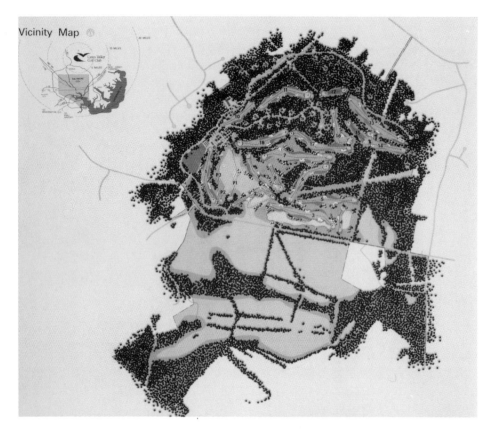

Above: The Baltimore Country Club at Five Farms. The reconstruction of the 18-hole west course, home of the 1988 U.S. Women's Open, was achieved in conjunction with golf professional Tom Kite and Bob Cupp Designs, Inc.

Left: The Caves Valley Golf Club is a 900-acre site located in the pastoral Caves Valley. A showcase for "The Maryland Experience," the site includes a world-class, championship course designed by golf course architect Tom Fazio and club-facilities architect Jack Rinehart.

Far Left: The 17th hole at Caves Valley Golf Club. DMW creates challenging golf routing while protecting the environment.

Left: DMW performs extensive environmental pre- and post-construction investigations, assessments, and monitoring required by the Corps of Engineers and state and local agencies regarding wetland and wildlife habitats, pesticide methodologies, and groundwater quality protection.

customized solutions to client problems. Stand-alone workstations permit fast, efficient, "what-if" modeling for environmental planning, land use, and infrastructure modeling. The workstations are connected to VAX mini-computers via an Ethernet (communications) network that allows diverse professionals access to up-to-date information simultaneously.

In collaboration with golf course architect Tom Fazio, DMW's Caves Valley team created a world-class championship 18-hole course that showcases the Maryland environment. Land planning for the Baltimore County project with extensive environmentally sensitive areas required responsible design in both routing the course and balancing it with "envelopes" for a limited number of residential lots. Daft-McCune-Walker's design preserves the integrity of the property's trout streams and wetlands while utilizing these natural assets as

both course challenges and visual amenities.

Golf course planning is a DMW specialty. The firm was retained by the Baltimore Country Club at Five Farms, site of the 1988 U.S. Women's Open Golf Championship, to work with Tom Kite and Cupp Designs on implementing schematic plans for the reconstruction of the club's 18-hole west course. As landscape architects and environmental planners, DMW provided construction drawings to

comply with local environmental regulations. In addition to the reconstruction, DMW plans called for upgrading the appearance of the new clubhouse area, including vehicular and pedestrian traffic zones.

To fulfill its mission, the firm relies on a broad-based group of professionals—not only landscape architects and civil engineers but also wildlife biologists, hydrologists, industrial hygienists, and environmental engineers. Before the design process is begun, these specialists perform a multitude of surveys and tests. They investigate the impact of such factors as building-related air and water quality, noise impact, surface and ground water, wetlands, wildlife habitats, and urban forestry.

Utilizing a unique combination of mainframe, mini-frame, and stand-alone workstations, DMW effectively provides computer modeling for numerous planning and construction phase applications.

firm was able to make additions and revisions as needed, incorporating new building shapes, parcel delineations, and specific prospective purchasers' buildings. DMW was also able to satisfy another client need—for mass mailings of the plan—by providing the offset printer with computer-generated color separations.

In addition to this plan, DMW prepared master landscape plans for the entire Meadowridge property as well as entrance feature designs, signs, and graphics. The firm also established the design criteria for the park's development.

Through the efforts of DMW's environmental staff, Meadowridge's usable land area has been increased. The strategy was to pro-

Left: Environmental staff members investigate, assess, and document essential natural features that impact site options and effect solutions with DMW planners and landscape architects.

Right: The Cove in Columbia is a multifamily housing community for The Rouse Company.

Below: Meadowridge Business Park is a 125-acre business development and joint venture of Winchester Commercial, Inc., and Crystal Hill Investments Incorporated.

vide specialized mitigation areas within the project's open space system.

Now a major force in environmental studies, DMW has always understood that growth can occur while the environment remains protected. The firm recognizes that increasingly strict environmental regulations are here to stay, and it embraces environmentally sensible and sound development proposals. DMW's environmental staff provides a full range of services. These highly qualified professionals work closely with landscape architects, engineers, and surveyors and legal counsel, lending institutions, and government agencies in planning, surveying, assessment, and management. From identification of land-use restrictions through development of plans for managing or mitigating environmental

DMW provides its specialists with the most sophisticated tools available, including two mainframe computers. Accounting, design work, project scheduling, surveying, desktop publishing, and graphics are all on the computer. This gives the firm an edge from which clients benefit. It can produce plans in a fraction of the time and with far greater detail and subtlety than conventional methods allow. With mundane, time-consuming chores such as drawing taken off their hands, DMW's professionals have more time to think and invent creative solutions to client problems.

Meadowridge Business Park, 125 acres at the intersection of U.S. Route 1 and State Route 103 in Howard County, is a mixed-use project under development by Winchester Commercial, Inc., and Crystal Hill Investments Incorporated. DMW, retained as land-development consultants, prepared the project's master plan. A unique feature of its computer-generated plan was flexibility: the

conditions, the staff provides skilled, cost-effective leadership.

DMW has developed master plans for 4,000 acres around the WISP ski area in Garrett County's Deep Creek Lake resort community. Prominent in the plans, in addition to the downhill ski facilities, are cross-country ski and equestrian trails, a 27-hole golf course, 150-room conference center, and 1,500 residential units. Contract documents for these units include slope-side townhouses, condominium villas, and lakeside single-family homes.

One measure of DMW's service is the multitude of awards its clients have earned from such organizations as the American Society of Landscape Architects, National Association of Industrial and Office Parks, National Association of Home Builders, U.S. Army Corps of Engineers, and National Recreation and Parks Association. "Our work is recognized as being based on sound land planning and environmental design principles," says Robert C. Galvin, president.

Just as it uses the team approach professionally, DMW also applies it to community service. Volunteers from the firm work together for several charitable and cultural organizations including the Kennedy Center, Special Olympics, Woodbourne Center, and Toys for Tots.

Working in a stewardship way, Daft-Mc-Cune-Walker, Inc., is convinced its involvement in the land makes a difference. "There is not only an initial return to the client, but a long-range legacy to the community," Galvin says.

Above: Interactive computer design workstations increase accuracy, speed, and delivery of construction drawings.

Right: The collective spirit of land planners, environmentalists, landscape architects, engineers, and surveyors brings DMW clients' dreams, visions, and goals to completion. This is the Broadmead Life Care Community in Cockeysville, Maryland.

Below: Creativity of design is essential to each project and is a cornerstone of the philosophy and work ethic of DMW.

PRICE WATERHOUSE

Price Waterhouse is the preeminent accounting and business advisory firm in Baltimore, the choice of many of the city's major corporations as well as many middle-market businesses, entrepreneurs, and individuals. Under the direction of managing partner H. William Acker, Price Waterhouse maintains a team of more than 150 highly skilled professional business advisers dedicated to seeking innovative, practical solutions for clients.

The firm serves as auditors for clients in diverse industries, including financial services, health care, food processing, distribution, retail, and a variety of other services. Price Waterhouse also provides highly specialized technical advice and consultation to some of the largest public corporations in Maryland, and it offers specialized services to rapidly growing middle-market companies and entrepreneurs.

Baltimore's business community often calls on the firm's more than 60 Management Consulting Services specialists. MCS consultants, led by partner J. Christopher Everett, assist in the design of information systems, acquisition of computer hardware and software, management of the information system resource, strategic planning, quantitative analysis, human resources management, litigation assistance, and manufacturing and cost management.

The firm's tax specialists, under the direction of partner John J. Pauliny, have the capability and expertise to render a wide range of services, including tax planning and compliance. Price Waterhouse takes pride in its ability to identify tax savings opportunities for corporate and individual clients.

The Baltimore staff, with support from technical specialists around the nation, also serves clients in such areas as executive compensation, mergers and acquisitions, employee benefits, and valuing companies.

Price Waterhouse serves the entire community. It is a strong supporter of many local civic and charitable activities. Partners and managers occupy leadership positions in such organizations as the Red Cross, Salvation Army, and Kennedy Institute. In addition, partners and staff are active in and provide financial support to United Way and the Baltimore Symphony, among other groups. The firm is also a member of the Greater Baltimore Committee, Maryland Economic Growth Association, and Washington-Baltimore Regional Association.

Worldwide, Price Waterhouse is known as the preeminent professional accounting firm with 4,000 offices in more than 100 countries and 33,000 total staff.

Since the origin of Price Waterhouse in nineteenth-century England, its hallmark has been the rendering of superior and distinctive client service by outstanding professional people. From its Baltimore office opening in 1955 with a total staff of six people, that legacy has been maintained by the outstanding professional people of its Baltimore branch.

The Baltimore office of Price Waterhouse, which opened in 1955, is equipped with state-of-the-art technology for the benefit of its clients and staff. Since 1986 Price Waterhouse has been located in the heart of the Baltimore community at 7 Paul Street.

FRANK, BERNSTEIN, CONAWAY & GOLDMAN

One of the oldest and largest law firms in Maryland, Frank, Bernstein, Conaway & Goldman practices in virtually every major area of legal representation. The firm's nearly 200 lawyers are committed to furnishing clients with the highest quality legal services. According to its responsiveness ethic, clients' needs are paramount, and their calls are answered immediately. The firm perceives its function as that of counselor. It has a strong tradition in that line.

Frank, Bernstein traces its origins to 1879, when one of its founders, John Carter Rose, took up the practice of law. Rose initiated a number of Frank, Bernstein customs, including involvement in public affairs; he helped reform the election laws in 1890 and 1896 and, two years later, became President McKinley's U.S. Attorney. Rose also started the tradition of bringing in highly qualified young people and giving them the training and guidance to become top-flight professionals.

Over the years the firm's name was changed several times, reflecting departures, often to public service, as well as arrivals and mergers.

In 1966 it became Frank, Bernstein, Conaway & Goldman, a small firm with 11 partners and nine associates.

Since then the firm has grown rapidly, in staff, offices, geographical coverage, and specialties. In addition to lawyers, the Frank, Bernstein team includes 35 paralegals and 250 technical, secretarial, and clerical assistants. The main office occupies five floors of the 300 East Lombard Building. In 1978 it opened its first office outside the city, in Columbia. Today it also has offices in Baltimore County, Frederick, Bethesda, and Washington, D.C., facilitating its coverage of the Baltimore/Washington common market.

Moving beyond that area, Frank, Bernstein has acquired an international capability. It is part of a network of foreign law firms, located in Canada, London, Luxembourg, Brussels, Amsterdam, Rotterdam, Frankfort, Stockholm, Japan, and Hong Kong. This enables Frank,

Frank, Bernstein's main office occupies five floors of the 300 East Lombard Building.

Bernstein to represent American clients overseas, in conjunction with local law firms, and, under reciprocal arrangements, to represent their clients in business dealings in the United States. With these well-established relationships, the firm can work comfortably worldwide.

A long list of legal specialties distinguishes Frank, Bernstein. Each one is headed by a thoroughly experienced partner or team and supported by outstanding associates who undergo continuous training in a unique in-house legal education program.

The firm's business department counsels manufacturers, distributors, wholesalers, retailers, franchisers and franchisees, financial institutions, health care providers, and service organizations operating in a broad variety of fields domestically and internationally. The department's lawyers work closely with clients in all aspects of business planning and problem-solving, from start-up and initial financing to mergers, acquisitions, sales, and liquidations. They also deal with public offerings, security compliance for public companies, partnerships,

ERISA, and government regulation, among other areas affecting business clients.

Frank, Bernstein's environmental and land use specialty is growing increasingly important as these issues permeate nearly every deal today. The firm assists clients, including major corporations, in identifying and solving environmental problems. It also represents clients before local, state, and federal courts, environmental agencies, and legislative bodies to obtain permits, to clarify the scope of existing regulations, and to minimize the adverse financial impacts of environmental conditions.

The real estate department is recognized nationally for its expertise in handling sophisticated real estate transactions, including land use. Among the many clients are national and local developers, banks, insurance companies, and retailers. The department regularly handles myriad transactions, including structuring of joint ventures, land acquisition, planning and zoning, and commercial leasing.

Litigation department lawyers, with varied and extensive trial and appellate experience, deal with all aspects of civil litigation in all courts. The cases, generated by the firm's diverse clientele, extend to a wide variety of fields, including complex business litigation, real estate law, constitutional law, franchise cases, relationships between suppliers and dis-

tributors, antitrust and securities matters, and trade secrets.

Frank, Bernstein's labor department represents management in labor/management disputes, Equal Employment Opportunity Commission cases, wage and hour issues, immigration cases, and union organizing situations. Bankruptcy department lawyers handle the full range of debtor/creditor relationships, including workouts. Estates and trusts lawyers are involved in every phase of estate planning as well as trust, estate, and guardianship administration; contested estate and trust matters; and all other components of this specialty. Banking and financial services department attorneys represent lenders and borrowers in banking, savings and loan, and financial services industries.

In its more than 110 years, Frank, Bernstein has provided the city, state, and nation with many distinguished public servants. The number of judges among them is impressive. Many, starting with John Carter Rose, have served on the faculty of the University of Maryland Law

School. One—Reuben Oppenheimer—wrote the famous Hoover Commission Report on Deportation. Eli Frank, Jr., son of the firm's original Frank, served as chief counsel to the U.S. Customs Department. Frank, Bernstein has also produced 10 presidents of the Maryland State Bar Association, 11 members of the American Law Institute, a state attorney general, and a dean of the University of Baltimore Law School.

As a longstanding Baltimore establishment, Frank, Bernstein, Conaway & Goldman is deeply involved in community issues and institutions. It has been especially concerned with downtown revitalization, representing developers and banks. Many firm members serve on state and municipal commissions, appointed by the governor and mayor. Members also serve on boards of education, work with charitable and religious groups, and are active in public service on issues such as hunger. The firm contributes significant money as well as time to a variety of cultural institutions, including museums, orchestras, and theaters, and to universities and hospitals.

According to partner Wilbert H. Sirota, "Frank, Bernstein has a commitment to remain a very strong, regionally based law firm. We are committed to this area's growth and prosperity."

THIEBLOT, RYAN, MARTIN & FERGUSON, P.A.

A medium-size law firm with broad expertise in many areas, Thieblot, Ryan, Martin & Ferguson believes that attention to detail is far more important than dazzle. In consequence, the firm enjoys a solid reputation for being thoughtful and careful, which it works hard to maintain. Competence and integrity are the hallmarks of Thieblot, Ryan's reputation, stemming from its determination to do its best work for every client.

The firm was founded in 1964 with a staff of four people—three lawyers and a secretary—and originally specialized in insurance and maritime work. While it still represents many

Right: Commercial attorneys (from left) Robert Harwick, Donna Raffaele, and Anthony Ryan.

Below: Senior Partner Robert Thieblot.

land and the District of Columbia. Thieblot, Ryan also serves out-of-state clients, from Vermont to California, sometimes handling all of their work, and employing local counsel nationwide, when necessary.

Thieblot, Ryan is a modern, state-of-the-art law firm, which has computerized all aspects of its practice. The attorneys find that computerization has been a great benefit to their clients, making for accuracy and the easy access to current information.

The professionals at Thieblot, Ryan include both specialists and generalists in the practice of law. Every senior partner has specialized legal experience. Robert J. Thieblot practices business

insurance companies and corporations in the defense of personal injury actions, it handles a variety of other specialties and has seen a substantial increase and diversification in its clients and work. One of the first tenants to move into Baltimore's World Trade Center on the Inner Harbor, Thieblot, Ryan today occupies its entire fourth floor. Its staff has expanded to more than 10 times the original number and includes seven partners and eight associates.

In addition to its traditional insurance and

maritime work, Thieblot, Ryan now handles extensive corporate work; a growing real estate practice; construction and banking law; estate and tax planning; and toxic tort litigation. It has also become one of the region's leading creditor rights firms and handles extensive accounts for its commercial, bankruptcy, and foreclosure clients. Members of the firm are active in litigation in every county in Maryland, in the state courts of Delaware, in the local courts in the District of Columbia, and in the federal trial and appellate courts in Mary-

law and works in the area of estate planning and management. Anthony W. Ryan is a specialist in creditors' rights and commercial litigation. J. Edward Martin practices primarily in the fields of real estate development, investment syndications, and business litigation. Robert L. Ferguson, Jr., heads the firm's department of civil litigation and maritime law.

The firm is deeply involved in major issues of the day and has been called upon to perform services of statewide interest. In 1985 the circuit court appointed Robert Thieblot as special

Litigation Partners Thomas Schetelich (left) and Robert Ferguson.

counsel to a failed savings and loan association. The challenges presented by the assignment included ongoing litigation in several states and came to involve the entire firm. Many attorneys turned their energies to savings and loan issues, in addition to carrying on their regular work, for the six months that it took to complete the task.

Beyond the law office and the courtroom, the firm and its members are prominent in a variety of local and state-wide professional activities. Among them, they have drafted bills for the Maryland General Assembly, chaired the Baltimore Bar Associations Committee on Professional Ethics, served on the state's Appellate Judicial Nominating Committee, taught at the Judicial Institute of Maryland, chaired the Litigation Section of the Maryland State Bar Association, helped revise the *Annotated Code of Maryland,* and presented continuing legal

education seminars to the legal community. Thieblot, Ryan lawyers are also members of the Maritime Law Association of the U.S., the Maryland Association of Defense Trial Counsel, the Defense Research Institute, and the American Association of Creditor Attorneys—associations which keep them in the forefront of national legal developments. Robert Thieblot is the longest in service as a director, and past president, of the Library Company of

the Baltimore Bar, a private library for lawyers founded in 1840 and housed in the Mitchell Courthouse.

The civic and charitable contributions made by the firm and its members are equally varied and extensive. Thieblot, Ryan has been involved from its outset in 1984, in helping to fund the National Aquarium, including its latest addition. Members hold or have held leadership positions in such cultural organizations as the Baltimore Life Museums (which includes the Peale Museum and the Mencken House), the B&O Museum, and the Commission for Historical and Architectural Preservation. They are concerned with education, participating in fund-raising for schools, and one served as a Baltimore City School Commissioner.

Now well established and representing a broad range of clients, the firm is interested in only modest growth. It believes that there are valuable benefits to remaining a medium-size firm, including the ability to give individual attention and better service to clients, while generating more internal loyalty than a large, impersonal firm can manage. The firm's partners plan to keep the tradition of care and attention to detail which has been its road to success. They expect that Thieblot, Ryan, Martin & Ferguson will remain a respected and confident member of the Baltimore legal community well into the twenty-first century.

Corporate Partner J. Edward Martin.

KAPLAN, HEYMAN, GREENBERG, ENGELMAN & BELGRAD, P.A.

The story of the law firm of Kaplan, Heyman, Greenberg, Engelman & Belgrad, P.A., parallels the success of its long-standing clients, the City of Baltimore, and the State of Maryland. Although Kaplan, Heyman's roots span more than 65 years, most of its well-managed growth has taken place within the last two decades.

Kaplan, Heyman's culture has been one of personal involvement by its partners. By design, the firm remains small enough to continue to make personal service possible while growing large enough to meet the most complex needs of its clients.

The firm's genesis, similar to Baltimore's, was based on a burgeoning maritime industry. Constantly changing and evolving with the city and state, the firm evolved in recent years into a broadly based general-practice law firm.

As one of Baltimore's top 20 law firms, Kaplan, Heyman today offers a wide range of legal services to its diverse client base. In addition to the firm's significant presence in the real estate community, general and commercial litigation, public utility law, labor and employment law, business and corporate law, administrative law, family law, and trusts and estates are all important areas of practice.

Kaplan, Heyman's client base is as broad and diverse as the growing region it serves. Clients include prominent real estate develop-

ers, financial institutions, utilities, automobile dealerships, restaurants, retail establishments, nursing homes, and a wide variety of other businesses in the professional, manufacturing, and service sectors. While the firm primarily practices in the greater Baltimore-Washington region, it is regularly called upon to serve national and international clientele.

Many of Kaplan, Heyman's clients are closely held family businesses. Based on many years of experience, the firm has special counseling expertise in this field; its lawyers understand the legal aspects of the businesses as well as the cultural and personal issues that characterize family enterprises. This special expertise has grown over many years of serving both the business and personal needs of Maryland's finest families. Many of its clients are now in the second and third generations of the founding families and have been represented by Kaplan, Heyman from the very beginning.

Being a counselor often means much more than acting as legal advisor. It also means being a sounding board for business ideas, dealing with sensitive succession issues as families mature, and being available when crucial decisions need to be made. The firm is not driven by what the lawyers want to do, but rather, by the needs of the clients.

The firm takes pride in being an integral part of the City of Baltimore and the State of Maryland and is known for its distinguished

The Baltimore Orioles are about to get a new playing field. Kaplan, Heyman's Herb Belgrad, in his role as chairman of the Maryland Stadium Authority, has been instrumental in assuring Baltimore's prominent future in professional sports. He recently took some time to point out to a group of his Kaplan, Heyman colleagues some design features of the new baseball stadium at Camden Yards.

service to both. Its attorneys take part in a multitude of professional, civic, and charitable activities. The firm has long been active in zoning and land use, helping to plan for orderly growth as the revitalization of Baltimore was envisioned, launched, and realized.

One partner, a nationally recognized expert on lotteries, has served as director of the Maryland State Lottery. Active in the American Bar Association, the firm has produced two city bar association presidents and one president of the Maryland State Bar Association.

Partners are active in an impressive list of civic and community organizations. They have held high leadership positions in many organizations including the presidency of the influential Mt. Washington Improvement Association, Baltimore City Planning Commissioner, president of the Baltimore Legal Aid Bureau, and most recently chairman of

Above: Kaplan, Heyman attorneys are regular visitors to the region's courts. The newly renovated Baltimore City Courthouse has been the scene for many trials handled by the firm's litigators.

Right: Baltimore has recently experienced a dynamic period of real estate and commercial growth. Charles Heyman (left), senior partner, and Searle Mitnick, managing partner, are two Kaplan, Heyman attorneys who have been guiding the firm's growing real estate and commercial practices.

typifies the kind of thing Kaplan, Heyman has always done; it has been in tune with the city right from the start.

The firm's pursuit of civic achievement includes membership in the prestigious Greater Baltimore Committee as well as the Home Builders' Association and other organizations associated with the real estate industry. Special charitable efforts center on leadership in various religious communities and agencies. All of these activities with local civic, charitable, and philanthropic organizations continue a long tradition, keeping Kaplan, Heyman in the forefront of endeavors that enhance Baltimore's quality of life, in both leadership and financial support.

In the future as in the past, this law firm will be closely linked to the needs of the region it serves. As its clients and the region look forward to continued dynamic growth and prosperity, so does the firm. Kaplan, Heyman, Greenberg, Engelman & Belgrad, P.A., is proud of its heritage of service to its clients and the community. But it won't rest on the past as exciting challenges of the present and future drive the firm toward the next century.

the Maryland Stadium Authority. This intimate knowledge of its market has always allowed the firm to better serve the needs of its clients.

One attorney is the only chairman the Maryland Stadium Authority has ever had. Under his leadership, the authority began construction of the new stadium complex at Camden Yards, ensuring many years of enjoyable professional sports for the enthusiastic fans of the region. He has also led the vigorous effort to bring professional football back to Baltimore. Involvement in these activities

RTKL ASSOCIATES INC.

One of the most comprehensive architecture/engineering firms in the nation, RTKL Associates Inc. is also the largest one by far in Baltimore. The firm, which also maintains offices in Dallas, Fort Lauderdale, Los Angeles, Washington, D.C., London, and Tokyo, provides a full-service, in-house staff of more than 600 professionals. They include architects; planners; civil structural, mechanical, and electrical engineers; interior architects; landscape architects; programming architects; and graphic designers. The firm has been using CADD (computer-aided design and drafting) since 1977, and all its offices are linked.

RTKL is a leader in the design and engineering of urban and suburban office buildings, and large-scale retail, mixed-use, medical, and hotel projects. As the winner of more than 75 awards, the firm is known for creating buildings and projects that make a strong, lasting statement while achieving a high level of occupancy and economic success.

Part of the Maryland tradition for more than 45 years, RTKL was founded in 1946 by Archibald C. Rogers (then newly discharged from the U.S. Navy) in his grandmother's Annapolis basement. Rogers' company was innovative from the start. One early achievement was the design for the East Coast's first enclosed shopping mall, Harundale Shopping Center in Glen Burnie. In the nearly four decades since then, RTKL has stood at the forefront of retail architecture, with projects dotting the continent and overseas as far away as Brazil and Australia.

By 1960, when it relocated to Baltimore,

Above: The Owings Mills Town Center, for which RTKL provided architectural and engineering services, is illuminated primarily with natural light, and its interior is accented by luxurious finishes, palm trees, and Victorian-inspired topiary. Photo by Ron Solomon

Right: The Bank of Baltimore Building, 25 stories of granite and glass, establishes a powerful presence in the city's financial district. Photo by David Whitcomb

Below: For USF&G, one of the nation's largest insurance companies, RTKL transformed a nineteenth-century college campus into a state-of-the-art data processing and education center. Photo by Richard Anderson

the firm had become involved in the redevelopment of the city's waterfront. Its role was pivotal. RTKL coordinated the public improvements and designed the pedestrian spaces for the Charles Center Urban Renewal area, just two blocks north of the Inner Harbor basin. It also designed Charles Center South, the center's last major office building.

The project's success won RTKL commissions to design the downtown plans for more than a dozen cities. It also renewed interest in the Inner Harbor area, and the firm went on to prepare a pedestrian circulation plan delineating a broad range of street malls, skywalks, arcades, and street crossings to link major activity centers. RTKL also designed four major structures in the waterfront area, which acted as catalysts to development—the Baltimore Hyatt Regency Hotel, Edward Garmatz Federal Building and Courthouse, Inner Harbor Center, and C&P Telephone Co. headquarters.

After several name changes to reflect the addition of new partners, the firm took on its present name in 1968. It expanded rapidly over the next 15 years, opening branch offices and looking toward international markets. In 1986

Above: Occupying one and a half floors in a prestigious office tower, the Center Club, designed by RTKL, provides its members with an elegant yet comfortable setting for dining. Photo by Ron Solomon

Left: With its intricate combination of facets and setbacks, the RTKL-designed Signet Tower, 24 stories tall, etches a distinctive signature on Baltimore's skyline. Photo by Victoria Lefcourt

RTKL moved into Los Angeles, largely to reach a growing audience in the Pacific Rim. At that time international work accounted for just 5 percent of its business. Today, with all seven of its offices serving international clients, the figure is 12 percent, and RTKL has projects in Japan, Indonesia, and Portugal as well as the U.K., Australia, and Brazil. It does more work in Japan than any other architecture firm.

The firm's noteworthy accomplishments overseas result from the unique package it offers, says chairman Harold L. Adams. "Whether it's language, cultural differences, or even things as simple as introductions, listening, and being sensitive to the unspoken are key to our success abroad. Combine this with expanded services and quality design, and you have a firm that's

become a major player in the global arena."

While serving clients all around the globe, RTKL is based in Baltimore and will continue its long-time involvement in the city. Its major local works include health care, such as Johns Hopkins Hospital Redevelopment and Francis Scott Key Medical Center; retail, such as the Owings Mills Town Center; and commercial projects, including Signet Tower and the Bank of Baltimore Building. The firm also did the interior architecture for the Bank of Baltimore, opening its large windows to flood the space with natural light and installing a new coffered ceiling, open mezzanine, and marble counter that holds state-of-the-art teller equipment.

Committed to the city, RTKL is a major force in such local betterment groups as the

Greater Baltimore Committee and Baltimore Economic Development Council. In 1959 the firm helped launch the committee. Founder Archibald Rogers took a leave of absence from his duties to help organize the civic project.

In 1982, when little progress was being made on the renewal of the Inner Harbor, RTKL relocated to 400 East Pratt Street. Its move to the area made a difference, and the redevelopment project soon gathered new momentum. Seven years later the firm had outgrown that space and announced a new move, to a 30-story, 450,000-square-foot building on Commerce Place. The $90-million building, which RTKL designed, is a joint venture in which one partner is Japanese, the Kajima Development Corp. The building's lead tenant, RTKL is taking 100,000 square feet for its 350 local employees.

Looking ahead, the firm envisions expanding into the international arena by setting up additional offices overseas. As it conducts its international business, RTKL Associates Inc. is pleased at the chance to spread Baltimore's reputation around the world.

WALPERT, SMULLIAN & BLUMENTHAL, P.A.

Alfred M. Walpert, Managing Director

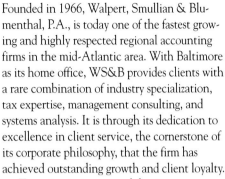

Bernard M. Smullian, Director

Jay M. Blumenthal, Director

Jacob J. Cohen, Director

Arnold R. Scheinberg, Director

Alfred L. Whiteman, Director

Brian S. Meritt, Director

M. Patrick Tracy, Director

Founded in 1966, Walpert, Smullian & Blumenthal, P.A., is today one of the fastest growing and highly respected regional accounting firms in the mid-Atlantic area. With Baltimore as its home office, WS&B provides clients with a rare combination of industry specialization, tax expertise, management consulting, and systems analysis. It is through its dedication to excellence in client service, the cornerstone of its corporate philosophy, that the firm has achieved outstanding growth and client loyalty.

To maintain its regional dominance, WS&B, years ago, replaced the traditional audit department with industry audit teams that would focus their training and talents on the needs of particular industries. The team concept was a result of the firm's professionals viewing their role as the client's management advisor. By taking an industry specialist approach, these professionals could pool resources and take advantage of considerable experience and expertise in their clients' increasingly complex operations.

The firm carefully planned the pattern for its industry teams. Professionals within the firm's Tax Department would become tax liaisons to the industry groups, focusing on the complex tax transactions of each industry. In today's economic environment, WS&B continues to be successful in guiding clients through the complex tax maze of forms, regulations, and statutes. By developing creative strategies and pinpointing opportunities, WS&B is an aggressive advocate of the client's point of view.

Management consultants provide another dimension of the industry team concept. For clients with complex management problems, WS&B draws on the talents and skills of professionals with backgrounds that include engineering, marketing, personnel, and systems design. These consultants complement the industry teams by providing high-quality, results-oriented support as clients implement their strategic plans.

Today WS&B has dominance in a variety of industries. Areas of specialization include automotive dealerships and leasing operations; bankruptcy and workouts; construction; government services; health care; home building; insurance companies; litigation support; manufacturing; medical/dental practices; mergers and acquisitions; personal financial planning; real estate development and management; recruiting; retail; tax planning; and wholesale distribution.

WS&B is particularly knowledgeable on the special needs of fast-growing businesses. For these companies, growing profitably requires a great deal of skill and operational involvement. WS&B consultants provide affordable growth planning, work flow planning, and labor efficiency analysis. Most important, WS&B becomes a member of the client's management team, providing a sounding board for their interests and concerns. In a recent independent survey of Baltimore-area fast-growing companies, WS&B was identified as having more fast-growing companies as clients than any of the other certified public accounting firms in the survey, including Big 6, national, regional, and local firms.

WS&B shares the international perspective of Europe 1992 as an opportunity for its clients to expand into global markets. In addition to in-house expertise, WS&B is a member of Summit International Associates, Inc., an association of major independent accounting and consulting firms in the United States, Canada, and many foreign countries. These firms combine their resources to provide national and international expertise for clients involved in multistate and foreign markets. The presence of affiliate firms in major national and international cities will assist clients explore opportunities in and develop products and services for the global marketplace.

At WS&B, people make the difference. The firm recruits actively on the finest campuses. Students from major colleges and universities seek the practical experience of WS&B internships to complement their technical training. Many of the firm's interns remain with WS&B as staff accountants. A formalized, ongoing training program and hands-on experience in a variety of business situations strengthens their creativity and judgment. WS&B is proud that three of the firm's directors were student interns at one time.

Experienced professionals are also attracted to WS&B, where an entrepreneurial environment enables those with outstanding technical ability and practical business sense the opportunity to advance at a rapid pace. Multiple career tracks, a hallmark of this progressive firm, offer professionals with family care responsibilities the option of part-time arrangements and alternate work schedules. WS&B, proud of its atmosphere of challenge and opportunity, understands that only through the development of staff potential can the welfare of clients be assured.

WS&B is assured that its system of quality control meets the highest professional standards through participation in rigorous peer review, a standard that encourages investment bankers and credit grantors to recommend the financial statements of WS&B to their customers.

As a major accounting firm, WS&B is active in Baltimore, sharing its clients' pride and enthusiasm for the community by taking an active role in civic and charitable organizations. Directors and managers sit on the boards and serve in other leadership posts at several major associations. Some of these organizations are the United Way, The Greater Baltimore Committee, the Burn Center, the Jewish Community Center, the Associated Jewish Charities, the Associated Catholic Charities, the Community Foundation of Greater Baltimore, and the Poly Alumni Association. Recently, a WS&B director received the University of Baltimore's Alumnus of the Year Award.

On celebrating its 25th anniversary in 1991, WS&B looks ahead to a bright future. The firm views its current accomplishments as building blocks for tomorrow and looks forward to a future that will bring new challenges and opportunities.

Christopher C. Adler, Director

Martin P. Brunk, Director

Lynn S. Lazzaro, Director

Charles L. Stromberg, Director

SEMMES, BOWEN & SEMMES

While tracing its roots to the nineteenth century, Semmes, Bowen & Semmes is a forward-looking, multifaceted law firm with strengths in many areas and a reputation for delivering first-class legal services. The breadth and depth of its regional practice is enhanced by a growing national and international presence. With more than 150 lawyers in its Baltimore, Towson, Wilmington, and Washington offices, Semmes goes wherever its clients' needs dictate—throughout the United States, Europe, and the Pacific Rim.

The practice of law was very different in 1887, when John E. Semmes joined two other lawyers to form Steele, Semmes & Carey on Charles Street in downtown Baltimore. Practice then was strictly local, even though, by the turn of the century, the firm had grown into one of the largest law partnerships in the state. When the Great Baltimore Fire of 1904 destroyed its offices, along with much of the city's downtown, the firm was dissolved. John Semmes continued in practice with an associate, Jesse N. Bowen, until 1909 when his son, John E. Semmes, Jr., joined them and the firm took on its present, well-known name.

Throughout its long history, Semmes, Bowen & Semmes has been one of Baltimore's most highly respected law firms, although it chose to grow slowly until 1962. Over the next decade, the number of lawyers (20 lawyers in 1962) doubled, and the pace of growth has continued to increase. Today Semmes has a total staff of about 200 people.

For all the changes, some things remain the same, starting with the firm's emphasis on honesty and integrity. Jesse Bowen once recalled that when he was hired in 1904, John Semmes told him, "There is one thing I insist upon above all others. You must be honest."

The firm's commitment to the community and the profession of law has also endured over more than a century. John Semmes, Sr., served

as Baltimore city solicitor and head of the school and water boards. In that tradition, Semmes, Bowen & Semmes still encourages lawyers to become involved in local charitable, civic, and religious groups. Many of them serve as heads of community and neighborhood associations; several have been presidents of the Baltimore School Board. The firm's members are also involved in a variety of other organizations, such as the Maryland Food Committee and the Baltimore Symphony. The orchestra receives substantial contributions from the firm as well as individual members.

(From left) Maxine Adler, Anthony W. Kraus, and JoAnne Zawitoski.

Pro bono work is a Semmes priority. Lawyers are encouraged to participate in the Maryland Volunteer Lawyers Service, and they have provided legal services to youths in need of assistance for juvenile court proceedings and groups helping battered women and neglected children. All partners are members of the American Bar Association, Maryland State Bar Association, and Bar Association of Balti

Kathleen Howard Meredith (left) and Franklin J. Caudill.

more City. Many belong to the Federal Bar Association, District of Columbia Bar, and Baltimore County Bar Association.

Responsiveness and innovation are Semmes hallmarks. Committed to providing service in anticipation of clients' needs, it is among the most advanced law firms in its use of computers. It was first in the state to bring computers in for administration purposes and first to hook up to Lexis. Semmes also operates a fully equipped word-processing department with remote systems to link all offices.

To enhance its international operations, the firm runs a three-month internship program, bringing over a young foreign attorney with one to three years experience. Its interns have come from Taiwan as well as various European countries. Semmes facilitates research by maintaining one of the finest law libraries in the region, with a collection of more than 20,000 volumes. For work that does not require a law degree, the firm has trained paralegal specialists in various law-related disciplines. Much of the support staff has been

with Semmes for years, easing the way for lawyers and helping them give clients better service.

A general-practice firm, Semmes has strengths in many challenging and diverse fields of law. These include banking and finance, corporate and securities law, creditors' rights, commercial and bankruptcy litigation, estates and trusts, health law, workers' compensation, employers' liability, self-insurance, environmental law, public finance,

(From left) Benjamin R. Goertemiller, E. Bernard Justis (standing), Donna L. Jacobs, and Cleaveland D. Miller

trademarks/copyrights/patents, trade regulation, maritime and international law, real estate, construction and design law, tax law, family law, employee benefits, labor and employment, business litigation and arbitration, general litigation, insurance coverage and regulation, and product liability.

Many of these specialties, including labor law and litigation, transcend local issues and have provided the impetus for the firm's expansion around the nation. Its strong international position grew out of its extensive maritime practice, which involves private international law. The pursuit of alternate dispute resolution methods has enhanced this position, taking the firm into international arbitration.

Semmes also offers a full spectrum of legislative services, including lobbying on clients' behalf before the Maryland General Assembly. In addition, the firm monitors all state legislative and regulatory activities.

Both innovative and practical in the delivery of legal services, Semmes is also flexible. It has seen many changes in the practice of law during its time, and proved its ability to keep up. Semmes, Bowen & Semmes will continue to put its clients' needs first and provide service that meets the same high standards of quality and integrity set by its founders.

(From left) Rudolph L. Rose, William R. Levasseur, and Michael W. Lower.

STEGMAN & COMPANY

One of the largest regional public accounting and management consulting firms in Maryland, Stegman & Company is rich in Baltimore tradition and history. Founder Edward John Stegman was born to German immigrants John Henry and Anna S. Stegman in 1882. His father's position as an accountant for the former Bauernschmidt Brewery may have inspired the young Stegman to enter the profession. Edward J. Stegman first worked as secretary to the president of Provident Savings Bank while attending college classes at night.

His first accounting job was with the Roland Park Company, developers of one of the first planned communities in the United States. In 1915, the year he became a certified public accountant, he founded his own business. Edward J. Stegman & Company opened offices at 814-816 Equitable Building, on the corner of Calvert and Fayette streets. With his real estate expertise, his firm attracted several large local developers as clients.

Among the leaders of the movement to develop professional standards for certified public accountants, Stegman served as secretary/treasurer of the Maryland Association of Certified Public Accountants in 1920, vice president from 1921 to 1923, and president from 1923 to 1924. During this time he was also appointed chairman of the Maryland State Board of Public Accountancy by the then-Governor Albert C. Ritchie. The board prepared, administered, and graded the state examination for certification. Reappointed by

Edward John Stegman, founder.

five governors, Stegman served as chairman for more than 30 years.

As clients grew in size and numbers, the firm hired additional accountants and in 1927 Harold House was named a partner. The firm became Stegman, House & Company, until House's departure in 1948. In 1949 the firm totaled five partners—Louis A. Judges, Bertrand C. Welch, Edward J. Stegman, and his two sons, Edward R. and C. Donald Stegman—and seven staff accountants. Both sons retired in the late 1970s.

Today Stegman & Company's 60 profes-

sionals, including 14 directors provide services from offices in Baltimore, Columbia, Greenbelt, and Towson. The engagement team is determined both by area of expertise and proximity to the client. Stegman & Company provides a small-firm atmosphere—personalized attention to clients' concerns and continuity of staffing—while offering the large-firm expertise needed by clients.

As members of the client's management team, Stegman professionals seek to increase efficiency, productivity, and profitability. They evaluate the strengths and weaknesses of each client's operation and custom-tailor recommendations. The process is often a collaborative effort with the client's staff.

Stegman & Company's areas of specialization include services for manufacturing and construction companies; government contractors; law firms; real estate developers and brokers; wholesalers, distributors, and retailers; financial institutions; municipalities and government agencies; and nonprofit, trade, and professional organizations. Stegman provides expertise in accounting and auditing services, management information systems, and strategic business and tax planning.

The firm's management information systems specialists install computer hardware and software, provide computer consulting and training, conduct internal control studies, and design and program accounting and database systems. The Office of Tax Services consults with businesses on the tax implications of decisions such as mergers, acquisitions, reorganizations, and liquidations; advises both businesses and individuals on executive compensation, benefits, and financial planning; and provides representation before the IRS and other tax authorities.

Stegman & Company offers several consulting specialties. Its real estate services team tailors services for the specific needs of real estate product developers, service providers, and investors. These include accounting, auditing and tax services; management advisory services; cash-flow projections; documentation and loan structure reviews; financial/economic analyses; and financial and market risk assessments. Stegman's litigation support services team provides expertise in business valuation

Stegman & Company provides a small-firm atmosphere—personalized attention to clients' concerns and continuity of staffing—while offering the large-firm expertise needed by clients.

As important members of the client's management team, Stegman professionals work to find the most effective methods of increasing efficiency, productivity, and profitability.

providing self-funded group health insurance programs.

Professionalism, quality, and integrity, standards that have been the Stegman & Company hallmark for 75 years, are reflected in its achievements and activities. As a member of the AICPA's SEC Practice Section, Stegman submitted to peer reviews in 1981, 1984, 1987, and 1990 and received unqualified opinions.

To encourage accounting students to strive for excellence, the firm has established a scholarship at Johns Hopkins University. Stegman employees contribute their time and money to charitable organizations, such as the Juvenile Diabetes Foundation, Baltimore County Jaycees, and United Way. Professional staff are also actively involved in civic, community, and professional organizations as members of the Greater Baltimore Committee, Downtown Partnership of Baltimore, The Entrepreneurship Institute, the Rotary Club, and the Baltimore, Carroll, Hartford, Howard, and Prince George counties and Baltimore city chambers of commerce.

One of the area's oldest public accounting firms, Stegman & Company attributes its longevity and success to the professionalism and integrity of staff, quality of service provided to clients, and degree of expertise and specialized services for growing businesses and nonprofit organizations in the Baltimore/Washington corridor.

and forecasts, damage theory and calculation, fidelity and surety, financial and tax planning, product liability, and record organization to a growing number of law firms.

The firm's government contracting specialists assist clients with proposal development, contract negotiations (rates, "ceilings," and "floors"), annual incurred costs submissions (rate justification) for audit agencies such as the Defense Contract Audit Agency (DCAA), pre-award audits, and accounting systems development, implementation, and certification.

A Stegman affiliate, Health Claims Administrators, is a third-party administrator

PIPER & MARBURY

Edward O. Clarke, Jr. (left), and L.P. Scriggins, co-chairmen of the firm's business division.

Piper & Marbury is a general practice law firm with major offices in Baltimore, Maryland, and Washington, D.C. In 1989 the firm opened an office in Easton, Maryland, to serve its important Eastern Shore clients. In 1990 the firm established an office in London to enable it to enhance its capability to represent its U.K. clients and U.S. clients with European interests, and in early 1991 an office in New York City was established to serve the firm's institutional clients in that city.

The firm is among the 100 largest firms in the country. Formed in Baltimore by the 1952 union of two long-established firms—Piper, Watkins, Avirett & Egerton and Marbury, Miller & Evans—Piper & Marbury can trace its predecessors back to the nineteenth cen-

tury. The firm has grown from 14 lawyers in 1952 to 258 lawyers today. There are 193 lawyers practicing in the Baltimore office and 65 in the Washington office.

The firm has a broad regional and national practice and serves as general counsel to many major Maryland-based companies. Regular clients for which the firm does a significant amount of work as general counsel or in specific areas include *Fortune* 500 companies, commercial banks, major investment bankers and investment advisers, many regional and local firms, closely held enterprises, state and local governments, and individuals. The firm represents clients and handles matters throughout the country and abroad.

Over the years Piper & Marbury has partic-

ipated broadly in Baltimore's growth and development, representing Baltimore-based companies and commercial and investment banks, as well as state, county, and municipal agencies and authorities in financial and other capacities. It has served as issuers' or underwriters' counsel in a great many corporate finance transactions and is recognized as one of the leading firms in the country involved in initial public offerings of securities. The firm has a very strong mergers and acquisitions practice in which its corporate lawyers are teamed with tax, employee benefit, and other specialists to provide complete legal coverage for the transaction.

Piper & Marbury has one of the largest public finance practices in this part of the country. It serves as bond counsel to the State of Maryland, many subdivisions of the state, and several important public financing agencies. In 1969 the firm served as finance counsel for the creation of the Maryland Open Space Program, which funds acquisition of open land for public use and was one of the first such state-funded programs in the nation. Piper & Marbury has also served as finance counsel for the separate financing of the City of Baltimore water and sewer systems and its off-street parking program. The firm has developed outstanding expertise in waste-to-energy projects and is regarded as one of a very small number of firms with national prominence in this important field.

Piper & Marbury has been significantly involved in the financing and organization of Baltimore hospitals, notably the city's two teaching hospitals, the Johns Hopkins Hospital and the University of Maryland Hospital. One partner has served as chairman of the Hopkins Hospital board, and another created the corporate structure for the University of Maryland Hospital when it changed from a public to a private institution in 1984.

The firm has a very large controversy practice, with particular emphasis on products liability and commercial litigation and on environmental law matters. The firm represents Occidental Chemical Company in the Love Canal case, one of the most significant environmental controversies in history, as well as a national group of utilities in environmental regulatory matters. Its products liability practice includes representation of a number of automobile manufacturers, and its commercial litigators have been involved in a broad range of cases involving trade regulation, securities claims, and banking and thrift controversies.

Piper & Marbury believes that it has responsibilities to the community to provide legal services to those unable to afford them and for many years has sponsored programs to enable its lawyers to discharge these responsibilities. In 1969 the firm established a branch office in East Baltimore where badly needed legal services could be made available to poor people. As circumstances changed, this commitment evolved into major support of the clinical programs at the University of Maryland Law School and participation in a number of community programs for the delivery of pro bono legal services.

Many of the firm's lawyers have taken leadership positions in national, state, and local legal organizations and in civic and charitable institutions. In recent years its partners have

Above: Joseph G. Finnerty, Jr. (left), and Thomas H. Truitt, co-chairmen of the firm's controversy division.

Left: Decatur H. Miller (left), chairman, and Andre W. Brewster, former chairman, stand before a portrait of William L. Marbury, Jr.

held board chairmanships at the Baltimore Museum of Art, the Baltimore Symphony Orchestra, the Peabody Institute, the Enoch Pratt Free Library, the Maryland Institute of Art, and the Alvin Ailey Dance Theater Foundation of Maryland. The firm's lawyers serve on the boards of virtually every major nonprofit institution in the city. For many years the firm has been a significant contributor to charitable and cultural institutions in the city and considers itself to be a leader among law firms in its support of community causes.

Woven into the fabric of Baltimore over the decades, Piper & Marbury can point to an impressive number of alumni presently or formerly in prominent public service positions. For example, the present mayor and city solicitor of Baltimore were Piper & Marbury lawyers, as were a number of state and federal judges. The firm, looking to the future, sees itself as one of the half-dozen leading law firms in the mid-Atlantic region and among those firms recognized in this country and abroad as having the capacity and expertise to represent their clients in the most challenging legal engagements.

BALTIMORE RESCO

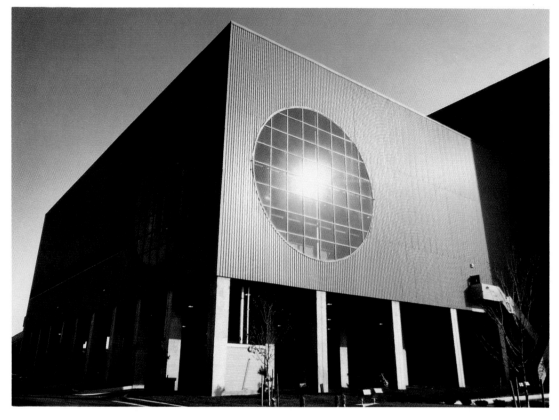

Above: The Baltimore RESCO facility.

Below: Repopulating Chesapeake Bay with endangered rockfish bred at the Baltimore plant.

Operating out of a contemporary plant building that is well suited to its downtown location, Baltimore RESCO provides dependable, environmentally safe disposal of up to 2,250 tons per day of the city's and county's solid wastes. The plant, built on the site of an earlier unsuccessful Baltimore recycling effort, incorporates the latest trash-to-steam technology. It is an industrial showplace, regularly welcoming groups from all over the world. Thousands of visitors have been taken through since the plant opened in 1985.

An aerial view of the Baltimore RESCO facility.

The RESCO facility is owned and operated by New Hampshire-based Wheelabrator Environmental Systems Inc., the nation's leading waste-to-energy company. With plants in many East Coast states from New Hampshire to Florida, Wheelabrator also operates cogeneration facilities and other small power plants as well as systems that purify water, treat wastewater, and control air pollution.

The Baltimore operation is simple. Incoming trucks dump refuse into an enclosed receiving pit from which it is transferred by overhead cranes to furnace feed hoppers. The refuse is moved on reciprocating grates through the furnaces, as air from the refuse pit area is blown in above and below the grates. This fuels a complete combustion process in the furnaces while maintaining negative pressure over the pit, preventing odors from escaping. A waterwall boiler above the grate area produces superheated steam that drives a turbine-generator to produce electricity for Baltimore Gas and Electric Company. Steam is also supplied to Baltimore Steam Co.'s downtown heating loop. Energy recaptured by the plant—60,000 kilowatts of power every hour—can power 40,000 homes. It is sufficient to satisfy downtown Baltimore's heating needs and a significant portion of its air conditioning needs.

An environment-conscious company as well as a good corporate citizen, RESCO maintains excellent relations with its Westport community. It has entered into a partnership with Westport Elementary School, sending employee volunteers in as computer and reading tutors and sponsoring perfect-attendance awards to classes. The company also runs a summer learning calendar for the school, with special projects tied into environmental themes.

Among many other local contributions, RESCO was a major donor for the relocation of the Seven Foot Knoll Lighthouse to the Inner Harbor, and the firm is a major sponsor of the Lady Baltimore project. In a unique effort, RESCO runs a fish hatchery on its premises, breeding endangered rockfish in cleaned water that has served as a coolant. The fish are used to restock Chesapeake Bay.

Baltimore RESCO looks ahead to maintaining its position as one of the nation's most efficient recycling plants, upgrading and modernizing as newer technology becomes available.

Photo by Roger Miller

13

QUALITY OF LIFE

Medical and educational institutions contribute to the quality of life for
Baltimore area residents.

▪ ▪ ▪

Photo by Roger Miller

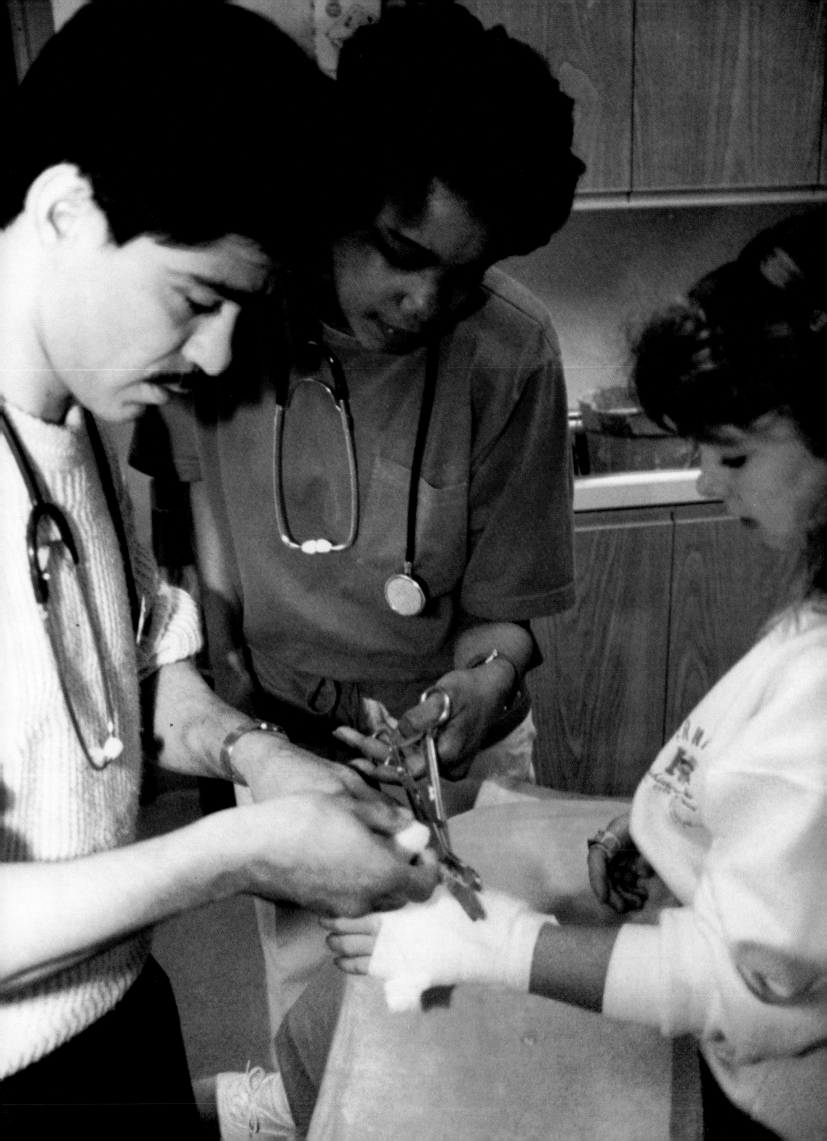

SHEPPARD PRATT HEALTH SYSTEM

The Main Hospital Building.

One of the nation's premier centers for psychiatric treatment, education, and research, Sheppard Pratt cares for people of all ages, from children to the elderly. Its philosophy of healing, rooted in a profound respect for the individual, appreciates the complexity of human behavior. The hospital does not confine itself to any single approach to healing but designs and staffs programs to suit individual needs. The range of programs is wide. It includes outpatient counseling and therapy; partial, day, and short-term hospitalization; residential treatment; and special long-term treatment for the chronically mentally ill.

Some of the best and brightest psychiatric health care professionals to be found anywhere comprise the Sheppard Pratt staff. Among them are 140 physicians, 25 psychologists, 200 registered nurses, 50 social workers, and scores

of other therapists and technicians. All of them share the belief in the human spirit that underlies the hospital's programs, engendering its national reputation.

Chartered in 1853, the private, not-for-profit Sheppard Pratt owes its start to the concern for the mentally ill shown by Moses Sheppard, a Quaker who devoted much of his life to helping the needy, including prisoners and slaves. When Sheppard died in 1857, he left his estate to the board of trustees to whom he had assigned responsibility for establishing the Sheppard Asylum. He wished the trustees not dip into the principal but wait for it to grow, necessitating that trustees proceed slowly. They began by purchasing the property where the hospital now stands, then the Mount Airy farm. In the ensuing years the trustees constructed several homelike buildings with

pleasant, comfortable interiors. The first patients were admitted to the Sheppard Asylum in December 1891, and Sheppard Pratt counts 1991 as its centennial year of patient care.

The institution received a new infusion of money in 1896, on the death of another prominent Baltimore philanthropist, Enoch Pratt. Pratt left $1.6 million to the trustees asking only that they change the asylum's name to the Sheppard and Enoch Pratt Hospital. The trustees welcomed the change; replacing the word "asylum" with "hospital" signaled a new era in which the stigma attached to mental illness would begin to fade as patients were no longer simply housed, however humanely, but helped or even cured with the development of new medical treatment.

The hospital's original policy called for it to be self-sufficient. It retained the farm's orchards and vegetable fields, kept livestock, and housed its entire staff. That changed after World War II, although the president and others still live on the grounds. In the 1960s the trustees chose to sell premium acreage at a modest yield to the Greater Baltimore Medical Center, St. Joseph's Hospital, and Towson State University to form what is regarded as a major academic/medical complex. The 322-bed hospital remains an attractively landscaped parcel of 100 rolling, wooded acres. Its trademark remains the stone gatehouse, built in 1859, which stands at the entrance to the property.

Today the fully accredited hospital, a member of the Sheppard and Enoch Pratt Health System, Inc., is a place where patients are both healed and, no less important, helped to assume control of their own lives. The hospital's therapeutic environment encourages growth and increasing self-reliance by means of graduated reentry into the community. Through counseling and group interaction, patients learn to trust themselves. At the same time they learn to improve communications with their families, whom Sheppard Pratt regards as key figures in the therapeutic process.

For the community, the hospital serves as a mental health resource and place of learning. Sheppard Pratt sponsors a variety of programs for the public, professions, and business. An institution of people helping people, it also publishes widely circulated newsletters for both the public and the psychiatric profession.

The hospital's roster of patients is diverse. About one-third are children and teenagers, while the elderly also constitute a significant

Moses Sheppard

Enoch Pratt

percentage. More than half are under treatment for mood-related illnesses, including depression and bipolar disorder; others suffer from such problems as chemical dependency, schizophrenia, eating disorders. For all its patients, Sheppard Pratt provides every service essential to initiating the healing process. Its staff includes experts in psychopharmacology, psychogerontology, and child and adolescent behavior. Its activity and occupational therapy programs are among the most highly sophisticated in the nation.

As a hospital, Sheppard Pratt wants its patients in their homes. In every case, its emphasis is on eliminating or shortening hospital stays. Instead of the months or even years of hospitalization that mood-related illnesses required not long ago, the average stay has been reduced to 30 to 45 days. Underlying this accomplishment are new insights in psychotherapy and advances in psychopharmacology. A leader in both areas, Sheppard Pratt hospitalizes only people who cannot be successfully treated as outpatients, and only until they can be stabilized. As a matter of policy, discharge planning begins within 24 hours of admission. Patients, once discharged, continue working with their therapists. Both medication and therapist are carefully selected to meet individual needs.

For patients who do not require hospitalization or are ready to leave the hospital but not to return home yet, Sheppard Pratt has created a variety of innovative transitional programs. The Mount Airy quarter-way house, opened in 1988 to offer 24-hour supervision and more structure than a halfway house, teaches both social and vocational skills. The 16 residents of its well-furnished single and double rooms are afforded access to shops, banks, and other elements of everyday life, as well as to such special activities as gardening. Maintained on medica-

tion, patients may stay up to two years before being discharged. They may even be able to work during their Mount Airy residence, with help from a special career counseling service, transitional occupation programs (TOPS). Mount Airy has proved so successful, with costs only 25 to 30 percent as much as full hospitalization, that Sheppard Pratt envisions a village of such group homes.

The adult day hospital, geared to patients aged 18 to 60 who require intensive psychiatric treatment, is a multidisciplinary partial hospitalization program. Open from Monday through Friday, it allows patients to spend evenings and weekends at home. For continuity of treatment, many begin day hospital activities before leaving the inpatient unit. Attending half or full days according to need, patients are encouraged to help design their own treatment plans.

Sheppard Pratt's emphasis on minimizing hospital stays extends to the chronically mentally ill. One vehicle for accomplishing this goal is New Ventures, a community rehabilitation program designed to help patients learn or recall social skills and normalize their behavior. The only such program in Maryland administered by a private psychiatric hospital, New Ventures gives patients the opportunity to develop their natural abilities, enhance their

The National Center for Human Development.

Above: Activity therapy, child and adolescent division.

Right: Activity therapy, geriatric day hospital.

For the general public, NCHD offers free lectures as well as a variety of enrichment and preventive mental health courses, which are aimed at increasing individuals' control over their own lives. These courses cover such areas of common concern as starting over after divorce, alcohol/chemical dependence recovery, and self-hypnosis for stress management. Other programs address the needs of parents, teachers, and children.

The NCHD's Business and Management Institute customizes management consulting and training programs for business, and offers a full range of psychological services. Among its areas of special expertise are stress management, managing difficult people, and handling drug abuse. Sheppard Pratt also offers skills assessment services, a nationwide employee assistance program, and a series of packaged programs that cover the whole realm of interpersonal relations. They include teaching managers to spot drug problems as well as management training for sales and middle managers and one-on-one training sessions for high-level managers.

Embedded in Baltimore County for over a century, Sheppard Pratt is always looking for ways to help the community. The career counseling offered by TOPS is not restricted to patients but is also available to others in the community who want to change careers.

The hospital's quarterly consumer newsletter, *Hearts and Minds*, is another public service, mailed out to 30,000 local residents. It keeps readers informed on such subjects of common interest as preventive mental health care, eating disorders, and depression in children and adolescents. The hospital's

autonomy, and become productive members of the community.

Sheppard Pratt also administers the Northern Baltimore County Community Mental Health Center (NORCOM), a private/public partnership of Baltimore County and the State of Maryland. This community-based program provides comprehensive outpatient services, including crisis intervention, evaluation, and short-term treatment. NORCOM works with individuals, groups, and families, according to clinical need, and supplies chemotherapy and alcoholism services as well as post-hospitalization and community-support systems for the severely mentally disabled.

To help those with chronic mental illness, who may have been labeled treatment resistant, leave the hospital for good, Sheppard Pratt has created the mobile treatment team (MOTT). Operating since 1988, MOTT blends community psychiatry, supportive therapy, and sound case management. Teams make house calls to check on use of prescribed medications and provide additional care and supervision as needed.

To spread its reach to the entire community and beyond, Sheppard Pratt now runs an educational division, the National Center for

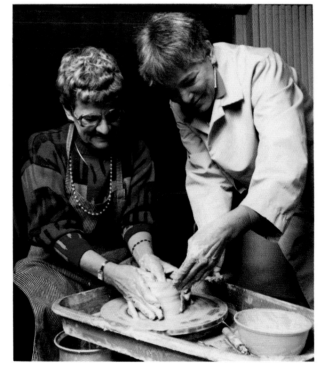

Human Development (NCHD). Housed in a new multimillion-dollar building equipped with the latest educational technology, the center served more than 10,000 people in its first year (1988). They included health and human service professionals, the public, and the business community. Programs for professionals, conducted by well-known authorities, center on keeping up with new developments in the field.

professional newsletter, *Psychiatric Review*, is published six times yearly. Presenting mental health information and commentary, it is distributed to the 33,000 psychiatrists in the United States.

In further outreach efforts, Sheppard Pratt runs a speakers bureau that local organizations call on for experts to address meetings, and a counsel line to help educate callers on mental health topics. As part of its service to local

Above: The Mt. Airy quarter-way house.

Right: Group therapy session.

schools, it sends counselors out to help children deal with their feelings after disturbing events. Sheppard Pratt also supports various community projects. During the Multiple Sclerosis Walk each April, the hospital opens its grounds and provides rest stops for walkers.

Moving into its second century of service to Baltimore, Sheppard Pratt applauds the changes in psychiatric treatment that make people functional faster. The hospital anticipates additional progress as therapy is further improved and medicine is further refined.

Its own constant growth and development over the years have consistently enabled Sheppard Pratt Hospital to give patients the best that science and medicine have to offer. That was what Moses Sheppard wanted and what the hospital he founded is pledged to go on giving.

THE FRANCIS SCOTT KEY MEDICAL CENTER

An affiliate of Johns Hopkins Health System, The Francis Scott Key Medical Center serves as a major teaching hospital in both acute and long-term care services. The 581-bed center comprises three health-care business lines: a full service, community, acute care hospital; skilled nursing facility; and chronic hospital. The outpatient services it provides are especially important to the community. Each year Baltimore city and county residents make 36,000 emergency room visits and 150,000 hospital clinic and grant-funded visits.

The medical center's impact extends beyond its immediate community. It provides extensive regional referral services, including burn care at the Baltimore Regional Burn Center, the only one of its kind in the state. Key, which does renal transplants, also has Mary-

years in its initial location on Eutaw Street, the almshouse moved to Lexington Street; in 1866 it moved once more, to its present site on Eastern Avenue, overlooking the Chesapeake Bay. Known as the Bay View Asylum, it developed a system of student and resident training under the supervision of three local medical schools, including Johns Hopkins. In 1925 its name was changed to Baltimore City Hospitals and, 10 years later, it came under the jurisdiction of the city's Department of Public Welfare.

The institution adopted its present name in 1984 when the city transferred control to the not-for-profit Johns Hopkins Hospital and University. The Johns Hopkins Health System is now the parent organization. Its role is to formulate policy and provide centralized management along with treasury, marketing, pur-

land's largest hospital-based dialysis program; it performs 25,000 treatments every year. The institution serves as a state-designated area-wide trauma center. The facility also has one of Maryland's six high-risk neonatal intensive care units as well as a nationally known sleep disorder center. Two important federal agencies are located on the campus: the National Institute on Drug Abuse and the National Institute on Aging. They contribute to Key's national and international reputation for research in crucial areas of modern medicine. In addition to substance abuse and geriatric care, which have been long-standing Key specialties, programs of distinction also include digestive diseases and clinical immunology, pulmonary medicine, and cardiology.

A pre-Revolutionary War origin distinguishes Key, which traces its roots to a 1773 decision by the Maryland legislature to finance an almshouse for the poor and infirm. After 50

Above: Newest neighbor on campus, the Johns Hopkins Asthma & Allergy Center is part of Hopkins' Bayview redevelopment program and home to Key's pulmonary medicine division.

Right: Severely ill newborns are transported from all over Maryland to Key's state-of-the-art neonatal intensive care unit.

chasing, materials management, clinical laboratory, audit, and legal services.

The privatization of Key has resulted in a remarkable turnaround. In just a few years, the institution reverted from annual losses of $8 million to profits averaging $3 million, enabling it to fund its own much-needed redevelopment. The center had long been deteriorating by the time Johns Hopkins took over. While it continued to provide excellent medical care and retained a highly qualified and

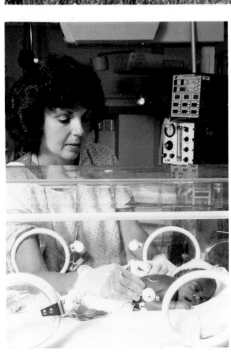

Above: Residents of Key's geriatrics center make crafts for the annual summer festival.

Below: The Baltimore Regional Burn Center treats an average of 300 patients a year and has a success rate in excess of 90 percent.

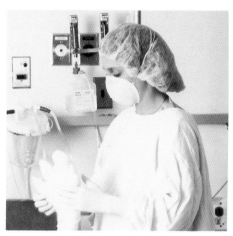

Bayview Community Park is located on the Hopkins Bayview campus, home of The Francis Scott Key Medical Center.

dedicated staff, as activities grew more complex, management was found lacking and the aging physical plant was taking its toll.

Extensive changes implemented by the new management hinge on a major redevelopment program designed to build on the institution's strengths. The first phase, completed early in 1991, included a new central utilities plant and a $17-million long-term care facility that replaced a Civil War-era structure. Named the Johns Hopkins Geriatrics Center, the state-of-the-art building serves as the home of Johns Hopkins Health System programs in geriatric medicine. It was designed as a national model for teaching nursing homes, incorporating chronic hospital and skilled nursing facility

beds. The facility's innovative design and physical environment encourages residents to maintain their independence and remain part of the community.

The second phase of redevelopment, an acute hospital tower, is scheduled for completion in the fall of 1993. Replacing 190 of the acute hospital's 315 beds, including 72 beds for burn, coronary, and medical and surgical intensive care, the nine-level, two-pod addition also provides space for radiology, trauma and emergency rooms, and operating rooms. Plans have been carefully drawn to keep the part of the existing facility that is structurally sound for lower-technology activities while redoing all the high-technology areas.

As a full-service community teaching and research institution, Key offers nearly all medical and surgical services. Its digestive diseases division, with three fully equipped endoscopy suites for diagnosis and treatment, ranks among

the best in the region. And the chemical dependence program with a 26-bed inpatient unit, and outpatient, rehabilitation clinical research beds, ranks among the state's largest. Most Key staff physicians are on the faculty of the Johns Hopkins University School of Medicine.

The medical center and its employees are vital partners in good corporate citizenship as well as health care. Among the charitable activities they support are the semi-annual Red Cross blood drive, an annual food drive, and United Way, for which Key recently led Maryland hospitals in per capita giving.

Well into its third century of serving Baltimore, the Francis Scott Key Medical Center has "the resources to provide a wide range of innovative health care services to our community," says Ronald R. Peterson, president. He expects the redevelopment program to enhance those resources.

TOWSON STATE UNIVERSITY

Towson State University, part of the University of Maryland System since 1988, is dedicated to providing quality education at a reasonable cost. Towson State is highly regarded around the nation. It has been cited for excellence several times in *U.S. News & World Report*'s annual survey of America's best colleges, in which it was most recently mentioned as one of the 12 rising stars of American higher education.

Founded in 1866 in Baltimore as the State Normal School, it relocated to Towson in 1915. In 1935 the school began to offer a bachelor of science in education, changing its name to Maryland State Teachers College at Towson. An arts and sciences program was introduced in 1946 and expanded in 1963, and the institution became Towson State College. By 1976 the college had evolved into a comprehensive institution of higher learning and was granted university status.

Today Towson State is the largest provider of baccalaureate degrees to students in the Baltimore area. The university provides a strong, liberal arts-based education to students in its 40 undergraduate major programs. Spread out over a 306-acre campus, it enrolls about 9,800 full-time and 3,700 part-time undergraduates as well as 1,500 graduate students. Undergraduate colleges and schools include Allied Health Sciences and Physical Education, Continuing Studies, Education, Fine Arts and Communication, Liberal Arts, Natural and Mathematical Sciences, and Business and Economics. They award bachelor of arts, science, and fine

Towson State University's women's studies program is nationally recognized.

arts degrees. The graduate school, begun in 1958, offers 24 programs leading to the master of arts, science, fine arts, and education degrees. The university also offers, in conjunction with the University of Maryland, the doctor of education degree.

The School of Business and Economics, with 35 percent of the total enrollment, provides a broad-based professional education with a solid foundation in liberal arts and sciences. Degrees are granted in accounting, economics, and business administration, which includes finance, management, and marketing. Through the school's Center for Area Resource Development, working relationships with the greater Baltimore business community have

been strengthened. The College of Education also offers services to business, including daycare center consultation to help companies establish and operate centers.

Fine arts is among Towson State's major strengths. The only institution in Maryland to confer a BFA degree in dance, it also runs an exchange program in dance and music with the Leningrad State Conservatory in the Soviet Union. The art department offers many innovative programs, such as a sculpture conference, performance art course, and corporate art program, which offers opportunities for students to sell to business. The Music Department sponsors more than 200 performances each year; its faculty includes many acclaimed concert artists. Classical and experimental theater productions are staged each year in the Fine Arts Center's superb facilities. A collaboration with Baltimore's Theatre Project is providing new opportunities for exposure to international theater.

Among its unique programs, Towson State offers the state's only master's degree program in professional writing. Writing is also the core of several College of Education programs. Through an Abell Foundation grant, Baltimore teachers are trained to improve their writing instruction. Support from the Center for the

Teaching and Study of Writing enhances the programs of the Maryland Writing Project, a statewide program based at Towson State.

In 1984 the College of Education initiated an overseas student-teaching program that includes internships and seminars in England, travel study courses in England and Italy, and faculty exchanges with China and England. The college also sponsors a Gifted and Talented program for children around the state and one of the East Coast's finest model centers for parent education and infant development.

Other ongoing and new programs have also earned honors for Towson State. The university's highly regarded women's studies program has been involved in a project to integrate the study of women's issues into the traditional curriculum. The university also hosted the 1989 National Women's Studies Conference, which brought 2,000 people to campus. Tow-

Founded in 1866 as a teacher-training school, Towson State University is a comprehensive university today, offering 40 undergraduate and 24 graduate degree programs.

son State's international studies major offers travel study opportunities and special events. Students from nearly 60 countries study at the university, which has formal faculty/student exchange agreements with many European and Asian institutions. The Center for Suburban and Regional Studies, founded in 1989, is the first such academic institute in the nation. It serves as a clearinghouse for information, promoting research, education, and publication in suburban issues. Still newer, the Center for the Study of Adult Development and Aging also encompasses a clinic, the University Life Center. The center explores how adults adapt to the physical and mental changes of aging, and

utilizes research and education to foster positive adaptations, enhancing quality of life.

Among a multitude of community outreach programs, Towson State operates a national Center for the Study and Prevention of Campus Violence. The university began studying the problem in 1985 and formally established the center three years later as a clearinghouse for current information and statistical data. Towson State also participates in the city's Adopt-a-School and At-Risk Student programs, while its Future Teachers Club and College Kids Club encourage Baltimore elementary schoolchildren to continue their education.

Maryland's second-largest university, Towson State University looks forward to continued growth in reputation as it reaches out not only to the surrounding community but to the world.

UNIVERSITY OF MARYLAND MEDICAL SYSTEM

Nearly half of all the physicians in the state of Maryland are trained at the University of Maryland Medical System (UMMS), which comprises three downtown facilities for patient care plus three community affiliations. An academic medical center, UMMS also trains dentists, nurses, pharmacists, and social workers.

The system brings together hundreds of the best and brightest in medicine to provide the most advanced and compassionate care available anywhere. Every physician on the staff has the expertise required for a faculty appointment at the university's School of Medicine. Clinical care is enhanced by continual research, and diagnostic equipment is state of the art. UMMS's role as a referral center, which extends beyond Maryland's borders, confers specialized knowledge and experience, enabling it to treat the most complex illnesses.

University surgeons are pioneers in the use of the laparoscope in general surgery, which eliminates the need for large incisions. As a result, hospital stays after gallbladder or other types of surgery are drastically reduced to only one night, and patients return to their normal activities within one week.

In the course of a long history, UMMS has achieved many firsts. Founded in 1823 as the Baltimore Infirmary, the University of Maryland Hospital's forerunner, it is considered the nation's first hospital to be built by a medical school for clinical instruction. The school also offered the nation's first intramural residency training.

When it moved to a new building in 1897, the Baltimore Infirmary became University Hospital. The creation of the state university system in 1920 turned the hospital into a public institution. It retained that status until 1984, when it became the second academic medical center in the United States to change its governance from public to private status. In spite of the fact that UMMS is private and the School of Medicine is public, these entities are naturally intertwined. They use the umbrella name, University of Maryland Medical Center, to tie together clinical research and education functions.

Today UMMS is a large and growing complex with an annual operating budget of more than $200 million. It has 747 beds and a total staff of 5,000 people, including 800 medical staff members and 1,000 nurses. The down-

The new $44-million R Adams Cowley Shock Trauma Center treats the most severely injured of Maryland's trauma patients, most of whom are injured in motor vehicle accidents. Because of its expert care, 92 percent of the center's patients survive their injuries.

town campus, made up of University Hospital, the R Adams Cowley Shock Trauma Center, and the University of Maryland Cancer Center, admits 23,000 patients each year while handling 186,000 visits by outpatients.

Among the hospital's many special centers and programs are the Maryland Center for Multiple Sclerosis; Maryland Epilepsy and Stroke centers; Sudden Infant Death Syndrome Institute; and in vitro fertilization and high-risk pregnancy programs.

University surgeons are known worldwide for their pioneering work in laparoscopic surgery for gallbladders, ulcers, and hernia repair, as well as for their skill in bone lengthening techniques. The Heart Center employs innovative techniques to clear blocked arteries and prevent unnecessary surgery, including coronary laser angioplasty.

The Cancer Center, a miniature hospital with 56 beds, received its designation from the National Cancer Institute in 1981. It has since expanded the scope of its research and services to become one of the country's leading cancer centers. The UMMS center is one of just a few in the nation to be awarded grants by the National Institutes of Health to test new drugs and new uses for existing drugs; its patients are given medication unavailable elsewhere.

UMMS's best-known unit, the R Adams Cowley Shock Trauma Center, is widely regarded as the world's most sophisticated center of its kind. From its start in a one-room laboratory in 1964, the center has grown into the clinical hub of Maryland's trauma system, and it is housed in a $44-million building opened

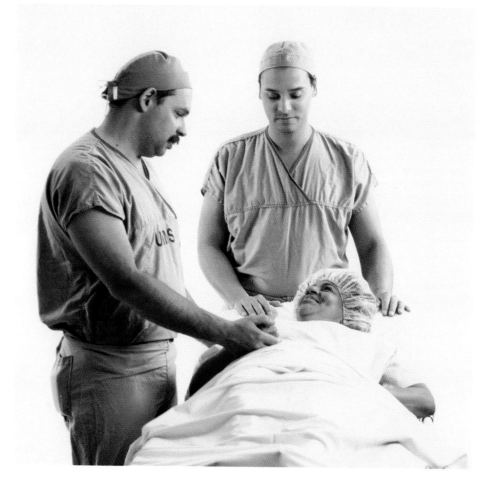

University is an important part of the revitalization of downtown Baltimore's west side. A new inpatient tower and ambulatory care center will be built near the hospital, just a few blocks away from the new Camden Yards stadium.

in 1989. The 138-bed facility is named for R Adams Cowley, M.D., who treated trauma as a treatable illness. Although it cares for the most critically ill and injured patients with life-threatening trauma, the center has a survival rate of 92 percent.

The 183-bed Montebello Rehabilitation Hospital is one of UMMS's community affiliations. The hospital treats head and spinal cord injuries, stroke, amputations, polytrauma, and neurologic and orthopedic conditions. Montebello is the largest free-standing rehabilitation facility in the state.

UMMS is also affiliated with the James Lawrence Kernan Hospital, which specializes in acute rehabilitation and supportive care. Together, UMMS, Kernan, and Montebello form the University of Maryland Rehabilitation Network, providing patients with a total spectrum of coordinated care that allows them to achieve the fullest recovery possible.

The third community affiliation is with the Maryland Kidney Stone Center, which is connected with five local hospitals and houses a $1.8-million lithotripter, or kidney stone crusher. The instrument eliminates the need for surgery or incisions of any kind, diminishing the pain, convalescence time, and costs of kidney stone treatment.

As an integral part of Baltimore since early in the nineteenth century, UMMS sponsors various outreach programs and supports local nonprofit groups. One outreach effort, Health-talk, is a free series of lunchtime talks on such

timely topics as eating disorders, cholesterol, stress, and drugs. United Way is among the charitable organizations receiving enthusiastic support from UMMS and its staff, who work with the umbrella group's agencies every day in the course of helping their patients. Each year, a United Way campaign kickoff is held on the downtown campus, and an increasing percent-

age of employees participate in the fund-raising.

Looking ahead into the next century, UMMS is organizing a $210-million capital improvement plan. It will encompass both a new inpatient tower and ambulatory care center and renovations of older space. Both state support and private philanthropy will fund these projects.

As the physicians for all of Maryland, University of Maryland Medical System lives by the slogan, "We touch Maryland's life everyday." At the same time, it maintains its position as a pioneer in medicine, determined to be not just a survivor of the profound changes taking place in the health care environment but a leader shaping those changes.

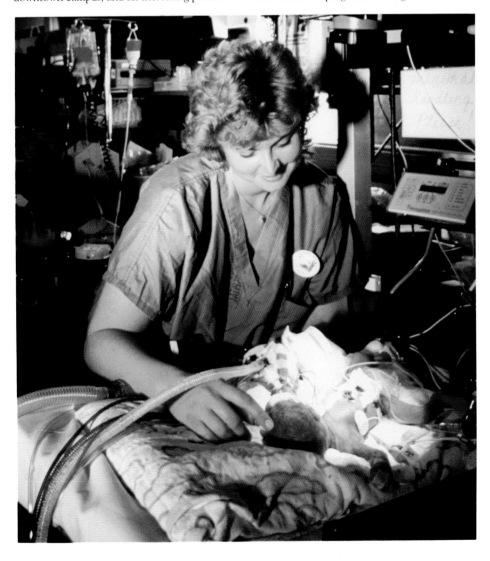

Critically ill and premature infants receive tender loving care combined with the most up-to-date medical treatment at University's neonatal intensive care unit. University is a statewide referral center for high-risk pregnancy and cares for critically ill newborns from all over the region.

WOODBOURNE

For nearly 200 years, Woodbourne has been caring for Baltimore children. It is one of the five oldest child care facilities in the nation, fulfilling a mission to provide quality mental health and educational services to children and families. The private, nonprofit organization is committed to sharing its leadership and expertise with the community in helping to rebuild troubled families today while laying the foundation for stronger families tomorrow.

Founded in 1798 as the Female Charity School, it was originally an orphanage. One hundred years later, as the Nursery and Child's Hospital, it was annually treating some 80 children on an operating budget of under $3,500. Today Woodbourne serves nearly 2,000 clients and 500 families a year on an operating budget of almost $10 million.

Woodbourne's services are extensive; its clients' needs prodigious. Referred by local child-care agencies, virtually all are from dysfunctional families. Many have been physically or sexually abused, and severe learning disabilities are common among them.

For these children in need, Woodbourne offers a variety of inpatient and outpatient programs. The 48-bed Children's Diagnostic/Treatment Center takes in infants to 14-year-olds who have been removed from crisis situations at home. They may stay for up to 60 days while their immediate educational, psychological, and medical needs are met and their long-term care prescribed.

Accredited by the Joint Commission on the Accreditation of Health Care Organizations (JCAHO), the Residential Treatment Center, housing 32 children aged 11 to 16, provides comprehensive therapy for their emotional problems while offering special education and a structured program of activities. A short-term, 12-bed unit of the Residential Treatment Center, Woodbourne's newest program, treats adolescents in crisis and provides diagnosis and recommendations for long-term treatment.

The Day School makes special education and treatment programs available to 60 junior high school-age children who cannot cope in a

Above: Personal attention and stimulating activities are vital when working with children who have been ignored or abused by their parents.

Below: Students with learning disabilities gain confidence and academic skills when working with computers in Woodbourne's educational programs.

regular school setting. Woodbourne also administers a specialized foster care program, training 36 prospective foster families to care for troubled children in their homes; an in-home intervention program for 60 adjudicated adolescents; and programs to help parents in jeopardy of losing their children learn positive parenting skills.

Exemplifying Woodbourne's progressive approach, its Community Services Center

Woodbourne board members and senior staff study plans to enhance facilities. From left: Elias A. Dorsey; Patricia K. Cronin, executive vice president; John Hodge-Williams, Ed.D., president; Marcia Hall, chairman; William Daniel White; and Michael J. Chesser.

Williams, with its first statewide Leadership of Distinction Award, in 1989.

Approaching its 200th anniversary, Woodbourne anticipates expanding its prevention programs. High on the agenda is working with families by providing short-term residential treatment and follow-up services to whole families, and in-home services with emphasis on prevention to families of children in day treatment programs. In the 1990s Woodbourne looks forward to serving the broader community as well.

represents a first for the region—an independent outpatient program with JCAHO accreditation. The center furnishes children and their families with outpatient mental health services, including individual, group, and family counseling; expressive arts therapies; and in-home visits.

Expressive arts therapies, initiated in 1981, typify Woodbourne's creative responses to its clients' difficulties. A form of psychotherapy that uses spontaneous artistic expressions as a means of communicating, art, movement, and drama help the children break through barriers to expressing thoughts and feelings. This and other innovative services help ensure that clients at Woodbourne get the continuity of care they need to reintegrate into the community.

Convinced that early intervention produces stronger families, Woodbourne has launched a program to teach bonding techniques to teenage mothers and their children. Another program helps pregnant teens get the prenatal care they need to assure healthy babies and prepares the young girls to shoulder their new responsibilities as mothers.

Providing all these services is a highly motivated staff of about 325 full- and part-time workers whose commitment and resourcefulness are what make Woodbourne different. Many have bachelor or graduate degrees, and all are still learning, for Woodbourne channels its resources into constant training opportunities. At the top, Woodbourne is distinguished by "outstanding leadership and management." United Way used these words in honoring its president, John Hodge-

Jerome and some of the other boys on his hall spend time building friendships and learning to get along with each other.

For Jerome's mother, the decision to send her son to Woodbourne's residential treatment program was not easy. It meant separating him from family, friends, and familiar surroundings. But 12-year-old Jerome's clinic visits and sessions with his social worker and school counselor were not enough. He continued to run away from home. He was failing in school where, frustrated by his inability to concentrate or learn, he took out his anger on those around him. His mother, used to sullenness, was growing frightened by his sudden outbursts and threatening gestures.

As Jerome's emotional problems became too much for the family to handle, his mother recognized that, without help, he was headed for more serious trouble. The Department of Social Services referred Jerome to Woodbourne.

At Woodbourne, he was placed in a residential treatment unit with others his age who had similar problems. He is now being helped through a variety of clinical and educational resources. Family sessions, an integral part of his treatment, allow Jerome and his mother to work on family problems. It will take time for him to progress to the point where he can return home, but he is one of Woodbourne's more fortunate clients: Jerome has something and someone to return to.

SINAI HOSPITAL

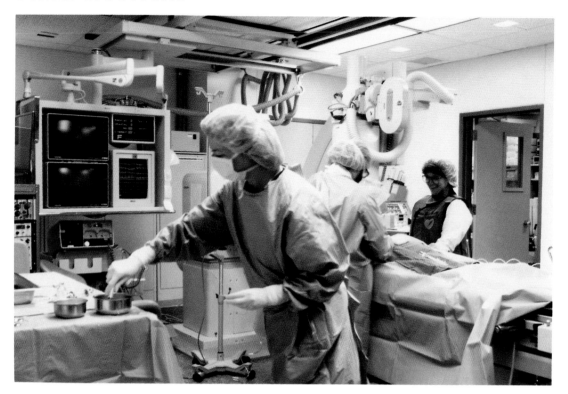

One of Baltimore's oldest hospitals, celebrating its 125th anniversary in 1991, the nonprofit Sinai Hospital is dedicated to continuing its twin traditions of caring for the community and teaching/research. Sinai offers a full range of acute medical and surgical specialties along with preventive, primary, and rehabilitative care.

As the third-largest teaching hospital in Maryland, it remains in the forefront of medical knowledge and practice, honing professional skills and striving for perfection. One advantage for patients is expert 24-hour care from highly trained physicians. In 1980 it was Sinai physicians who developed and introduced the first automatic implantable cardio-verter defibrillator, used to prevent certain types of cardiac arrest. Still a leader in cardiology, Sinai began performing open-heart surgery in October 1990.

The 463-bed hospital, located on 29 landscaped acres at Belvedere Avenue and Northern Parkway, has come a long way from its beginnings in 1866, as the Hebrew Hospital and Asylum, in a 10-room structure on Monument Street. The hospital's name was changed to Sinai Hospital in 1926, reflecting growth and expanded services. Moving with the population, Sinai opened its present facility in 1958, aided by the Associated Jewish Charities.

In the same year the hospital established the Blaustein Obstetrical/Gynecological building to initiate excellence in women's services. Today,

The cardiology staff proceeds with an electrophysiologic heart catheterization study to evaluate the cause of a patient's syncope (fainting episodes).

Sinai offers one of the area's largest, best-equipped obstetrics/gynecology departments, including a fertility center, family-centered birthing program, and genetics counseling. The hospital delivers almost 4,000 babies per year—one of the highest totals in the state.

Other on-site centers of excellence, all es-

tablished in the 1980s and 1990s as community needs changed, include an Emergency Services Center and trauma unit, neonatal intensive care unit, inpatient psychiatric unit, and Ambulatory Surgery Center. Sinai's 10-bed head trauma unit, opened in 1989 in the continually expanding rehabilitation center, is one of the state's largest. In 1990 still another addition to the Sinai campus, a second medical building, was opened. It houses doctors' offices; the new Krieger Eye Institute; a pharmacy; and an optical shop.

The second-largest employer in northwest Baltimore, with 2,400 employees, Sinai extends its geographical outreach with such new projects as the multispecialty Women's Health Center and Pediatric Care Center at Belvedere Square, and the SurgiCenter of Baltimore, an ambulatory surgical facility run in conjunction with Health Specialists, P.A., in Owings Mills. The hospital also offers free community programs ranging from annual health screens to positive parenting programs and the Premier Years senior membership program.

At Sinai Hospital health care is dynamic. The hospital, for 125 years a healthy influence, is well-positioned to meet its community's needs in the future.

NEW COMMUNITY COLLEGE OF BALTIMORE

A strong affiliation with local businesses distinguishes the New Community College of Baltimore, the city's "opportunity college." Its new Business and Industry Center, located in the midst of the thriving hub of Baltimore, is dedicated to meeting industry's learning needs for the next decade and next century.

Opened in 1947, CCB had an initial enrollment of 47 students, mainly newly demobilized World War II veterans. The first classes met at Baltimore City College High School.

From that modest beginning, the college has developed into a major educational institution. The New Community College of Baltimore, accredited by the Middle States Association of Colleges and Schools, has a daytime enrollment of more than 6,000 students and an evening enrollment of 4,500. Along with its two primary campuses, the new one downtown and the Liberty campus in northwest Baltimore, New CCB offers programs in 125 community educational centers while providing fieldwork experience at 130 training sites.

Well over 75,000 persons have attended CCB, enrolling in associate in arts degree programs, which prepare students for transfer to four-year schools, and in career programs. Among its alumni are many college professors and successful business people as well as city officials and members of Congress. New CCB's most famous alumnus is director Barry Levinson, whose films include *Diner*, *Tin Men*, and *Good Morning, Vietnam*.

The Business and Industry Center, officially opened in 1989, is housed in the college's Inner Harbor building, redesignated for the purpose. In cooperation with the Greater Baltimore Committee, many of the city's largest companies have become involved in the center's programs, which include training courses in the subjects and skills business needs most. Courses include secretarial science, computer science, law enforcement, fashion merchandising, legal assistance, busi-

New CCB's Business and Industry Center, opened in 1989, is located in the Inner Harbor district.

ness, telecommunications, and biotechnology. A wide range of one-day seminars is also offered, in conjunction with Dun & Bradstreet, on such timely topics as Managerial and Leadership Skills for Women.

New CCB degree programs include arts and sciences, with specialties in humanities, math, science/health sciences, and social and behavioral sciences; business administration; engineering; nursing; telecommunications; and a wide range of others.

The college provides many services to the city. Its radio station, WBJC-FM, broadcasts classical music to a steadily growing audience, counted by Arbitron at 170,000 per week—far ahead of any other area public radio station. New CCB also offers a large program to senior citizens, at local schools, libraries, and senior centers. Several thousand Baltimore seniors sign up each year for free courses in politics, arts, culture, and health, among other topics.

Accessible, affordable, and accredited, New Community College of Baltimore looks forward to a bright future, built in partnership with Baltimore citizens.

14

BUILDING GREATER BALTIMORE

Developers, contractors, and real estate professionals all help to shape the
Baltimore of tomorrow.

■ ■ ■

Above and facing: Photo by Greg Pease

MIE INVESTMENT CO.

Long prominent in Baltimore real estate, MIE Investment Co. is in the development, construction, leasing, and land acquisition businesses. Today its name is also becoming known in Denver and Milwaukee, as MIE looks toward expansion.

In 1967 Edward St. John completed his first 16,000-square-foot warehouse with Leroy Merritt, one of many the two partners developed in their four years together. In 1971 he formed MIE and continued to build high-bulk distribution centers. In 1981 the office/flex building evolved to become MIE's primary product. During the 1980s MIE constructed more than 1.5 million square feet of office/flex space.

Today MIE owns and manages 6 million square feet of office, shopping center, and

warehouse space, and approximately 2,000 apartments, some acquired in partnership with other companies. Several of its projects have won the prestigious Awards of Excellence given by the National Association of Industrial Office Parks. Among MIE's winners are BWI

Below: Beltway West Corporate Center, a low-rise suburban office park, consists of four buildings with a total of 75,400 square feet.

When phase one, 201,000 square feet of MIE's Caton Research Center, was fully leased, the company began to build phase two. It was completed in 1989.

Commerce Park; Yorkridge Center North in Hunt Valley; and the First American Bank Building.

BWI Commerce Park, one of MIE's major projects, is a 55-acre park with 500,000 square feet of space. Adjacent to Baltimore-Washington International Airport, it is a master-planned business community encompassing three single-user buildings and 13 multi-tenant, high-tech buildings.

In 1985, MIE broke ground for the Caton Research Center, a 480,000-square-foot research and development facility. Located near the intersection of 695, the Baltimore Beltway, and I-95, the interstate highway to Washington, D.C., the center has nine one-story red brick buildings. The buildings are designed for a variety of uses in addition to research and development; they also hold service centers, data processing units, communications centers, and light assembly and manufacturing.

Above Right: About 30 percent of the nearly 500,000 square feet in BWI Commerce Park is used for offices. Completed in 1988, the project is adjacent to Baltimore-Washington Airport.

Above: Phase one of Ownings Mills is made up of 101,700 square feet in two buildings. These buildings are examples of MIE's primary product, the flex building.

Right: MIE completed phases four and five of its Owings Mills North project in 1990.

Among MIE's newest projects are Owings Mills North, at Crondall Lane, Owings Mills South, at Deer Park, and Riverside Center. MIE is currently developing the I-97 business park, which when completed will have almost 300,000 square feet of office/flex space.

MIE Investment Co. has grown conservatively since its origination but has taken significant steps in recent years to widen its scope in terms of product and community development.

RIPARIUS CORPORATION

Providing quality services and prompt response are two objectives of Riparius Corporation, a holding company engaged in the real estate development, construction, environmental, and engineering businesses through its subsidiaries.

Founded in 1984, Riparius can trace its history 51 years before that to 1933, when F. Jordon McCarthy came to Baltimore from Riparius, New York, to start a liquor distribution business. His company, McCarthy-Hicks, Inc., grew into one of the nation's largest liquor distributorships. But by the time his grandson, Michael J. McCarthy, was brought in to manage the business, the outlook was changing. Concluding that the liquor business had little growth potential, Michael McCarthy set up a parent company, Riparius Corporation, and established Riparius Development Corporation. Since the company already owned various parcels of land in the thriving Timonium-Hunt Valley area, real estate development looked most promising.

After selling McCarthy-Hicks in 1986, Riparius established another subsidiary: Riparius Construction, Inc. In 1987 it acquired Century Engineering, Inc.

Riparius Development is a full-service real estate firm committed to long-term, high-quality development. It is actively engaged in a broad mix of office and industrial projects, site acquisition, land development, build-to-suit, sale leaseback, joint venture, property management, and mixed-use development.

Riparius Construction is a full-service construction company offering design/build construction management and general construction services. In addition to building for Riparius Development, the construction company works with other prominent developers and businesses in the region.

Century Engineering, Inc., provides professional engineering services to clients in both the private and public sectors. Its clients include the State of Maryland. The company, combined with Century Mechanical and Electrical and Century Engineering International, provides expertise in the areas of land development, land surveying, geotechnical and transportation engineering and facilities, shipyard and marine design, and environmental engineering.

Riparius Development's first major project was the conversion of a McCarthy-Hicks warehouse, set on 12 acres in Timonium, to an office building. The conversion, which involved adding a mezzanine level to the single-story warehouse, resulted in a handsome brick and glass building with 100,000 square feet of first-class office space. Named the Atrium, it was completed in 1986 and leased quickly.

In December 1987 Riparius broke ground for a second office building, 9690 Deereco Road, on the same site. A striking eight-story glass and steel structure with 150,000 square feet of space and nine-foot high ceilings, it offers such special features as executive offices with outside balconies and an upscale restaurant on the lobby floor. The new building, com-

This site plan of Riparius Center at Owings Mills shows the arrangement of corporate office buildings and parking structures relative to surrounding green areas. The plan emphasizes vistas and focal points, as well as pedestrian accessibility to amenities.

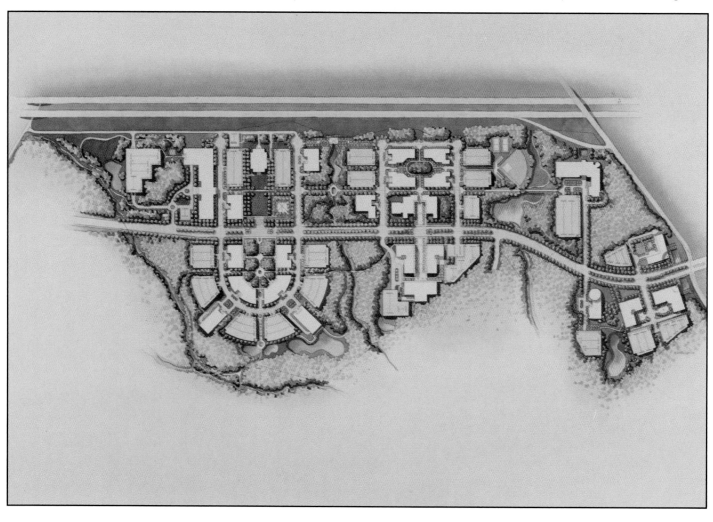

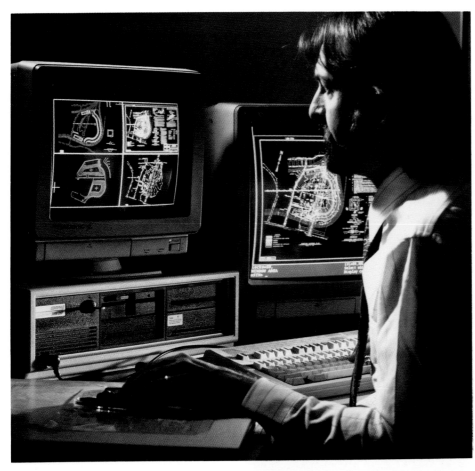

ment that we would like to be in ourselves," Michael McCarthy says.

A Baltimore company and there to stay, Riparius has long supported a variety of local nonprofit organizations mainly through the McCarthy Family Foundation. The foundation makes contributions to educational institutions and to Baltimore cultural organizations and hospitals. Riparius executives are involved in such causes as Project Sail, Johns Hopkins Children's Center, United Way, Kennedy Institute, Greater Baltimore Committee, Maryland Economic Growth Associates (MEGA), and area chambers of commerce.

Left: Century Engineering, Inc., located in Towson, boasts state-of-the-art technology as illustrated here by a CADD (computer-aided drafting and design) operator. Century provides expertise in land surveying, geotechnical, environmental, transportation, and shipyard engineering.

Below: 9690 Deereco Road, in Timonium, is Riparius Development Corporation's flagship building. Eight stories of striking blue glass with a four-story atrium lobby clad in granite and brass, the structure creates an inviting place for business. Photo by Ron Haisfield

pleted in 1989, was also leased in a short time.

Other Riparius projects are located in Holabird Industrial Park in Baltimore and Business Center at Owings Mills. The Holabird building offers 20,000 square feet of decorator-finished, first-class office space as well as 63,000 square feet of warehouse space. The Business Center is a five-building complex, completed in 1990, with a total of 130,000 square feet of elegant office space, laboratory space, and loading docks. These facilities have attracted biotechnology and pharmaceutical companies, among other tenants, and helped make the complex successful.

The company's biggest project is a corporate office park, Riparius Center at Owings Mills, which will create more than 3.5 million square feet of space on 180 acres. Office space, according to the master plan, will be laid out in mid-rise buildings while parking space will be in structures, not lots. Anticipating an early 1993 opening to coincide with the completion of Red Run Boulevard, the park will provide a pleasant workplace for 14,000 people.

The concept behind Riparius Center, which won county development approval in 1989, is to create the ambience of a village where peo-

ple have many amenities and services readily available to them. Pedestrian-oriented, Riparius Center will include a food court, dry cleaners, banks, a 150-room hotel, a community center with child care and a library, a dining and racquet club, and conference facilities—services not usually found in suburban corporate office parks. "We want to build the kind of environ-

A Baltimore native, Michael McCarthy wants Riparius Corporation to concentrate on providing development, construction, and engineering services in the greater Baltimore metropolitan area. "Thirty years from now we're going to be the same organization as today. And in these businesses, you can accomplish a lot in that amount of time."

RYAN HOMES

matic as they are practical. With Ryan's guaranteed quality interiors, customers can depend on a lifetime of easy comfort in rooms designed for better living. Ryan homes are also energy efficient; Ryan's standard energy package, one of the most comprehensive in the housing industry, is designed to save the home owner money with lower utility bills.

Single-family homes offer available features such as formal entrances with open foyers and hardwood floors, center island kitchens, and master suites with whirlpool baths and spacious

Left: Ryan's popular Nantucket Traditional home has more than 2,000 square feet of well-designed living space.

Below: The New Haven Colonial home, great for a growing family, has the diversity to expand to five bedrooms and three full baths.

As a customer-oriented company, Ryan Homes aims to set new industry standards for quality of both services and products. Ryan, a new-home builder for more than 40 years, operates on the principle that demonstrating its commitment to quality and customer service will make it the builder of choice in the markets it serves.

Ryan's demonstration of commitment to quality begins with the initial customer contact and continues not only until the sale is made but long afterward. Ryan puts its commitment in writing, in a notice prominently displayed in every model home: ". . . We believe there's more to home building than nails and lumber. Ryan is a philosphy at work: 'Give people the most for their money.' We back up our philosophy with a service program that includes two inspections, one when you move and another six months later."

Its responsibility does not end there. A 10-year limited warranty comes with each home. Ryan promises to complete routine service within 10 days of its inspections and complete emergency service immediately.

The commitment to meeting customer needs goes back to 1948, when Ryan Homes was founded on that principle by Ed and Jim Ryan in Pittsburgh, Pennsylvania. The Ryan brothers' idea was to build affordable single-family homes, townhomes, and multi-family garden homes for first-time buyers. With the emphasis on quality as well as affordability, the idea caught on and the company branched out into new locations, coming to Baltimore in 1980. Today, in addition to Maryland and Pennsylvania, Ryan operates in Delaware, New

York, North Carolina, and Virginia.

A merger completed in June 1987 incorporated Ryan Homes under its parent company NVR of McLean, Virginia. NVR is the nation's largest builder of new homes for sale. NVR also has operations in building products and financial services. It owns NVR Savings Bank, a four-branch institution based in McLean, and NVR Mortgage, which provides affordable financing for home buyers.

No longer just for first-time buyers, Ryan Homes serves the entire spectrum of consumers, including those moving up for the fourth or fifth time. It markets a variety of homes at a wide range of prices. Ryan floor plans are designed to take advantage of natural light and to create living spaces that are as dra-

walk-in closets. Townhome buyers choose between three bedrooms or two master bedroom suites. Decks, skylights, and fireplaces are also available.

Such features, along with innovative designs, have won Ryan recognition and awards. Among the honors it has received are two Finest for Family Living awards and the Award of Excellence sponsored by the Home Builders Association of Maryland. The public recognized this excellence: in 1990 Ryan continued to be the leader in home building in the Baltimore/Washington area, with 1,850 sales.

Intensifying its efforts to ensure that buyers get exactly what they want, Ryan created a new customer-involvement program in the fall of 1989. Ryan strives to develop a personal relationship with each customer. The customer meets with the construction supervisor when the home is sited and again before the drywall goes in. These meetings are intended to show the customer just how their new home is built. Ryan encourages customers to visit any Ryan community and talk with Ryan home owners. The company is confident that after a thorough comparison with other builders, Ryan's extraordinary value will be apparent.

Ryan Homes offers a pre-settlement orientation to introduce customers to their new home with a post-settlement questionnaire to listen to any comments and concerns of new home owners. The Ryan homeowner's manual provides thorough in-hand information, and an in-house quality assurance and customer service department is always ready to serve the owner. Ryan's six-month post-settlement inspection and 10-year limited warranty makes for peace of mind at settlement as well as years later.

Now building for the move-up market as well as first-time buyers, Ryan Homes offers a diversity of homes and services. The firm assures the sale of the customer's present home, offers below-market financing, and it even helps with closing costs in many of its communities. The company, now in its fifth decade, has perfected the craft of home building. Each home is built on what Ryan has learned by consulting with home owners. Putting the customer's needs first and foremost, it guarantees quality and value with every new home.

Left: The elegant Newcastle Colonial Grand home boasts a first-floor library. A bright and airy sun-room may also be added.

Below: The Fairfax Townhome is a three-level home boasting cathedral ceilings, whirlpool tubs, and marble fireplaces.

15

THE MARKETPLACE

Baltimore's retail establishments, service industries, and products are enjoyed
by residents and visitors alike.

■ ■ ■

Photo by Greg Pease

CORT FURNITURE RENTAL CORPORATION

Cort Furniture Rental Corporation is the nation's leading provider of high-value rental furnishings services for both home and office. Cort offers excellent quality and a wide selection of styles along with a service guarantee and flexibility driven by customer needs.

Cort has six showrooms and three retail/clearance centers in the Baltimore/Washington area. Founded in 1972, Cort was a subsidiary of the Mohasco Corporation until 1981. It is now privately owned, with headquarters in Fairfax, Virginia, and has more than 80 showrooms and retail outlets in 53 metropolitan areas nationwide.

Cort employees are dedicated to service. Unique in their field, Cort's trained professionals are committed to serving in close partnership with customers and are available to work on-site to assist customers in evaluating space and furnishings options. The company encourages a "can do" spirit and offers every customer a written guarantee. Cort guarantees that furniture will be picked up or delivered on the date promised and that the furniture will arrive in a clean, undamaged condition, comparable to the furniture on display in the showrooms. Unavoidable substitutions will be of the same or higher value than the item ordered at no additional charge. Cort also guarantees prompt exchanges on request.

One of Cort's primary goals is to meet the multiple needs of business. Start-up companies can furnish offices in a wide range of styles without large cash outlays. Growing companies with changing needs and firms awaiting delivery of newly ordered furniture look to Cort for immediate service. Corporate transferees who need to settle in quickly find their lives both more comfortable and more efficient thanks to Cort. For them, the company's services are virtually unlimited. With the aid of professional consultants, Cort helps find living quarters; offers decorating advice; and supplies towels, linens, housewares, area rugs, VCRs and microwaves, and even artwork. Cort also serves apartment management companies by providing quality furniture for model apartments and rental units.

Residential clients turn to Cort for home furnishings for many reasons: temporary needs due to moving, life-style changes, short-term

Cort Furniture Rental Corporation provides beautiful and elegant furnishings in a wide variety of styles for the home or office.

special needs, natural disaster damage, or other personal needs. Cort's wide range of furniture styles, from classic eighteenth-century reproductions to California contemporary, offers great choice. Clients can rent a few pieces or a house full for a short time or a few years.

Another key element in Cort's management philosophy is its sincere dedication to good corporate citizenship. Cort was a sponsor of Hands Across America and is now a national sponsor of Special Olympics International and of the 1991 Summer Special Olympic Games. Cort has pledged to raise $250,000 for Special Olympics.

Whether for a single room or a building, for a need in 48 hours or next month, in Baltimore or San Francisco, for office or home, customers turn to Cort Furniture Rental Corporation for unparalleled service and value.

TREMONT SUITE HOTELS

A small, luxuriously furnished hotel with a continental flavor, the Tremont Hotel stresses impeccable personal service for every guest. Located on a quiet side street downtown, it is just a few blocks from the Inner Harbor. The hotel's 62 suites, all with fully equipped kitchens, including microwave ovens, are equally well suited to the corporate travelers who make up most of the weekday clientele and the out-of-state couples who take advantage of the romantic weekend packages. Genuine suites, not just two adjoining rooms, the Tremont's accommodations are sufficiently comfortable and homelike for visitors on extended stays.

The Tremont was renovated in 1983 by William C. Smith & Co., Inc., a family-owned company that also operates the Tremont Plaza Hotel. The two are known as the Tremont Suite Hotels. Special features of the 12-story, red-brick Tremont include wood-paneled ele-

vators, a well-appointed lobby, elegant dining place, and intimate cocktail lounge. The restaurant, 8 East, with its pink-suede upholstered chairs and seafoam-green linens, won first place in a national interior design competition. Open for breakfast, lunch, and dinner, 8 East serves fine continental cuisine.

For the traveler accustomed to luxury, the Tremont offers its unique Concierge Club. Guests who elect to pay a small extra charge receive a passport entitling them to such courtesies as happy hours in the cocktail lounge, full breakfasts, downtown transportation, and Downtown Athletic Club privileges. Tremont guests can be treated to nightly turndown service, nightly cordials and chocolates, terry cloth robe, complimentary morning newspaper, fully equipped kitchens, bath supplies, and valet parking. Wake-up calls come complete with the latest weather report, and each suite's kitchen contains coffee beans and grinder

The Tremont Plaza's lobby is elegantly decorated with marble, limestone, and mahogany.

along with an automatic coffeemaker.

For meetings or banquets, the hotel has specialized facilities accommodating up to 80 people. Distinctive quarters for smaller groups include the Boardroom Suite, which is designed around a spacious meeting area with a handsome wood conference table, and the Mayor's Suite, furnished as an elegant living room with such extras as a stereo system and presentation center.

While striving to give clients a memorable hotel experience, the Tremont Suite Hotels also serve the community. One of their finest suites has been designated the Johns Hopkins Family Suite, and it is offered at no charge to the families of children with cancer who are being treated at Johns Hopkins. The Tremont

Above: The Plaza's rooms are spacious and comfortable, with polished wood dining tables, soft upholstered furniture, and ample closet space.

Left: The Tremont Hotel stresses impeccable personal service for every guest.

Suite Hotels are also among the four major business sponsors of the Ed Block Courage Awards, which benefit abused children.

The Tremont prides itself on providing warm, efficient service in an atmosphere of luxury at competitive rates.

The Tremont Plaza Hotel is a 37-story, white stone and brick building, offering 228 suites plus several well-equipped conference centers and boardrooms, all with outside windows for natural light. The Plaza, on a quiet street near the Inner Harbor, caters to corporate travelers and, especially on weekends, out-of-state families on short vacations. Baltimore residents also find the Tremont Plaza just the place for myriad social functions from wedding receptions to Christmas and retirement parties.

Opened in 1986 after a two-year renovation, the Tremont Plaza is all marble, limestone, and mahogany, bespeaking elegance and warmth. Suites come with panoramic skyline views, sometimes with the harbor in the background. The large bathrooms offer various sup-

The Tremont Hotel's warmly appointed lobby.

plies and accessories, including a hair dryer in some suites. Kitchens contain a refrigerator, range, and dishwasher, along with china, pots and pans, as well as a toaster and coffeemaker. Televisions in the bedroom and living room, polished wood dining tables, soft upholstered furniture, and ample closet space all demonstrate the Tremont Plaza's hallmark for spacious, comfortable quarters.

The Plaza also goes to some lengths to pro-

vide all the comforts of home. Amenities include valet parking, concierge services, complimentary in-house movies, morning newspapers, and privileges to the nearby Downtown Athletic Club. During the summer an outdoor pool and sauna, with poolside food service, adds another dimension.

Dining choices include Tug's Restaurant, which specializes in American cuisine, mainly steaks and seafood, and offers popular weekend buffet breakfasts. The Plaza Deli, a gourmet delicatessen, offers a variety of quality gourmet foods, as well as custom-made gift baskets and personalized catering services. Tables are available, but many guests order takeout food or buy pasta or other specialties to cook in their own kitchens. Open from 6:30 a.m. to 10 p.m. seven days a week, the deli is a winner of *Baltimore Magazine*'s Best Deli Sandwich in Baltimore award.

Celebrities, a cocktail lounge, takes its name from the hotel's famous guests whose pictures line the walls. Many are film stars, reflecting the Tremont Plaza's frequent use as production headquarters for the considerable number of movies filmed in Baltimore.

The hotel's policy is to treat celebrities and other guests alike to the utmost in personalized service and comfort.

PEABODY COURT HOTEL

The Peabody Court Hotel is an elegant hotel with a distinct continental flavor. It is located in Mt. Vernon Place, a fine residential neighborhood that is also Baltimore's historic and cultural center. The hotel, with its columned entrance, period furniture, and crystal chandeliers, embodies the charm and luxury of an earlier time. Similar to the buildings around it, the Peabody is listed on the National Register of Historic Buildings.

Standing on the site of the original Baltimore Museum of Art, the Peabody Court was built as an apartment house in the 1920s, to the majestic standards of the day. Later, it housed students from the Peabody Institute, one of the nation's most prestigious conservatories, which is just across the square. In 1982 the plan to turn the classic structure into a hotel was implemented and renovation begun. The meticulous work, which maintained the facade, and the custom decoration of the interior, took three years. The Peabody Court

opened as a luxury hotel in April 1985.

The 12-story hotel has 79 guest rooms, 25 suites, 12 function rooms of various sizes, and 2 fine restaurants along with 2 cocktail lounges. With its hand-loomed carpeting, original art works, opulent marble bathrooms, exceptional personal service, and limousines to downtown destinations, the Peabody is a favorite among celebrities, executives, and sophisticated travelers alike.

It is a quiet place, with only 12 rooms to a floor, six on each side of the elevator. The lobby, too, has an air of quiet grandeur imparted by the marble floors, dramatic six-foot Baccarat crystal chandelier, antique furnishings, and glass-fronted bookcases. The shelves are lined with leather-bound editions of Dickens, Scott, Gibbons, and other classics of literature.

The Conservatory piano lounge has a mahogany bar with a marble top. Bar stools are upholstered in genuine leather.

One floor above the lobby, with a street as well as inside entrance, is Peabody's, a cheerful, amusing restaurant with big, comfortable leather chairs and marble tables that are covered for dinner with white linens. Open from 7 a.m. to midnight, Peabody's is an American grill. It is versatile and accommodating, always ready to serve a full-course meal or a light repast. Peabody's superbly prepared, sensibly priced fare ranges from gourmet pizza—topped with escargots or Cajun green tomatoes—to softshell crab sandwiches, gourmet hamburgers, and such specialties as Norwegian salmon, rosemary grilled lamb chops, and blackened porterhouse steak.

The Conservatory, the hotel's glass-enclosed rooftop restaurant, offers sweeping views from all tables of the Mt. Vernon Place, which are among the finest remaining examples of nineteenth-century American urban planning. Tables are covered in creamy linen and set with fine china and crystal, and chairs are up-

holstered in a discreet paisley, blending in with the patterned carpet. Overhead lighting is designed specifically for each table. Well-known for its French cuisine, the restaurant draws its clientele not only from Peabody guests but also from other hotels' guests and Baltimore residents. In the Conservatory piano lounge, the centerpiece is an original Joseph Sheppard painting. A marble-topped, mahogany bar encircles the painting; bar stools with backs are covered in leather.

Each guest suite is furnished with fine antiques and tapestries. The spacious living and dining area is complete with a crystal chandelier and fully stocked bar, making it a gracious setting for dining with friends or cocktails and hors d'oeuvres with business associates. Like the living room, the beautifully appointed master bedroom has its own television set. The adjoining bathroom features a whirlpool bath, towel warmer, and hair dryer. The hotel's largest suite, the Presidential Suite, has a full kitchen as well as a

blackboard with pulldown screen. It is often reserved by celebrities or businesses for dinner parties or board meetings. Other suites are flexible; two-bedroom, three-bath arrangements are possible.

Guest rooms are almost suite-size themselves; most of them, like the suites, have king-size beds. Tastefully fitted with handcrafted European furniture, the rooms are lit by lamps hand painted to match their decor, which includes patterned carpeting. Every room has a two-line telephone, with an extension in the marble bathroom, and television with satellite channels and remote controls.

The Peabody Court's function rooms accommodate groups of 12 people to 300 for training sessions, conferences, banquets, and receptions. Business services include secretarial assistance, teleconferencing, facsimile communications, and limousine.

To assure guests' privacy and security, the hotel provides electronic locks, video cameras, and security guards. It also provides such complimentary extras as guest privileges at the nearby Downtown Athletic Club, a full-service facility.

As an integral part of historic Baltimore, the Peabody Court supports a variety of local charitable and civic projects, including the American Cancer Society and United Way. It also works with smaller organizations, helping to get things done on the community level. Hotel services, such as dinners or overnight stays, are often contributed to serve as prizes.

The Peabody Court Hotel is conscious of its place in the overall development of the city, and aware that nothing like it will be built in the future. Enjoying a reputation for attention to detail and personal service, it is determined to maintain and constantly improve its standards and remain a Baltimore landmark.

Above: Twelve stories above historic Mt. Vernon Place, the glass-enclosed Conservatory Restaurant serves fine French food.

Left: Displayed on the walls of Peabody's Restaurant, an American brasserie, are old photographs from the Peabody Institute, Baltimore's internationally known conservatory.

Below: The commodious Presidential Suite includes a dramatic dining room as well as a living room, bedroom, and marble bath.

BALTIMORE STATIONERY

A longstanding, stable company, Baltimore Stationery is oriented to serving people and meeting their needs in the office supply field. The company still observes two rules set down by its founder, Calvert Randolph Jones, Jr.: provide high-quality service and products for all customers and make sure employees are well trained and motivated. Following these rules has helped Baltimore Stationery grow each year and become the leader that it is today.

Founded in 1930 as a stationery supplier, the company prospered despite the Depression, and two years later the firm added a line of office furniture, enhancing growth opportunities. Baltimore Stationery incorporated in 1943 and during the next several years expanded its business. When the founder died in 1966, his brother, William W. Jones, who had worked alongside Calvert almost since the company's founding, took over. Under his leadership, the company continued to thrive, establishing Interplan, a new inte-

Since its founding in 1930, Baltimore Stationery has grown to become one of the largest office supply and furniture dealers in the country.

rior design division, and expanded into the region.

Today, under William W. Jones, Jr., president since 1984, Baltimore Stationery has become one of the largest companies in its industry, with branches in Newark, Delaware, as well as in Salisbury and Rockville, Mary-

land. Employing more than 200 people, the company also does business in Pennsylvania, Virginia, West Virginia, and Washington, D.C. The business offers open office systems, computer supplies, printing, and other services, in addition to office supplies, furniture, and interior design.

Baltimore Stationery dedicates itself to find ways to respond to customers' needs. "That is not just lip service or an advertising ploy," Bill Jones says. "We have created departments and various services over the years in a constant attempt to find better ways to serve our customers. For example, computer-aided design capabilities."

A full-service dealer, the company maintains a service department, interior design department, installation coordinators, showrooms, and more. "We are not a mail order or budget operation," Jones says.

The company strives to fulfill a four-step mission: to honor God; serve customers in the finest possible way; provide fair pay, good benefits, comfortable working conditions, and job security for employees; and earn a reasonable return on investment. "Our corporation is our people," Jones says. "Our employees are treated like family." To mark its 60th anniversary in 1990, Baltimore Stationery sponsored an Employee Appreciation Family Day, highlighted by a luncheon and sightseeing aboard a ship cruising the harbor.

Demonstrating care for all community members, the company supports numerous local groups, including the United Way, the Baltimore Symphony, Johns Hopkins University, Christian churches, and the Christian Businessmen's Committee.

Baltimore Stationery, which has never laid off an employee, plans to remain a concerned, dependable employer, to keep growing, and to find better ways to serve customers' needs.

An important part of Baltimore Stationery's business is the sale of open office systems furniture. This trendsetting design is by Haworth, one of the premier manufacturers.

EXCLUSIVE INTERIM PROPERTIES

Dedicated to providing "great homes away from home" for everyone from transferred executives and their families to movie crews on location, Exclusive Interim Properties offers fully furnished residences in the Baltimore, Annapolis, and Washington, D.C., areas. "Fully furnished" means every imaginable amenity, according to Melanie R. Sabelhaus, president. She specifies linens, china, place settings for eight, microwave oven, iron, towels, and maid service.

Sabelhaus founded the company in 1987. The idea for the business grew out of her own experience; transfers had kept her on the move for years. After starting out in Cleveland, her family went on to Annapolis, Miami, and New York, among other places, before settling in Baltimore. "We moved eight times and always found ourselves with the children, a dog, and a nanny in a hotel suite," she says. "It was very

Exclusive Interim Properties offers fully furnished residences featuring all the comforts of home, making hotel living unnecessary for those in need of extended temporary accommodations.

difficult to live this way for three or four months while we looked for a house."

EIP makes hotel living unnecessary. Working closely with area realtors, the company leases houses, town houses, and condominiums in the finest locations for varying periods, according to need. In Baltimore, these locations include Federal Hill, overlooking the Inner Harbor, and Greenspring Valley—out in the country but only 25 minutes from downtown. In Annapolis homes are available overlooking Chesapeake Bay, and in Washington, clients can live in the Georgetown and Washington Circle areas.

Sabelhaus finds she is often the first step in the relocation process, but her clients also include people on temporary assignment or building their own homes, fire victims, divorcing couples, Johns Hopkins patients and their fami-

lies, and the Hollywood contingent.

"Everything we do is quality," Sabelhaus says. "The properties are elegantly done." Proving her point, she cites an impressive list of clients, including chief executive officers, bank presidents, consultants from around the nation, international visitors, and such movie luminaries as Paulina Porizkova and Jessica Lange.

Since making her home in Baltimore, Sabelhaus has taken on a variety of civic and charitable activities. She teaches Sunday school, belongs to the Junior League, and has served on the President's Circle of the Baltimore Opera. In 1990 she chaired the WMAR TV-2 Children's Miracle Network Telethon for the benefit of the Johns Hopkins Children's Center.

Stressing that EIP's essence is customer service, Sabelhaus makes sure her clients' stays are

"totally comfortable and enjoyable. If the faucet leaks or the phone doesn't work, we go out and fix it."

In order to further enhance the range of services provided, Sabelhaus has joined with partner and neighbor Liz Schroeder to start a real estate brokerage company specializing in longer-term unfurnished rentals in the Baltimore area. The new company, Exclusive Rental Properties, Ltd., offers relocated executives and their families an alternative to home buying. "This gives people a chance to get their feet wet in the Baltimore/Annapolis market prior to settling on a neighborhood and life-style," says Schroeder.

For Exclusive Interim Properties and Exclusive Rental Properties, Sabelhaus anticipates steady growth and expansion into the Washington, D.C., and Virginia marketplace.

PATRONS

The following individuals, companies, and organizations have made a valuable commitment to the quality of this publication. Windsor Publications gratefully acknowledges their participation in *Baltimore: Jewel of the Chesapeake*.

AAI Corporation*
Alexander & Alexander Services Inc.*
Baltimore Business Journal*
Baltimore Gas and Electric Company*
Baltimore RESCO*
Baseline Software Group*
Baltimore Stationery*
Black & Decker*
Blue Cross and Blue Shield of Maryland, Inc.*
Chicago Title Insurance Co. of Maryland*
City Paper*
Cort Furniture Rental Corporation*
Daft-McCune-Walker, Inc.*
The Daily Record*

Environmental Elements Corporation*
Exclusive Interim Properties*
FMC Corporation*
The Francis Scott Key Medical Center*
Frank, Bernstein, Conaway & Goldman*
IBM*
Kaplan, Heyman, Greenberg, Engelman & Belgrad, P.A.*
Locke Insulators, Inc.*
Mercantile-Safe Deposit and Trust Company*
MIE Investment Co.*
NCNB National Bank of Maryland*
New Community College of Baltimore*
Peabody Court Hotel*
Piper & Marbury*
The Poole & Kent Company*
Price Waterhouse*
Riparius Corporation*
RTKL Associates Inc.*
Ryan Homes*

Semmes, Bowen & Semmes*
Sheppard Pratt Health System*
Sinai Hospital*
Stegman & Company*
Thieblot, Ryan, Martin & Ferguson, P.A.*
Towson State University*
Travel Guide*
Tremont Suite Hotels*
T. Rowe Price Associates, Inc.*
University of Maryland Medical System*
Walpert, Smullian & Blumenthal, P.A.*
W.B. Doner & Company*
WLIF-FM*
Woodbourne*
The World Trade Center Baltimore*

*Participants in Part Two, "Baltimore's Enterprises." The stories of these companies and organizations appear in chapters 9 through 15, beginning on page 152.

SELECT BIBLIOGRAPHY

BOOKS

Beirne, Francis F. *The Amiable Baltimoreans*. Tradition Press: Hatboro, Pa., 1968.

——————, and Carleton Jones. *Baltimore: A Picture History*. Bodine & Associates, Inc., and Maclay & Associates: Baltimore, 1968.

Brugger, Robert J. *Maryland: A Middle Temperament, 1634-1980*. The Johns Hopkins University Press: Baltimore, 1988.

Greene, Suzanne Ellery. *Baltimore: An Illustrated History*. Windsor Publications: Woodland Hills, Calif., 1980.

Heye, Edgar. *I Didn't Know That! First Happenings In Maryland*. Maryland Historical Society: Baltimore, 1973.

Kelly, Jacques. *Bygone Baltimore: A Historical Portrait*. Donning Company: Norfolk, Va., 1982.

McClellan, Dennis M. *If It's Trivia About Baltimore It's Far From Trivial*. Schneidereith & Sons, Inc.: Baltimore, 1984.

——————, and Roger Miller. *Baltimore: A Portrait*. Image Publishing: Baltimore, 1983.

Nast, Leonora H., Laurence N. Krause, and R.C. Monk. *Baltimore: A Living Renaissance*. Historic Baltimore Society, Inc.: Baltimore, 1982.

Olson, Sherry. *Baltimore: The Building of An American City*. The Johns Hopkins University Press: Baltimore, 1980.

Owens, Hamilton. *Baltimore on the Chesapeake*. Doubleday, Doran & Co.: Garden City, N.Y., 1941.

Warren, Marrion E. and Mame Warren. *Baltimore: When She Was What She Used to Be*. The Johns Hopkins University Press: Baltimore, 1987.

MAGAZINES

Baltimore Magazine
Eastern Review
Holiday Magazine
Johns Hopkins Magazine
Maryland Magazine
National Geographic
New York Times Magazine
Sunday Sun Magazine
Warfield's

NEWSPAPERS

Baltimore Business Journal
The Daily Record
The Evening Sun
The Messenger
The News American
The Sun
Washington Post

DIRECTORY OF CORPORATE SPONSORS

INDEX